BUILDING INCLUSIVE
FINANCIAL SYSTEMS

THE WORLD BANK GROUP

THE BROOKINGS INSTITUTION

This book is based on the seventh annual financial markets and development conference held May 30–31, 2006, in Washington, D.C. The conference was jointly sponsored by the World Bank Group and the Brookings Institution.

The previous volumes in this series are available from the Brookings Institution Press:

Financial Markets and Development: The Crisis in Emerging Markets (1999)

Managing Financial and Corporate Distress: Lessons from Asia (2000)

Open Doors: Foreign Participation in Financial Systems in Developing Countries (2001)

Financial Sector Governance: The Roles of the Public and Private Sectors (2002)

The Future of Domestic Capital Markets in Development Countries (2003)

The Future of State-Owned Financial Institutions (2004)

Financial Crises: Lessons from the Past, Preparation for the Future (2005)

MICHAEL S. BARR
ANJALI KUMAR
ROBERT E. LITAN
Editors

BUILDING INCLUSIVE
FINANCIAL SYSTEMS

A Framework
for Financial Access

BROOKINGS INSTITUTION PRESS
Washington, D.C.

Library of Congress Cataloging-in-Publication data
Building inclusive financial systems : a framework for financial access / Michael S. Barr, Anjali Kumar, Robert E. Litan, editors.
    p.   cm.   — (Emerging markets series)
    "This book is based on the seventh annual financial markets and development conference held May 30–31, 2006, in Washington, D.C. The conference was cosponsored by the World Bank Group and Brookings Institution."
    Includes bibliographical references and index.
    ISBN-13: 978-0-8157-0839-1 (pbk. : alk. paper)
    ISBN-10: 0-8157-0839-4 (pbk. : alk. paper)
    1. Finance—Developing countries—Congresses.   2. Financial institutions—Developing countries—Congresses.   3. Microfinance—Developing countries—Congresses.   4. Credit—Developing countries—Congresses.   5. Financial services industry—Developing countries—Congresses.   I. Barr, Michael S.   II. Kumar, Anjali.   III. Litan, Robert E., 1950–   IV. World Bank.   V. International Monetary Fund.   VI. Title.   VII. Series.
    HG195.B84 2007
    332.109172'4—dc22   2007027761

9 8 7 6 5 4 3 2 1

Typeset in Adobe Garamond

Composition by Lynn Rivenbark
Macon, Georgia

Printed by R. R. Donnelley
Harrisonburg, Virginia

Contents

Acknowledgments

THE EDITORS WISH to thank the World Bank Group and the Brookings Institution for making this conference possible. ABN AMRO, CGAP, Citigroup Foundation, Temenos, the United Nations Capital Development Fund, and the World Savings Banks Institute also were key sponsors of the conference. In addition, sponsorships, materials, and speakers were contributed by ACCION International, ICICI Bank, and KfW.

At the Brookings Institution Press, Eileen Hughes and Anthony Nathe ably guided the manuscript to completion, and Carlotta Ribar proofread the pages. Linda Wielfaert provided essential editorial support for Michael Barr.

MICHAEL S. BARR
ANJALI KUMAR
ROBERT E. LITAN

1

Introduction

M ICROFINANCE—the extension of loans of small sums and other financial
services to the poor—is a hot topic. The founder of the field, Muhammad
Yunus, won the Nobel Prize in 2006 for his pioneering work in launching
Grameen Bank in Bangladesh. The United Nations designated the previous year,
2005, the International Year of Microcredit. More than $1 billion in microcredit
loans, made to nearly 30 million people, are outstanding. For-profit lenders have
discovered the potential profitability in microfinance, and they are now competing with the nonprofits that launched the field.

It is an opportune time, therefore, to take stock of what has been accomplished
and learned so far and to identify what further challenges remain in expanding
financial access, deepening markets for microfinance, and potentially linking
microfinance provision more closely with conventional financial institutions. To
that end, practitioners, academics, and policymakers convened in Washington
May 30–31, 2006, to attend "Access to Finance: Building Inclusive Financial Systems," a conference sponsored by the World Bank and the Brookings Institution.

That conference and this volume represent the sixth in a series of collabora-
tions on emerging markets finance between the World Bank Group and the
Brookings Institution. The 2006 conference differed from the earlier conferences
in some important respects. In previous conferences, authors presented completed drafts of the chapters that they had prepared for the volume based on the

conference, and they received comments from designated discussants and other invited participants. At the 2006 conference, however, presentations included a range of approaches by practitioners, government officials, and academics, and the presentations for each conference session were summarized in a single chapter, which also draws on the prevailing literature, to present a thematic overview of the topic of the session. Each session had an average of three or four authored presentations. This volume presents, therefore, a series of original survey articles that include summaries of presentations by multiple experts.

In the balance of this introductory chapter, we preview the questions and issues taken up by the authors of the chapters that follow. We purposely avoid summarizing the key findings of the chapters, which are found instead in our concluding chapter.

It is natural to begin by asking how much access individuals and firms have to financial services—to payments facilities and credit and savings vehicles. That question is important because evolving research has documented the significance of financial access in economic growth; in particular, growing evidence suggests a link between financial development and the reduction of poverty and income inequality. How, then, should access to finance be measured?

That question is taken up in chapter 2 by Anjali Kumar, with colleagues from the World Bank, the U.K. Department for International Development, and FinMark Trust of South Africa. The authors wrestle with questions such as whether access should be measured by type of financial institution, of financial service, or of financial product used (they suggest using institutions and services as measures); whether distinctions should be made between voluntary and involuntary exclusion from financial markets and institutions (they suggest that measures based on actual usage are the most transparent); what unit should be employed to measure access (individuals, households, and/or firms); and what differences in access arise when the supplier of financial services is "formal" (legally recognized) rather than "informal" (operating outside the purview of financial regulation or supervision) In answering those questions the authors pay special attention to the particular circumstances of developing countries, which are the focus of the conference and of this book and are the primary object of attention of suppliers of microfinance services and those who study them. The authors also highlight the special efforts to measure access by the World Bank and other international organizations, point out some of the limitations of current efforts, and suggest future directions for measuring access.

Chapter 2 hints at why access to finance matters—its link to growth and poverty reduction. In chapter 3, Xavier Gine delves into this important subject in greater detail, providing a thorough review of what already is known about it and drawing on presentations at the conference by a number of different experts. The predicate for the discussion is that financial access indeed does facilitate growth and reduce poverty; the issue is how best to provide access. Among the topics that Gine addresses are the kinds of government intervention in this area that have proven most effective; the differences in provision of access by various types of microfinance providers; the strategies taken by different microlenders in particular; the form of lending (whether to groups, as in the original Grameen Bank model, or to individuals); and the mechanisms that microlenders have used to ensure repayment of loans.

Can financial access be expanded by microfinance institutions? How sustainable and how profitable are these institutions? How profitable can they be? It is natural to ask such questions since microfinance began with grants from nonprofit organizations and foundations that did not expect a return on their investments. Yet because the supply of donor-provided funds is limited, the viability of microfinance in the long run depends on whether it can offer a reasonable, risk-adjusted return to private investors.

In chapter 4, Stephen Peachey approaches the profitability question by addressing the "double bottom line" of microfinance providers—the social as well as the private returns to investors. Private returns are well understood: they consist of the profits of a private enterprise. The social returns of microfinance, in this context, represent the broader value to society as a whole of increasing access to finance among those who otherwise would not have it or could not afford it. Peachey addresses the issue by looking at a wide range of microfinance providers, including nongovernmental organizations, nonbank financial institutions, cooperatives, and government-run policy lending institutions as well as private banks and savings banks around the world.

Peachey summarizes the three papers presented at the conference that address profitability, reporting that except for government-operated microlenders, providers generally have been able to return a profit while also enhancing financial access.[1] Indeed, the evidence suggests that there need be no trade-off between providing access and earning a profit; the two can go hand in hand if institutions are managed properly. At the same time, however, there seem to be economies of scale in the microfinance business, since much of the access around the world is provided by a relatively small number of institutions.

---

1. That finding is consistent with more recent evidence of the profitability of some major microlenders. See Tom Easton, "Time to Take the Credit," *Economist*, March 17, 2007, p. 16.

As microfinance has become more successful, it has attracted more established, formal financial institutions. In chapter 5, Ajai Nair and J. D. von Pischke document efforts by commercial banks to offer financial services to low-income individuals. Those efforts are relatively recent, since historically commercial banks have viewed the low-income market as risky or costly to serve and have left it to government-sponsored financial institutions or special directed credit programs. The chapter discusses the changing paradigm, documenting the activities of specific banks in specific countries, and then discusses innovations that banks have developed to enable them to serve the low-income market. Nair concludes with lessons for other banks, donors, and governments that are interested in expanding access to credit to poor people in developing countries.

Financial institutions and services are not provided in a vacuum; they require a certain technical and legal infrastructure to survive and grow. In chapter 6, David Porteous summarizes presentations by experts on developments in retail banking in particular, paying special attention to the role that information and communications technology (ICT) has played in the delivery of banking services. ICT has had an especially significant impact on retail banking, and, as Porteous argues, on delivery of banking services to low-income residents of developing countries. The key has been the development of infrastructure for electronic point-of-sale and mobile means of payment, both of which benefit from economies of scale, which in turn make the delivery of banking services affordable for a much broader class of people than would be the case through traditional brick-and-mortar branch offices. At the same time, however, because of the high fixed cost of the new infrastructure the investment risk is high and payback to investors is possible only through widespread use of the services. Nonetheless, with mobile banking, or "m-banking," parts of the developing world have the potential to leapfrog more developed economies in which banking systems still rely heavily on branch offices.

In chapter 7, Michael Barr explores possible government policy applications of some of the lessons learned from the papers discussed in the chapters above. He draws on the analysis in chapter 4, which suggests that even if some microfinance institutions can turn a profit—that is, provide returns to private investors—the fact that they also can provide social benefits suggests, at least in theory, that their services are undersupplied in a purely market setting. That is, if the total returns—social and private—exceed the purely private returns, then a role presumably exists for nonprofit institutions and governments to further expand financial access.

Barr notes that in the past, however, governments have become involved in their economy's financial sector for other reasons, primarily to direct lending toward favored industries or sectors. Such policies generally have failed, largely because directed lending is not constrained by market forces. Barr suggests that governments should focus instead on policy measures that they can and should take to encourage conventional financial institutions to serve lower-income households and individuals. He draws on successful models and policies in developed countries to help lead the way in developing countries. Barr's framework for analyzing different modes of government policy helps clarify the theoretical and practical assumptions underlying different approaches and the trade-offs among them.

The foregoing chapters provide a broad overview of the state of knowledge about recent efforts to expand financial access. What are the key findings of this volume? Perhaps even more important, what are the key lessons from the experiences so far and what challenges lie ahead—for both microfinance institutions and individuals and firms that can benefit from enhanced access to financial services? We conclude this volume in chapter 8 by suggesting answers to those questions, drawing on the findings of the authors of the previous chapters as well as of those whose work is summarized in the chapters. We conclude that microfinance is here to stay, that it is increasingly profitable and therefore likely to grow in scale and scope, and that it should help foster economic growth while increasing the income of the very poor throughout the world. The challenge for governments and for the private sector is to facilitate this financial revolution.

ANJALI KUMAR
MUKTA JOSHI
LORAINE RONCHI
KONSTANTINOS TZIOUMIS

2

Measuring
Financial Access

THERE IS GROWING recognition that increasing access to formal financial services has both private and social benefits, through growth as well as poverty alleviation. It is by improving the access of households and enterprises to financing, mobilizing savings, allocating credit, managing risks, and providing payment services that deeper and broader financial systems can promote growth and reduce income inequality.[1] The United Nations designated 2005 the International Year of Microcredit, affirming that the "greatest challenge before us is to address the constraints that exclude people from full participation in the financial sector" and formally adopting the goal of building inclusive financial systems.[2] And in 2006, Muhammad Yunus and the Grameen Bank were awarded the Nobel Prize for his contributions to microfinance.

Developing effective policy for expanding financial access has been constrained by difficulties in measuring access.[3] Basic data are unavailable on how many poor people have access to what types of financial services and at what cost, and reliable

---

1. For the relation between financial development and economic growth, see King and Levine (1993); Levine, Loayza, and Beck (2000); and Beck and Levine (2004). For the relation between financial growth and income inequality, see Beck, Demirgüç-Kunt, and Levine (2004). For the relation between financial growth and poverty, see Honohan (2004) and Beegle, Dehejia, and Gatti (2003).

2. UN Secretary General Kofi Annan, December 2003, quoted in "Building Inclusive Financial Systems" (generally known as the Blue Book) (New York: United Nations, 2006).

3. For a recent survey, see Stone (2005).

7

research on factors that may promote or hinder access has been scarce. A combination of conceptual and practical issues explains the historical lack of data on financial access. In developed countries, given the relatively widespread availability of financial services (more than 80 percent of the population, on average, has access), the debate has focused on the converse concept of financial exclusion.[4] While financial exclusion and the "unbanked" are now attracting policymakers' attention in developing countries, widespread financial exclusion in poorer countries has tilted the focus to financial access as an issue of policy relevance.[5]

This chapter examines recent progress in measuring access to finance for different economic agents, enterprises as well individuals and households.[6] While drawing on the broader work in this area, it focuses in particular on three papers presented at the May 2006 conference on financial access sponsored by the World Bank and the Brookings Institution.[7] The first is a paper by Thorsten Beck, Asli Demirgüç-Kunt, and Maria Soledad Martinez Peria on the supply of financial services across countries as recorded by regulatory officials worldwide. The next is a paper by Anne-Marie Chidzero, Karen Ellis, and Anjali Kumar that synthesizes recent measures of household financial access undertaken by various World Bank studies and the FinMark Trust in South Africa. The third paper, by Stijn Claessens and Konstantinos Tzioumis, points out some of the difficulties in measuring the financial access of firms. The chapter then looks briefly at additional perspectives on the measurement of financial access, especially in the area of microfinance, and concludes with comments on new directions in the measurement of financial access. Taken together, the efforts described here promise to provide a more complete picture of financial access than has hitherto been possible.

Conceptual Issues: Dimensions of Access

Issues that have challenged the measurement of financial access include, first, the question of the relevance of the distinction between access to financial services and actual use of services. It has been argued that because of voluntary exclusion, access

4. Peachey and Roe (2004) includes data on financial exclusion for developed countries. Barr (2004), Caskey (2002), and Dunham (2001) discuss the "unbanked" and excluded segments of society in the United States; Kempson and Whyley (1999) looks at financial exclusion in the United Kingdom. Caskey, Duran, and Solo (2006) studies the urban unbanked in Mexico and the United States, estimating the percentage of unbanked households in the United States and Mexico at 15 percent and 75 percent respectively.

5. Honohan (2006).

6. World Bank (2006).

7. Beck, Demirgüç-Kunt, and Martinez Peria (2005); Chidzero, Ellis, and Kumar (2006); and Claessens and Tzioumis (2006).

to financial services may be much wider than use.[8] However, it is difficult to measure the proportion of persons who voluntarily exclude themselves because voluntary exclusion is not generally directly observable in surveys of the use of financial services. Measuring use, on the other hand, is a more straightforward proposition.[9] In addition, the concepts of "voluntary" and "involuntary" may be indistinct in practice. For example, voluntary exclusion may include those who lack awareness of the products available or who believe that services are too expensive or that they may not be treated well by formal financial institutions. That is not the same as opting out of using known and affordable services. Similarly, involuntary exclusion may include not only those who have a poor credit history and who would rationally be excluded by informed financial institutions but also those who are irrationally discriminated against because they are perceived to pose greater risk. Difficulties in interpreting voluntary and involuntary exclusion are as relevant to enterprises, especially small enterprises, as to individuals. Because of the difficulties of disentangling such effects, the emerging consensus has been to measure access, in a first approximation, by actual use of services.[10]

A second stumbling block in measuring consumer access has been the issue of access for whom—the individual or the household? While much of the theory and practice regarding household income and expenditures centers on the household as the unit of response, intrahousehold structures are opaque and access cannot be assumed for everyone in a household because any single member has access. If the household is used as the unit, there is a risk of losing valuable demographic data correlating the use of financial services to characteristics such as gender, employment, age, and so forth. Yet household surveys such as budget surveys and income and expenditure surveys are the norm in the collection of other population characteristics and present an attractive opportunity for integrating information on financial access. Moreover, in some cultural situations it may be difficult to extract information directly from individual members of a household, especially female members. In practice, both forms of measures have been used.[11]

8. For example, a study in Brazil showed that 33 percent of those who did not have a bank account claimed to have voluntarily decided not to open one and that 70 percent of those who did not have a loan felt that they had no need for a loan (Kumar 2004).

9. Also discussed in, for example, Stone (2005), Kumar and others (2005b), and Claessens (2006).

10. One caveat in cross-country comparisons is that as societies grow richer, the use of some form of credit becomes widespread, even if not in the traditional form of a loan—for example, through overdraft facilities, lines of credit, and so forth. Thus with development and increased financial depth, the group of voluntarily excluded individuals presumably would shrink.

11. Family-level income and expenditure surveys are frequently the norm—for example, in the United States (Survey of Consumer Finances, Federal Reserve) and the United Kingdom (Family Expenditure

A third conceptual issue concerns the dimension on which financial access is to be measured. At least three broad dimensions could be considered: first, access to or use of the financial services of a particular *type of institution*, such as a bank, credit cooperative, or finance or leasing company, or of an informal entity such as a moneylender. A second alternative would be to measure access in terms of the *type of financial services* offered: access to payments and transactional services, which are probably the most important for consumer use; access to savings products; or access to credit (term transformation).[12] Additional services such as insurance (risk transformation) also could be included. In terms of the access of firms to finance, the spectrum of services would differ: credit would be more important than savings and the distinction between fixed and working capital credit, or between long- and short-term debt, would be useful. A third possible dimension of measurement could be the *type of product*—for example, debit cards, credit cards, life insurance, home mortgages, and so forth. However, these are highly country-specific measures and do not lend themselves to easy cross-country comparison.

Within each dimension, distinctions can be made in terms of *degree of access* (see figure 2-1). For example, at one end of the institutional spectrum are banks or near banks—formal financial institutions that can provide multiple financial services to their clients, including deposits, payments, and credit services. The attributes of banks and near banks are broadly comparable across countries. Other formal financial service providers include all other legal entities licensed to provide financial services. Such providers are registered and subject to some reporting requirements; their functions may be narrower and more specialized than those of banks and may vary across countries in terms of structure, form, and oversight and hence of comparability. Next are informal providers of financial services—other organized providers that are not registered as financial intermediaries and are not subject to oversight. They are likely to vary greatly between countries.[13]

Similar distinctions in degree of access can be drawn in terms of financial services. Savings, for example, can be measured in the simplest terms, such as having a deposit account; more complex savings products would be remunerated savings

---

Survey, Office of National Statistics). In contrast, the Eurobarometer surveys randomly select one individual per household, using a technique similar to that used by FinMark Trust of South Africa, discussed later in this chapter. The World Bank's Living Standards Measurement Surveys have used household surveys with specific questions addressed to all reporting members.

12. Also referred to as a functional basis for measuring financial access. The use of such a functional framework has been discussed, for example, in Ross Levine (1997). World Bank surveys using this broad construct include those in Brazil in 2002, as detailed in Kumar (2004); in India (Basu and Srivastava 2005); in Mexico (Caskey, Duran, and Solo 2006); and in Colombia (Solo 2005).

13. Described with definitions in Kumar and others (2005b).

Figure 2-1. *Degree of Financial Access, by Sector*

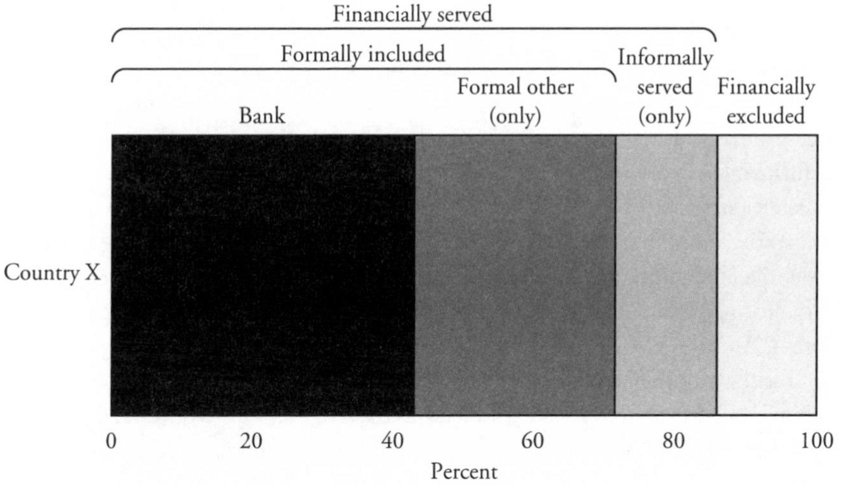

Source: Kumar and others (2005b).

accounts, fixed deposits, or sophisticated savings or investment instruments such as mutual funds, stocks, and bonds.

Once the dimension of measurement and the degree of differentiation or sophistication of the selected measures of financial access are chosen, one must determine whether data are to be collected from the perspective of the providers or the users of financial services. Provider (or supply side) data could include regulatory agency surveys or financial institution data on parameters such as the number of accounts maintained, number of clients, number of branches, regulatory requirements, and so forth. An alternative for measuring access is to question prospective users—firms/enterprises or individuals/households. Firm or household data usually require survey-based methods. Some information on firms also can be obtained by using information from business registrars, licensing authorities, or firms' annual reports or financial statements. Household surveys on financial access can be undertaken either as a part of an ongoing household survey or as a specialized survey on financial access.

There remains the issue that access to finance is multidimensional in nature. Generally, access to finance commonly refers to the availability of quality financial services at reasonable cost. However, the measurement of access to finance needs to take into account how one defines "quality" and "reasonable." Measurement of financial access is also influenced by the definition and priority of the various dimensions of access. For instance, one can distinguish the dimensions of reliability, convenience, continuity, and flexibility, with each requiring a different measure.

Especially in rural areas or for small entrepreneurs and small-scale businesses, financial access for the firm and household may be hard to distinguish, implying an overlap. Similarly, overlap between the household and the individual occurs if access for the entire household is channeled through one individual. A full picture of financial access could therefore involve each of these units of analysis and their possible combinations.[14]

Practical considerations also can drive data collection. Data tend to be relatively easier to collect from formal sources. But the poor are largely served by semiformal and informal institutions, and information for such institutions is more difficult to obtain. And there is a need for standardized or at least harmonized access indicators to allow for benchmarking and comparing data. A first core set of indicators of financial access was developed, for household surveys, at the World Bank in 2005, providing a standardized set of concepts to serve as a template for individual survey and data collection efforts in different countries.[15]

Determinants of access, whether for households or for firms, ultimately depend on both demand and supply side variables. The constraint of partial measures is that it is difficult to separate supply and demand effects. Most indicators used are partial; however, if their limitations are recognized, that should not impede the development of many useful alternatives to the "perfect" indicator.

Supply Side Measures of Access: Regulators and Financial Institutions

The first paper presented at this session of the conference, "Reaching Out: Access to and Use of Banking Services across Countries," reflected a major effort to collect and standardize supply side information on financial access through surveys of financial regulators.[16] While such surveys had been undertaken before, in the context of investigations of financial access in individual countries, the present paper represents the first effort to use regulator data to compare financial access across countries.[17] The financial research team of the World Bank collected information on banking sector outreach from bank regulatory agencies for some ninety-nine

---

14. Financial access measurement for households and individuals also can focus on special subsets of the population (for example, ethnic communities), rather than on the population as a whole. See, for example, Dunham (2001) and Townsend (1997).

15. Kumar and others (2005b).

16. Beck, Demirgüç-Kunt, and Martinez Peria (2005).

17. Kumar (2004) collects information from the Central Bank of Brazil on the parameters described.

Table 2-1. *Indicators of Banking Sector Outreach*

	Indicator	Definition
1	Geographic branch penetration	Number of bank branches per 1,000 kilometers
2	Demographic branch penetration	Number of bank branches per 100,000 people
3	Geographic ATM penetration	Number of bank ATMs per 1,000 kilometers
4	Demographic ATM penetration	Number of bank ATMs per 100,000 people
5	Loan accounts per capita	Number of loans per 1,000 people
6	Loan-income ratio	Average size of loans to GDP per capita
7	Deposit accounts per capita	Number of deposits per 1,000 people
8	Deposit-income ratio	Average size of deposits to GDP per capita

Source: Beck, Demirgüç-Kunt, and Martinez Peria (2005).

countries.[18] Through those surveys, data were assembled on branch and ATM penetration and on the number of deposit and loan accounts and their average size with respect to income. Those data have been used to develop a consistent set of cross-country indicators of banking sector outreach.

Indicators are constructed at two levels: first, access to and the possibility of use of financial services based on availability of banking outlets relative to population and geography, and second, actual use of financial services based on numbers of loan and deposit accounts and their average size relative to income per capita. Higher numbers of loan and deposit accounts indicate greater use of deposit and credit services by a larger population, while lower average loan and deposit sizes relative to GDP per capita indicate greater use of deposit and credit services by smaller clients.

The set of financial sector outreach indicators developed are presented in table 2-1. Indicators 1 through 4 measure the outreach of the financial sector as indicated by access to banks' physical outlets. Indicators 5 through 8 measure loans and deposits.

Going beyond the construction of such ratios, the paper finds that loan and deposit indicators are good predictors of the share of households with bank accounts and the share of small firms with bank loans. Geographic access to banking services is positively related to population density. And by linking the new outreach indicators to firms' reported financing obstacles, the paper observes that firms in countries with higher branch and ATM penetration and with more extensive use of loans report lower financing obstacles.[19]

18. Beck, Demirgüç-Kunt, and Martinez Peria (2005).
19. Using data from the World Business Environment Survey (1999–2000), which covers 10,000 firms in eighty-one countries and includes questions on firms' perceived obstacles to growth.

Results in terms of geographic and demographic penetration show large differences in access and use across countries. For example, the number of branches varies from barely one-tenth of a bank per 1,000 square kilometers for countries in the poorer African and Latin American countries (Namibia, Guyana, and Bolivia) to more than 300 for some sophisticated island economies such as those of Malta and Singapore, which enjoy more than 600 branches per 1,000 square kilometers. When branch presence is compared with population densities, findings range from less than one bank branch per 100,000 persons (Ethiopia, Uganda, and Madagascar) to fifty or more in Portugal and Spain.

Similar ratios are constructed for the number of ATMs per 1,000 square kilometers. A striking general finding is that the range of variation in access per capita is much greater than for income per capita. For example, Singapore's per capita GDP is twelve times higher than that of Namibia while its geographic branch penetration is more than 5,000 times higher. And South Korea's per capita income is more than fourteen times that of Nepal, but its geographic ATM penetration is more than 2,900 times greater.

Use indicators in the paper cover the number of deposit and loan accounts per 1,000 persons, which vary from as low as fourteen deposit accounts and just four loan accounts per 1,000 persons (Madagascar) to thousands for deposit accounts and hundreds for loan accounts in developed countries. Average deposit size is eight times GDP per capita in Zimbabwe, and average loan size is twenty-eight times GDP per capita in Bolivia, whereas the corresponding figures are equal to or less than GDP per capita in more developed countries. The authors suggest that these services are more affordable for poorer individuals and smaller firms in developed countries than they are in developing countries. Efforts to measure access have been further extended by the same team to encompass data collected from financial institutions themselves, which have been used to identify barriers to banking. This later work—Beck, Demirgüç-Kunt, and Martinez Peria (2006)—is valuable in understanding access to finance from the supply side. It is based on information on 193 banks from eighty-eight countries, constructed from a web-based survey sent to the five most important banks in each country.

Results were reported for countries in which information was obtained from banks that constituted at least 30 percent of the market in terms of total loans/total deposits or in which a response from the largest bank was received.[20] The bank surveys include questions on the costs (fees, minimum requirements, paperwork, documentation, and so forth) of opening and maintaining different types of accounts,

20. In practice, nonreporting of information has led to a substantial reduction in the numbers of banks and countries covered.

interest rates for the accounts, loan application procedures and documentation, interest rates and fees on different types of loans, costs associated with different payment services, and factors influencing credit and collateral decisions.

The indicators document the extent of barriers to the three types of banking services investigated (deposits, loans, and payments), across three dimensions (physical access, affordability, and eligibility). Physical access refers to number and convenience of points of service delivery. Affordability refers to the costs associated with the use of financial services, such as minimum balances or fees paid to open an account or obtain a loan. Eligibility refers to the requirements for obtaining services, such as documentation (for example, identification card, wage slip, or proof of residence). These three dimensions become especially important when access is measured.

High fees, high minimum balances, and strict documentation requirements can make financial products unaffordable for a large section of the population, while less convenient service delivery mechanisms and long loan application waiting times may lead potential clients to seek alternative financial service providers.[21] The authors examine the bank- and country-level factors explaining variation in indicators of bank barriers. They find that bank size and the availability of physical infrastructure are the most robust predictors of barriers and that banks in more economically and financially developed economies impose lower barriers. The authors' second work includes some interesting findings. For example, the majority of banks require clients to visit their headquarters to open a deposit account. In some poor countries, the minimum balance to open a checking account can exceed 50 percent to 100 percent of per capita income. Although the minimum balance requirement is zero for nineteen countries, it is one-third to one-half of per capita income in some African countries, and there seems to be a negative correlation between per capita income and minimum balance. Similarly, fees associated with maintaining a deposit account can be high in some poor countries, especially in Africa; however, other poor countries, such as India and Bangladesh, have no such fees. Documentation requirements also vary greatly, from a single piece of identification to multiple documents.

Together, these papers (Beck, Demirgüç-Kunt, and Martinez Peria 2005 and 2006) represent perhaps the most important standardized cross-country contributions to date measuring the supply of financial services. As in all research, there are limitations, especially with regard to getting adequate response rates. Such limitations should serve as a spur to extend these efforts and possibly use them to establish an ongoing database of comparisons.

21. Values for these indicators can be found in Beck, Demirgüç-Kunt, and Martinez Peria (2006).

Users' Perspectives: Individual and Household Access to Finance

A core limitation of supply side data for estimating access to financial services for individuals or households is the inability of the data to address the nature of the individuals who are the actual users of the services. The presence of branch banks in a given neighborhood does not say much about the clients who use the branches, and greater branch density need not imply that banking services are available to the poor. Apart from the lack of knowledge on the income or poverty level of users of financial services, other socioeconomic correlates of users also are unknown, and they may be critical determinants of financial access.[22] Another intrinsic limitation of supply side data is that the data necessarily focus on formal, regulated providers of financial services, about which regulators can offer information, whereas individuals and households use a broad spectrum of informal and semiformal sources, especially in developing countries.

New efforts based on surveys of individuals or households have been launched since 2002 in a series of countries to examine the actual use of financial services and the socioeconomic correlates of the users. The advantages of that approach are not only that it enables the correlation of information on the income, education, employment, and gender of the user but also that it captures the proportion of people who are excluded from formal financial services or all services, whether voluntarily or involuntarily.

A series of such specialized surveys on financial access were conducted by the World Bank in Brazil, India, Colombia, and Mexico during 2002–04, and several more are under way.[23] The U.K. Department for International Development (DFID) has supported surveys that are similar in many ways to the World Bank surveys through its establishment of the FinMark Trust in South Africa, an independent institution dedicated to measuring financial access through its FinScope surveys. DFID/FinMark have conducted surveys across many southern African countries. The pioneer survey was conducted in South Africa, followed by pilots in Botswana, Lesotho, Swaziland, and Namibia and by full-fledged surveys in Zam-

---

22. As pointed out by John Campbell in his presidential address to the American Economic Association in 2006, in which he showed that individuals' education and literacy level were key determinants of their use of financial services (Campbell 2006). Similar findings were reported in Kumar and others (2005a).

23. Kumar (2004) reports a survey in Brazil that was closely paralleled by studies in Mexico and Colombia (Caskey, Duran, and Solo 2006; Solo 2005) as well as by efforts in India (Basu and Srivastava 2005) and in Nepal (Ferrari, Shrestha, and Jaffrin 2007). New efforts at undertaking specialized surveys of financial access at the World Bank were under way in 2007 in Indonesia. Both the World Bank and FinScope are engaged in a joint survey in Pakistan.

so much research glazed over by de soto.

bia and Uganda. Additional surveys are planned for Tanzania and Ghana, and there is ongoing dialogue concerning other African countries.

There are a number of basic similarities in the approaches adopted by the World Bank and DFID/FinMark. Both have tried to measure present levels of access, using a mix of institutional, service, and product dimensions of financial access. Both have also tried to measure the informally served and the financially excluded, in addition to those served by formal financial institutions. Both try to capture information on obstacles to financial access. However, differences in the actual questions as well as in sampling techniques and scope suggests that results from the different surveys are not strictly comparable. The FinScope surveys place more emphasis on product-level measures, whereas the World Bank exercises have tended to emphasize institutional and functional access. The World Bank approach has not been internally uniform. Some of the World Bank studies, such as those undertaken in India and Nepal, have used the household rather than the individual as the unit of response.

Beginning in 2005, DFID and the World Bank jointly launched a major effort to harmonize the financial access survey work of the World Bank and FinMark Trust. The first part of the harmonization exercise was an agreement on a set of core indicators of financial access to serve as the basis for cross-country data collection. Those indicators are presented in table 2-2. The first three core indicators focus on measures of access in the institutional dimension; they cover access to banks, to all formal financial institutions, and to formal as well as informal financial institutions. The proportion of the population that is financially excluded is estimated as a residue. The next three indicators are functional, looking at payments, savings, and credit services. A final pair of supplementary indicators is added to capture the profile of the bottom quintile and to assess individual and household access.

In late 2005 the World Bank and FinScope, under the sponsorship of DFID, attempted to take the process of harmonization beyond the construction of core indicators to prepare a jointly agreed core questionnaire to be employed in any user-based survey of financial services.[24] Among the innovations of the questionnaire was its combination of questions for individuals and for households. Recognizing the communal nature of much family activity in poorer countries as well as the likelihood of indirect access through a household member, the agencies agreed that focusing on individual access may underestimate total access in a population.

24. Substantial progress was achieved with the standardization of the questionnaire, although standardized algorithms for the extraction of core indicators were not prepared.

Table 2-2. *Definitions of Core Indicators*

Indicator	Description
Institutional dimension	
A1	Percentage of total adult population with a bank account
A2	Percentage of total adult population that uses the services of any formal financial institution
A3	Percentage of total adult population that uses any formal or informal financial institution or both
Functional (service) dimension	
A4	Payments: percentage of adults receiving money regularly through formal financial instruments
A5	Savings: percentage of adults who keep money in formal financial instruments that allow them to safeguard and accumulate money, whether through transaction accounts, savings accounts, time deposits/CDs, bonds, stocks, funds, voluntary pension plans, and so forth
A6	Loans: percentage of adults who have outstanding or have obtained a loan or credit facility from a formal financial institution now or over the past twelve months
Supplementary indicators	
S1	Percentage of adult population in the bottom income quintile (based on the sample) that uses the services of any formal financial institution divided by the total adult population in that quintile, as a percentage
S2	Percentage of adult population formally served either directly or indirectly through another household member

Source: Kumar and others (2005b).

In the new survey instrument, a household representative, such as the head of household, is interviewed first and a randomly selected individual respondent within the household is interviewed next. This hybrid approach is being field-tested in Ghana, in conjunction with a randomized sampling initiative, to assess whether it adds any value to the process.[25]

It is possible to extract broadly comparable results on core indicators based on the definitions prescribed above even if a standardized core instrument is not used. Results from a selection of existing studies that span three countries in Latin America and four in Africa are presented in table 2-3, which is based on "Indicators of Access to Finance through Household-Level Surveys: Comparisons of Data from

---

25. Ronchi (2006). The Ghana experiment is being undertaken by Robert Cull and Kinnon Scott of the Research Department at the World Bank.

Six Countries," the paper written by Chidzero, Ellis, and Kumar for this conference.[26] Adjustments were made, as far as possible, to ensure equivalence in the indicators, despite differences in the underlying questionnaires.[27]

The first indicator (A1) suggests that the three African countries displayed here have more banked people than the Latin American countries shown. However, that may not be surprising, because Namibia and Botswana are closely associated with South Africa and enjoy relatively higher access to financial services than many other sub-Saharan African countries. Zambia's scores, at less than 15 percent, are strikingly lower than those for all other countries and may be more representative of Africa as a whole.

Within individual countries, results suggest highly variable differences between the formally included (A2) and the banked (A1), illustrating the different degrees of financial diversification across countries. In Brazil, 79.3 percent of adults are formally included and the percentage of the formally included is almost twice as high as that of the banked. Those figures reflect access to correspondent banks in Brazil, notably through outlets at lottery shops, which are permitted to house services that provide banking services (mainly transactions). In Mexico, with its obligatory and voluntary pension funds (AFOREs and SOFOLEs), the percentage of the formally included is more than twice as high as that of the banked. Even in Colombia, the figure for the formally included is approximately 9 percentage points greater than that for the banked. The difference between the banked and the formally included is lower for all the African countries, suggesting that formal services in Africa are heavily bank dominated and that there is lower diversification in financial service provision.

The third indicator, which includes informal finance, suggests that significant informal financial services are available in Mexico, where nearly 80 percent of the population is financially served. Much of that is due to the *cajas solidarias*, the savings clubs and cooperatives, as well as cooperative savings schemes such as the *tandas*. In South Africa, there is an 8 percentage point differential between the formally served and the financially served, suggesting a reasonably strong informal financial system. In contrast, in Namibia the informal system contributes only 2 percentage points to the financially served. These figures suggest some difficulties in capturing scale in informal service provision in certain countries.

The payments indicator on the use of the formal financial system for transactions such as sending or receiving money (A4) suggests that around a quarter of all

---

26. Chidzero, Ellis, and Kumar (2006).

27. For example, in the absence of directly available information on income in some surveys, measures of the bottom quintile were based on alternative proxies of wealth or expenditure.

Table 2-3. *Core Indicators of Financial Access*
Percent

Country	(A1) Banked	(A2) Formally served	(A3) Financially served	(A4) Payments	(A5) Savings	(A6) Loans and credit	(S1) Formally served (bottom quintile)	(S2) Direct and indirect access
Brazil	43.0	79.3	83.8	25.1	39.7	22.5	49.2[a] 43.2[b]	80.7
Colombia	39.2	48.1	50.6	24.1	36.4	6.4	n.a.	67.2
Mexico	23.0	52.0	78.6	20.8	44.1	7.4	16.8[c] 25.1[d]	67.3
South Africa	47.0	55.0	63.0	31.0	29.0	19.0	n.a.	n.a.
Namibia	51.1	53.9	55.8	41.1	51.3	22.7	n.a.	n.a.
Botswana	43.2	49.0	54.0	43.1	51.3	20.6	n.a.	n.a.
Zambia	14.6	22.4	33.7	14.4	21.9	5.5	n.a.	n.a.

Source: Authors' compilation based on Chidzero, Ellis, and Kumar (2006).

a. Quintile measure based on income.
b. Quintile measure based on bedrooms per person.
c. Quintile measure based on income.
d. Quintile measure based on rent.

adults in Brazil and Colombia receive income or remittances through formal finan-cial instruments. Mexico has a somewhat lower score, with a fifth of its population using such instruments.[28] The Latin American figures are much lower than the fig-ures in Namibia and Botswana (41 to 43 percent of the population) and in South Africa (31 percent). The higher percentage for the selected African countries can perhaps be attributed to their higher number of banked people.

Indicator A5 (savings) shows that more than half the population of Namibia and Botswana use financial instruments to safeguard money. Among the Latin American countries, Mexico has the largest number of people using formal saving instruments (44.1 percent), followed by Brazil and Colombia (39.7 percent and 36.4 percent respectively). The higher percent for Mexico could be explained by obligatory savings schemes through its AFOREs accounts.

As may be expected, formal access to loan facilities (indicator A6) is much lower in all countries than access to savings facilities.[29] In Brazil, Namibia, and Botswana, a little more than one-fifth of the population has access to loans and credit facili-ties. Access to formal loans and credit facilities is even lower in Mexico and Colom-bia, at less than 10 percent.

Subindicators also are available for the Latin American countries. The poverty subindicator (S1) shows that even though close to 80 percent of people are formally included in Brazil overall, that proportion falls by almost 30 percentage points when access for the people in the bottom income quintile is considered. When an alternative quintile measure based on bedrooms per person is considered, the num-ber of people formally included in the bottom quintile falls further, to 43.2 percent. In Mexico, where the figure is 52 percent for the country as a whole, less than one-third of persons in the bottom quintile are formally included (16.8 percent).

Data limitations and the paucity of relevant questions may explain the negligi-ble difference, less than 2 percentage points, between indicator A2 and subindica-tor S2 (indirect access) for Brazil. More data were available for Colombia and Mex-ico to construct indicator S2. Access to formal finance increased considerably in Mexico (from 52 percent to 67.3 percent) and in Colombia (from 48.1 percent to 67.2 percent) when household members' access was added as a measure of indirect access to formal financial services.

As mentioned, one limitation of the indicators used is the heterogeneity of the surveys on which they are based. The proposed standardized approach may change

28. Note, however, that more than half of Mexico's population (58 percent) receives income through checks. It is not known how they are cashed or deposited; hence checks are not counted as a formal pay-ment instrument.

29. The percentage of people with savings and loans facilities could be overestimated for African coun-tries as those indicators include informal service providers in A5 and A6.

that. One drawback of the common core instrument, however, is its huge cost of implementation if representative sampling is undertaken in each country. FinMark estimates that costs per survey report could range from $250,000 to $500,000. Undertaking such surveys for cross-country data collection would be expensive. At present such instruments are likely to be used only in individual countries where they clearly add value.

Users' Perspectives: Measuring Firms' Access to Finance

As in the case of consumers and households, knowledge of the degree to which financial services reach firms, small enterprises in particular, has been limited in most countries. A number of different measurement and data collection efforts have attempted to bridge the gaps in information. In the next paper written for this conference, "Measuring Firms' Access to Finance," Claessens and Tzioumis review the advantages and limitations of the existing approaches in measuring access to firms' finance.[30] They point out that both demand and supply side effects need to be addressed to frame public policies to broaden firms' access to finance.

As discussed in the paper, access to finance for firms has been measured either indirectly, by using data from financial statements, or directly, through enterprise surveys. In the first approach, data taken from firms' financial statements are analyzed for sensitivity of investments to the availability of internal funds. Evidence of higher sensitivity is taken as an indication of financing constraints and serves as a measure of financial access. Despite its wide appeal in the financial literature and its firm grounding in economic theory, this approach depends on strong theoretical assumptions and requires accurate and detailed financial statements.[31] Both the theoretical assumptions and the data requirements are difficult to meet in developing countries, where market frictions are severe and data from financial statements tend to be less reliable (because of the weak institutional environment) and less available (because small and medium-size enterprises account for the bulk of firm activity).

Surveys of enterprises provide a direct approach to measuring firms' access to finance. Enterprise surveys have been conducted by multilateral organizations, national statistical agencies, and central banks alike. By and large, while they have begun to fill some gaps on firms' access to finance, further work is required before consistent cross-country data can be obtained. Comprehensive financial access data for firms based on surveys conducted by governments or bilateral donors tend to be

---

30. Claessens and Tzioumis (2006).

31. In evaluating sensitivity, the literature has used either a reduced form q-model or an Euler equation for the capital stock (Schiantarelli 1996). See Claessens and Tzioumis (2006) for technical details.

conducted for one country at a time, in a cross-sectional fashion. Given their unco-ordinated execution by various governments and organizations and their differing concepts and definitions, merging these ad-hoc exercises into one multicountry dataset becomes difficult.

A number of surveys have been undertaken of firms in developing and transition countries to gauge their perspective on access to finance. The efforts range from including financial access questions for firms in wider household surveys to design-ing financial access survey instruments specifically for firms. In the first instance, questions aimed at firms or enterprises have been sporadically included in house-hold surveys across countries, including in the World Bank Living Standards Mea-surement Survey (LSMS). There has been some effort to bring the data together in one dataset, the Microdata for Financial Studies (MFS).[32] While most of the finan-cial access data collated by the MFS concern household access, data on a number of variables also have been collected for firms' access, mainly on sources and uses of loans. Even those limited variables, however, were collected only for a subset of countries.

While such efforts are valuable, there is clearly a need for enterprise surveys that are more specifically tailored to gather information on firms' finance across a large number of countries. The World Bank has been instrumental in that regard by developing in recent years several enterprise surveys specifically designed to measure financial access. While some of them have been limited to certain regions, others have wider coverage, namely the World Business Environment Survey (WBES), the Investment Climate Assessments (ICAs), and the Rural Investment Climate Sur-veys (RICS).[33] Each instrument surveys firms across multiple regions and explores questions of financial access. The surveys provide information on firms' perception of the degree to which access to and the cost of finance are obstacles to their oper-ations and growth. In that way, firms' financing obstacles can be measured directly, thus avoiding the use of financial statements to estimate financing constraints. (See table 2-4, based on data from the WBES and the ICA surveys.)

These World Bank surveys have been used extensively to identify the dimen-sions that affect firms' access to finance. For example, cross-country regression results have shown that access to finance tends to be the most binding constraint to firm growth in the overall business environment[34] and that the smallest firms are the most constrained.[35] Similarly, Kumar and others (2007) finds that in Middle

32. Gasparini and others (2005).
33. For example, the Business Environment and Enterprise Performance Survey—or BEEPS—collects data for eastern European countries only.
34. Ayyagari, Demirgüç-Kunt, and Maksimovic (2006).
35. Kumar and Francisco (2005); Beck, Demirgüç-Kunt, and Maksimovic (2005).

Table 2-4. *Data on Financing Obstacles and Collateral Practices in Developing and Transition Countries*

Financing is a major obstacle (percent of firms)[a]		Collateral required (as a percent of the loan made)		Loans requiring collateral (as a percent of all loans made)	
Top 5					
Tunisia	0.0	Pakistan	69.5	Slovenia	58.7
Namibia	1.7	China	80.8	South Africa	61.1
Egypt	10.8	Thailand	87.0	Cambodia	61.5
Slovenia	11.0	Bangladesh	92.5	Ethiopia	62.0
Cambodia	13.0	India	94.0	China	66.9
Median	38.5	Median	141.9	Median	86.1
Bottom 5					
Belarus	62.5	Bosnia and	196.4	Georgia	93.6
Moldova	64.4	Herzegovina		Bosnia and	95.9
Kyrgyz Republic	66.7	Nicaragua	204.0	Herzegovina	
Haiti	74.4	Syrian Arab	206.7	Macedonia	96.6
China	75.0	Republic		Albania	96.8
		Morocco	226.2	Morocco	98.9
		Zambia	311.3		

Source: Claessens and Tzioumis (2006).

a. For the calculations using WBES, firms with state or foreign ownership were excluded because they probably enjoyed preferential access to finance.

East and North African countries, younger, domestic, and exporting firms report higher finance-related obstacles to their growth and operations.

Nevertheless, when surveying firms themselves on their ease of access to finance, one has to be cautious regarding endogeneity issues and definition ambiguity. Dependent and independent variables in empirical analyses using data from survey responses often share a common parameter that is omitted in the survey and that usually is the result of self-selection. Also, the cross-sectional nature of most surveys does not allow tackling any simultaneity bias between survey responses that are used as dependent and independent variables. Specifically, better firms may not complain about their access to finance while worse firms do. Therefore complaints about access to finance cannot be used directly as an independent variable to predict firms' performance as a dependent variable. In addition, as pointed out previously, there are conceptual issues in defining access, which is a "bundle" of attributes. And the difficulties of separating access and use remain.

Given the importance of the institutional environment and financial development in firms' access to finance, the World Bank also has developed two indicator projects: doing business indicators and financial sector development indicators. The doing business indicators offer institutional information for a large number of countries regarding business regulations and their enforcement, as well as other relevant measures of the institutional environment. In a similar fashion, the financial sector development indicators (FSDI) provide a framework for assessing financial systems comprehensively by assessing the level of financial development in each country across various dimensions such as size, efficiency, and stability of the banking sector and capital markets. Corporate data also available from FSDI could be used in assessing corporate vulnerability, which may worsen firms' access to finance. The supply side of financing becomes more relevant when one examines firms' access to finance, which is more dependent on the level of financial development than is household access. For instance, using data from FSDI, Claessens and Tzioumis show that countries' corporate sector financing constraints (as measured by the median Kaplan-Zingales index across nonfinancial listed firms) and the share of informal financing (as reported by firms participating in the World Bank ICAs) are negatively related to countries' financial depth (see figures 2-2 and 2-3). That relation suggests that, while financial depth is not a perfect or sufficient measure, it does shed some light on the ease of access to finance.

Despite such efforts, there is room for improvement in research and data collection pertaining to firms' access to finance. Developing a conceptual framework to provide a sound foundation for benchmarking and coordinating data collection efforts is essential to identifying the demand- and supply-driven constraints to accessing financial services, designing appropriate interventions to improve access, and facilitating cross-country comparisons. Other approaches to improving our measurement and knowledge of firms' access to finance should include extending enterprise surveys to underrepresented regions like the Middle East and Africa.[36] An increase in both the scope and quantity of variables also is desirable. For example, extending the data to variables that include insurance, leasing, e-finance, and others would open new avenues of research. Finally, by using data from finance providers, one could analyze the process and timeline of firms' financing and examine the effect of institutional aspects of firms' financing on postcontractual behavior of firms receiving finance.[37]

---

36. A recent study on access to finance for firms in the Middle East region merges data from the Investment Climate Assessments with financial system data from the FSDI project and macro data (Kumar and others 2007). ICA data are available on only nine of the seventeen regional countries.

37. See studies undertaken in the field of consumer finance using contract data from credit providers (Karlan and Zinman 2005).

Figure 2-2. *Financial Depth and Financing Constraints*[a]

Kaplan-Zingales index

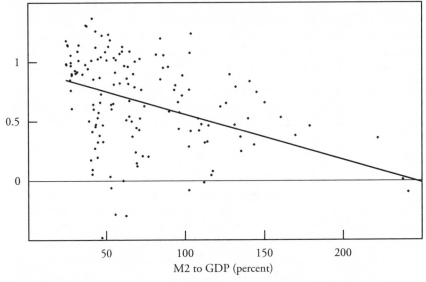

M2 to GDP (percent)

Source: World Bank, Financial Sector Development Indicators, various years.
a. Sample: thirty countries during the period 2000–04.

Other Measures of Financial Access: Microfinance Databases

Microfinance has gained a reputation as an effective tool for expanding financial access for the so-called "unbankables," and some recent measures of financial access have focused on that institutional segment. As a result of the increased interest in the topic, several data sources have recently been established that offer rich insights on microfinance activity around the world.

The Consultative Group to Assist the Poor (CGAP) has developed a database on microfinance that accounts for 148 countries covering many institutional types (for example, microfinance institutions, credit unions, credit cooperatives, postal savings banks, and commercial banks).[38] Nevertheless, as with earlier data collection attempts already described, the CGAP database cannot distinguish between numbers of clients and numbers of accounts.[39] Because some clients may have mul-

38. Christen, Rosenberg, and Jayadeva (2004).
39. A difficulty also faced by Beck, Demirgüç-Kunt, and Martinez Peria 2005, described above.

Figure 2-3. *Financial Depth and Informal Finance*[a]

Informal finance for investment (percent)

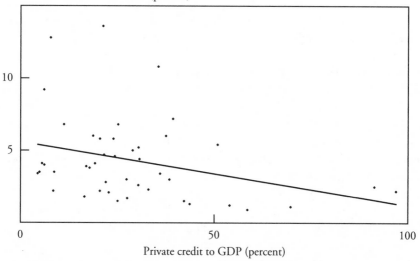

Private credit to GDP (percent)

Source: World Bank, Financial Sector Development Indicators and Investment Climate Assessments, 2004.
a. Sample: Forty-four developing and transition countries in 2004.

tiple accounts and some may have inactive accounts, the number of active clients could be less than the number of accounts. And some clients with savings accounts may have separate loan accounts. CGAP attempts to recognize the latter by netting out borrowers and lenders. Thus, for institutions reporting both savings and loan accounts, it counts only the larger number in the combined dataset. Although that procedure eliminates double counting of those who have a savings and a loan account with the same institution, it does not compensate for clients who have accounts in more than one institution, clients with multiple savings accounts in a single institution, or those with inactive savings accounts. Recently, the CGAP database has been enriched by Stephen Peachey of the World Savings Banks Institute with added data from savings banks that are members of the World Savings Banks Institute. That addition has increased the coverage of the CGAP database, especially in large countries like China and Russia.

Increasing numbers of microfinance institutions (MFIs) are reporting their performance to various international databases. Three popular databases include the Microcredit Summit database (MCS), which contains information from 2,153 reporting microfinance institutions on their number of borrowers, number of poorest borrowers, and profitability. Second, there is the Microfinance Information eXchange (MIX) database, established by the United Nations Conference on Trade and Development (UNCTAD) and CGAP, which currently contains information from 872 MFIs on financial and performance-related variables. Third, there is the MicroBanking Bulletin database (MBB), which contains information on 346 MFIs tracking a full range of financial indicators and information. These three databases have recently been combined into a single database that includes 2,600 MFIs serving approximately 94 million borrowers, after double counting has been eliminated.[40]

Gonzalez and Rosenberg analyze this extended version of the MIX database to examine the state of microfinance in terms of outreach, profitability, and client poverty. Microfinance predominates in Asia, but the Middle East, North Africa, Central Asia, and eastern Europe have relatively little microfinance. Governments continue to be the major providers of microcredit, followed by self-help groups and nongovernmental organizations. Private licensed banks and financial companies served approximately one in six microcredit clients in 2004.[41]

Finally, there has been a noteworthy attempt through the Central Bank of West African States (BCEAO) to create a microfinance database of the eight countries in the West African Economic and Monetary Union (WAEMU), which share a common currency. For each WAEMU country, the BCEAO has maintained over the past decade a database on formal microfinance institutions that contains a periodic qualitative assessment of the microfinance subsector as well as time series data on nineteen key indicators of microfinance performance and outreach.[42] While the BCEAO and other regulator data necessarily concentrate more on formal MFIs, other data collection efforts attempt to encompass informal providers as well. For example, the so-called "financial diaries" data of Stuart Rutherford offer an anthropological approach toward the detailed recording of the financial transactions undertaken by the very poor in South Asia.[43]

New Directions and Next Steps

It is worth mentioning some more recent attempts to measure access, such as Honohan's effort to combine information from different sources, both regulators and financial institutions, to develop a synthetic access indicator. Honohan observes that the data on bank account numbers and on average bank account size as a pro-

---

40. See Gonzalez and Rosenberg (2006).
41. Their paper is discussed in greater detail in chapter 5 of this volume.
42. These microfinance data are available at the BCEAO website (www.bceao.int/internet/bcweb.nsf).
43. Rutherford (2000).

portion of GDP are closely correlated with household survey data on the proportion of households with a bank account.[44] Using this method, based on "synthetic" access percentages, he develops a "composite" indicator for more than 150 countries. Scandinavian countries; western European countries such as the United Kingdom, Germany, and France; and the United States have higher values of the composite indicator than developing countries, ranging from a low of 91 percent for the United Kingdom and the United States to a high of 100 percent for the Netherlands. Not surprisingly, developing countries lag far behind, with access percentages in single digits for Armenia, Papua New Guinea, Nicaragua, Tanzania, and the Kyrgyz Republic.

Using the new database, the author examines whether financial access reduces poverty. He finds that access is negatively correlated with poverty rates but that the correlation is not robust. When per capita income is included in the regression, the results lose significance. While this is a useful construct in the absence of better cross-country data, it is limited in terms of the number of variables on which it provides information and its methodology is not easy to extend.

To summarize the findings discussed above, the new millennium has seen a radical change in the way in which financial systems are perceived. Size, depth, and stability are not the only criteria by which financial systems are evaluated; outreach and access are now recognized to be as important. Although there have been huge new efforts to collect data on financial access using a number of different techniques, current data collection efforts provide an imperfect and incomplete yardstick for policymakers to use to monitor progress in expanding access. That is due first of all to limitations of coverage in terms of supply side indicators and also to the difficulty in constructing sufficiently standardized demand side indicators across a wide spectrum of countries. Although survey-based approaches are growing in popularity, they have not achieved the standardization and annual repetition necessary for serious benchmarking.

New indicators on access to finance are being contemplated at the World Bank, with support from its partners in development. Proposals presently under discussion would build on and combine current supply side indicators, using information from regulators, industry associations, and financial services providers. Those would be augmented on the demand side by information compiled on users of different profiles, representing, for example, the "average" person of a given country or a poor person from the bottom quintile. Alternative profiles presented to a financial institution also could include a male or a female household head. That would enable the compilation of some demand side information with information from

44. See Honohan (2006) for technical details.

providers, thus simulating (at relatively low cost) information that could be gathered from household surveys.

Those concepts, however, are still in the design phase. Should such ventures prove to be successful, clearly there will be demand for their output. Meanwhile the search for better and more comprehensive measures of financial access and financial exclusion will continue.

References

Ayyagari, M., A. Demirgüç-Kunt, and V. Maksimovic. 2006. "How Important Are Financing Constraints? The Role of Finance in the Business Environment." World Bank Policy Research Working Paper WPS3820. Washington: World Bank.

Barr, Michael. 2004. "Banking the Poor: Policies to Bring Low-Income Americans into the Financial Mainstream." Brookings Institution Research Brief.

Basu, P., and P. Srivastava. 2005. "Scaling-up Microfinance for India's Rural Poor." World Bank Policy Research Working Paper 3646. Washington: World Bank.

Beck, T., A. Demirgüç-Kunt, and R. Levine. 2004. "Finance, Inequality, and Poverty: Cross-Country Evidence." World Bank Policy Research Working Paper 3338. Washington: World Bank.

Beck, T., A. Demirgüç-Kunt, and V. Maksimovic. 2005. "Financial and Legal Constraints to Growth: Does Firm Size Matter?" *Journal of Finance* 60, no. 1: 137–77.

Beck, T., A. Demirgüç-Kunt, and S. Martinez Peria. 2005. "Reaching Out: Access to and Use of Banking Services across Countries." World Bank Policy Research Working Paper 3754. Washington: World Bank.

———. 2006. "Banking Services for Everyone? Barriers to Bank Access around the World." World Bank Policy Research Working Paper 4079. Washington: World Bank.

Beck, T., and R. Levine. 2004. "Stock Markets, Banks, and Growth: Panel Evidence." *Journal of Banking and Finance* 28, no. 3: 423–42.

Beegle, K., R. H. Dehejia, and R. Gatti. 2003. "Child Labor, Income Shocks, and Access to Credit." World Bank Policy Research Working Paper 3075. Washington: World Bank.

Campbell, J. Y. 2006. "Household Finance." *Journal of Finance* 61, no. 4: 1553–1604.

Caskey, John P. 2002. "Bringing Unbanked Households into the Banking System." Capital Xchange Series. Brookings.

Caskey, J., C. Duran, and T. Solo. 2006. "The Urban Unbanked in Mexico and the United States." World Bank Policy Research Working Paper 3835. Washington: World Bank.

Chidzero, Anne-Marie, K. Ellis, and A. Kumar. 2006. "Indicators of Access to Finance through Household-Level Surveys: Comparisons of Data from Six Countries." Paper prepared for "Access to Finance: Building Inclusive Financial Systems." Brookings Institution and World Bank, Washington, May 30–31.

Christen, R. P., R. Rosenberg, and V. Jayadeva. 2004. "Financial Institutions with a Double Bottom Line: Implications for the Future of Microfinance." CGAP Occasional Paper 8. Washington: CGAP.

Claessens, S. 2006. "Access to Financial Services: A Review of the Issues and Public Policy Objectives." *World Bank Research Observer* (August).

Claessens, S., and K. Tzioumis. 2006. "Measuring Firms' Access to Finance." Paper prepared for "Access to Finance: Building Inclusive Financial Systems." Brookings Institution and World Bank, Washington, May 30–31.

Dunham, C. R. 2001. "The Role of Banks and Nonbanks in Serving Low- and Moderate-Income Communities." In *Changing Financial Markets and Community Development,* edited by J. L. Blanton, S. L. Rhine, and A. Williams, pp. 31–58. Federal Reserve Bank of Richmond.

Ferrari, A., S. R. Shrestha, and G. Jaffrin. 2007. "Access to Financial Services in Nepal." Directions in Development Series. Washington: World Bank.

Gasparini, L., and others. 2005. "Finance and Credit Variables in Household Surveys of Developing Countries." Washington: World Bank

Gonzalez, A., and R. Rosenberg. 2006. "The State of Microfinance: Outreach, Profitability, and Poverty: Findings from a Database of 2,600 Microfinance Institutions." Paper prepared for "Access to Finance: Building Inclusive Financial Systems." Brookings Institution and World Bank, Washington, May 30–31.

Honohan, P. 2004. "Financial Development, Growth, and Poverty: How Close Are the Links?" In *Financial Development and Economic Growth: Explaining the Links,* edited by C. Goodhard. London: Palgrave Macmillan.

———. 2006. "Household Financial Assets in the Process of Development." World Bank Policy Research Working Paper 3965. Washington: World Bank.

Karlan, D. S., and J. Zinman. 2005. "Observing Unobservables: Identifying Information Asymmetries with a Consumer Credit Field Experiment." Princeton University Working Paper.

Kempson, E., and C. Whyley. 1999. "Kept Out or Opted Out? Understanding and Combating Financial Exclusion." Bristol, U.K.: Policy Press.

King, R. G., and R. Levine. 1993. "Finance and Growth: Schumpeter Might Be Right." *Quarterly Journal of Economics* 108, no. 3: 717–38.

Kumar, A. 2004. "Access to Financial Services in Brazil." Directions in Development Series. Washington: World Bank.

Kumar, A., and M. Francisco. 2005. "Enterprise Size, Financing Patterns, and Credit Constraints in Brazil: Analysis of Data from the Investment Climate Assessment Survey." World Bank Working Paper 49. Washington: World Bank.

Kumar, Anjali, and others. 2005a. "Assessing Financial Access in Brazil." World Bank Working Paper 50. Washington: World Bank.

Kumar, Anjali, and others. 2005b. "Indicators of Financial Access: Household-Level Surveys." Policy Note. Washington: World Bank.

Kumar, A., and others. 2007. "Access to Firm Finance in Middle East and North African Countries." Washington: World Bank.

Levine, Ross. 1997. "Financial Development and Economic Growth: Views and Agenda." *Journal of Economic Literature* 35, no. 2: 688–726.

Levine, R., N. Loayza, and T. Beck. 2000. "Financial Intermediation and Growth: Causality and Causes." *Journal of Monetary Economics* 46, no. 1: 31–77.

Peachey, Stephen, and Alan Roe. 2004. "Access to Finance: A Study for the World Savings Banks Institute." Brussels: Oxford Policy Management.

Ronchi, L. 2006. "Measuring Access to Finance: Options for Survey Format and Approach." Background Note 2. Washington: World Bank.

Rutherford, S. 2000. *The Poor and Their Money.* Delhi: Oxford University Press.

Schiantarelli, F. 1996. "Financial Constraints and Investment: Methodological Issues and International Evidence." *Oxford Review of Economic Policy* 12, no. 2: 70–89.

Solo, T. 2005. "Financial Exclusion: A New Angle to Urban Poverty in Latin America." "En breve" Note. Latin America and the Caribbean Regional Office. Washington: World Bank.

Stone, R. 2005. "Financial Access Indicators Stocktake." London: DFID.

Townsend, R. 1997. "Formal and Informal Financial Services." In *Financial Access in the 21st Century: Proceedings of a Forum,* pp. 17–23. Washington: Office of the Comptroller of the Currency, U.S. Department of the Treasury.

World Bank. 2006. "Better Data Needed for Policy Research on Access to Financial Services." Washington: World Bank Finance Research (February 22) (http://econ.worldbank.org/WBSITE/EXTERNAL/EXTDEC/EXTRESEARCH/0,,contentMDK:20819859~pagePK:64165401~piPK:64165026~theSitePK:469382,00.html [June 1, 2007]).

XAVIER GINE 3

Why Does Access Matter?
Impact on Growth
and Poverty

THE EFFICIENCY WITH which financial markets and institutions overcome market frictions depends on the macroeconomic environment, market structure, and overall contractual and informational environment. Market frictions, namely transaction costs, agency problems, and uncertainty, are the key reason why institutions and organizations exist;[1] institutions offer financial contracts that take those frictions into consideration. In the case of credit, for example, lenders solve the problem of asymmetric information by resorting to different mechanisms, such as reducing the loan amount (credit rationing) and requiring collateral (for signaling and monitoring purposes) and certain types of information (for risk assessment).

The basic services offered by financial institutions typically are categorized into savings, credit, insurance, and payment services. Payment services reduce transaction costs in the exchange of goods and services between people and over time. Savings and credit allow efficient use of capital by delinking consumption from investment decisions. Insurance contracts allow households to hedge and diversify risks and smooth consumption.[2]

There exists a large variation across countries in the extent to which financial services are used. For example, while the percentage of households with a bank

1. North (1990).
2. See Levine (1997, 2006) for an overview.

33

deposit account reaches more than 90 percent in most high-income countries, in many low-income countries bank accounts still are restricted to a small number of firms and households.[3]

However, as Beck and de la Torre (2007) reminds us, low use of financial services need not imply a problem of access. On the demand side, potential users may have access to financial services but may decide not to use them. In that case, it would be inappropriate to argue that voluntary self-exclusion constitutes an access problem. On the supply side, creditors that cannot diversify risks properly or that face major difficulties in mitigating informational asymmetries and contract enforcement may decide to deny loans to certain borrowers—a prudent decision from the creditor's perspective. Whether this situation constitutes a problem of access also is debatable. In fact, if lenders made loans to certain borrowers under such circumstances, the whole financial system could be jeopardized, as many banking crises illustrate. The main point is that observed use of and restricted access to financial services creates the equilibrium that results from rational agents maximizing their utility and profit functions subject to the constraints imposed by existing market frictions.

Yet lack of access to financial services is a major concern for policymakers in developing countries. Implicit in their argument is the assumption that government intervention can alleviate some of the market frictions and propel the economy to a better equilibrium. A large theoretical and empirical literature lends supports to that assumption. Gine and Townsend (2004), for example, takes the model in the working-paper version of Lloyd-Ellis and Bernhardt (2000) and adds a sector with a perfectly functioning financial market to show that much of the growth that Thailand experienced from 1976 until 1996 can be explained by the expansion of the added sector, which mimicked the increase that occurred in Thailand during that period.[4]

This chapter gives an overview of the papers presented in the second session, "Why Does Access Matter? Impact on Growth and Poverty," of the 2006 conference on access to finance sponsored by the World Bank and the Brookings Institution. The first paper, Beck, Demirgüç-Kunt, and Levine (2006), employs a cross-country analysis to show that access to financial services does have a positive impact on growth and poverty alleviation. However, as the discussant Mark Schreiner put it, the paper is silent about the mechanisms by which growth and poverty alleviation are achieved. The rest of this chapter is devoted to exploring

3. Beck, Demirgüç-Kunt, and Martinez Peria (2007).
4. Other theoretical papers include, for example, Banerjee and Newman (1993) and Galor and Zeira (1993). Empirical papers include Rajan and Zingales (1998), Demirgüç-Kunt and Maksimovic (1998), and Beck, Levine, and Loayza (2000).

that topic. Early government efforts to improve access, which performed poorly, are reviewed first; attention then is turned to microfinance, which is seen by many as a promising and cost-effective tool for alleviating poverty.[5]

Zeller and Johannsen (2006), the second paper of the session, studies whether the type of financial institution delivering microfinance services—nongovernmental organization (NGO), private bank, public bank, or government institution—matters for access for the poor. The authors find different degrees of outreach among the different types of institutions, although by necessity their paper, which does not determine the particular attributes of the various financial structures that are best suited for serving the poor, is more descriptive than prescriptive.

Gine and Karlan (2006), the third paper of the session, studies the relative benefits of the two most prominent lending methodologies used in microfinance: group-liability loans, as in traditional microfinance, and individual-liability loans, as might be found at rural banks or in the revised Grameen system. The authors' findings provide evidence that joint liability can contribute to the growth of a microfinance program without jeopardizing its sustainability.

Finally, Rutherford (2006) examines how microfinance has adapted and exploited contract features typically found in informal financial contracts in the context of Grameen Bank's overhaul of its services under Grameen II. The author finds Grameen increasing the flexibility of its products and extending services by introducing products formerly unavailable to the rural poor.

Overall, the papers show that there is no simple recipe for fostering access among the poor. The success of a given policy intervention depends on the environment in which it occurs, because the constraints imposed by existing market frictions and faced by households are likely to vary. Advocates of microfinance refer to it as a "revolution" precisely because it provides financial contracts that are compatible with the incentives of clients in highly diverse contexts. The lesson to be drawn is that in order to increase access for the poor, the relevant constraints must be identified and incentive-compatible programs implemented to alleviate them.

Impact of Access on Inequality and Poverty

Although a significant relationship exists between financial deepening and macroeconomic growth, it is yet to be seen whether financial deepening has positive distributional effects for the poor. That is the focus of the first paper of the session,

---

5. Morduch (1999); Armendariz de Aghion and Morduch (2005); Microcredit Summit Campaign (2005).

by Beck, Demirgüç-Kunt, and Levine.[6] Using a standard measure of financial development—the value of credit issued by financial intermediaries to private firms as a share of GDP—the authors first show that countries with higher levels of private credit grow faster. But, noting that high levels of poverty and income inequality persist around the world, they argue that while economic growth can help reduce poverty, it is not by itself sufficient to eliminate poverty. Noting the differences between countries like Thailand (alluded to above), where poverty was reduced by 90 percent between 1981 and 2000, and Venezuela, where it doubled over the same period, they search for a cross-country comparison that can explain the impact of financial development on the poor. The authors used multiple cross-country datasets to examine the effect of financial development on changes in income inequality, changes in the growth of the income share of the poor (defined in the paper as the growth of the income share of the lowest quintile), and changes in the number of people living in poverty.

They argue that it is essential to determine the distributional effects of growth-enhancing policies, because, a priori, those policies can benefit the whole population, they can benefit primarily the poor, or they can benefit primarily the rich. To date, the issue has not been settled. Some theories suggest a negative relationship between inequality and growth, based on the fact that financial market imperfections such as information asymmetries, transaction costs, and contract enforcement costs may be especially binding on poor entrepreneurs who lack collateral, a credit history, and connections. For example, where credit market frictions prevent the poor from accessing financial markets, they may not be able to borrow to finance high-return projects or to send their children to school. Other theories, however, suggest that since the poor generally rely on informal sources of capital, most of the benefits of improvements in the formal financial sector go to the rich. Such models show that credit is channeled to those with the best connections, not to entrepreneurs with the best opportunities.

The dependent variables used in this paper are the average annual growth rate of the Gini coefficient, the average annual growth rate of the share of the lowest-income quintile, and the average annual growth rate in the poverty headcount (share of the population living on less than $1 a day) for two or three decades for fifty-two to fifty-eight developing and developed countries, depending on the sample.[7]

6. Beck, Demirgüç-Kunt, and Levine (2007). An earlier version of this article (Beck, Demirgüç-Kunt, and Levine 2006) was presented at the conference.

7. Analysis of inequality is based on data from fifty-two developing and developed economies averaged over the 1960–99 period; analysis of income growth of the poor is computed over the 1960–2005 period; and analysis of poverty alleviation is based on data on fifty-eight developing countries over the period from 1980 to 2000.

Figure 3-1. *Effect of Financial Development on Inequality*

Estimated change in the inequality coefficient[a]

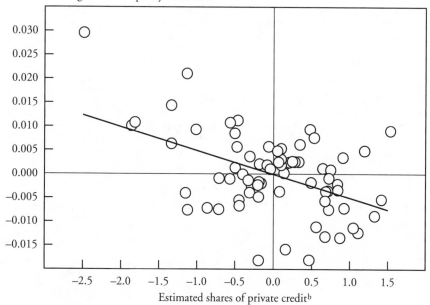

Estimated shares of private credit[b]

Source: Beck, Demirgüç-Kunt, and Levine (2007, table 2, reg. 1).
a. Axis Y = E (Gini growth/X).
b. Axis X = E (Private credit/X).

Looking next at the effect of financial development on inequality, the authors estimate that the Gini coefficient decreases by 0.004 for every percent increase in financial development. Figure 3-1 illustrates a strong negative relationship between financial development and the growth rate of income inequality. While clearly there is substantial variability in the data, removal of the outliers actually strengthens the relationship.

Figure 3-2 displays the positive relationship that exists between private credit and growth of the income share of the poor, defined as the lowest quintile of the population, when the authors control for GDP per capita growth. Controlling for GDP per capita growth allows for examining whether financial development benefits the poorest-income quintile relatively more than the overall population. They find that financial development is especially beneficial to the poor, whose average income rises approximately one for one with overall economic growth. The coefficient for private credit is 0.016, implying that for every percent increase in the share of private credit in GDP, income growth among the poorest quintile

Figure 3-2. *Relationship between Private Credit and Growth of Income Share of the Poor*

Estimated change in the lowest income share coefficient[a]

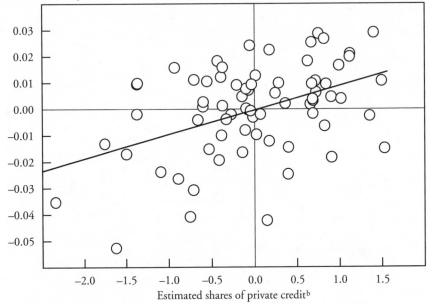

Estimated shares of private credit[b]

Source: Beck, Demirgüç-Kunt, and Levine (2007, table 3, reg. 1).
a. Axis Y = E (Gini growth/X).
b. Axis X = E (Private credit/X).

rises by 1.6 percent. To demonstrate the economic significance of that finding, the authors calculate that the income share of the poor in Brazil would have grown by 3 percent instead of 2.4 percent a year over the period 1961–2000 if Brazil had had the same level of financial intermediary development as Canada.

Finally, figure 3-3 shows the relationship between financial development and the number of poor people in a given country, illustrating that greater financial development is associated with less poverty. The authors find a 0.095 decrease in the annual growth rate of the percentage of the population living on $1 a day or less for every percent increase in the share of private credit in GDP.

According to some critics, the cross-country approach featured in the paper has limitations. They argue that it establishes clear patterns of correlation between many of the key variables of interest but that the policy take-aways often are quite limited because causality is not well established. In addition, this research approach often is too "black-boxy" to provide practical guidelines. In other

Figure 3-3. *Relationship between Financial Development and the Number of Poor*

Estimated change in the headcount coefficient[a]

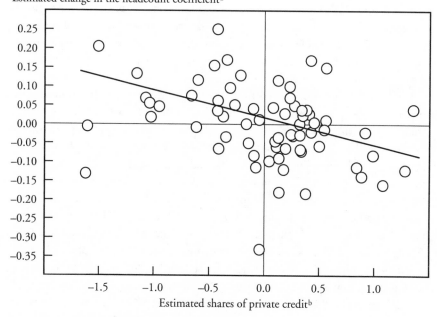

Estimated shares of private credit[b]

Source: Beck, Demirgüç-Kunt, and Levine (2007, table 4, reg. 1).
a. Axis Y = E (Gini growth/X).
b. Axis X = E (Private credit/X).

words, in the context of the paper the authors show that financial development is pro-poor, but it is not clear how to increase the access of poor people to financial services.

It is worth noting several recent and ongoing data collection efforts that the World Bank is conducting to open up the "black box" of the relationship between financial development and growth. Beck, Demirgüç-Kunt, and Martinez Peria (2007) constructs microindicators of the "reach" of the financial sector in an attempt to improve the understanding of the practical obstacles in accessing finance.

Government Early Interventions and Microfinance

Government efforts to deliver formal credit in rural areas included, among other policies, the establishment of special agricultural banks (development banks) and of requirements forcing commercial banks to lend a certain minimum percentage of their loan portfolio to targeted sectors. Those efforts, documented in Adams, Graham, and von Pischke (1984), Besley (1994), and Yaron, Benjamin, and Charitonenko (1998), generally have failed, for diverse reasons. The most important are low repayment rates, loan write-off decisions based on political considerations, policies that lead borrowers to believe that they do not have to repay loans, and the concentration of subsidized credit among wealthy farmers, since they can put up the most physical collateral.

While the recognition of the problems led to the gradual abandonment of such initiatives, Burgess and Pande (2003) uses the Indian experience to assess whether it had any benefit at all. From 1977 until 1991, the Indian government followed a policy of "social banking," which consisted of regulating bank activities through strict licensing rules: a bank could open a branch in a "banked" location (where branches of any commercial bank existed) as long as it opened four new branches in "unbanked" locations. Using a differences-in-differences analysis with data from before, during, and after the period of social banking, they find that it reduced poverty significantly.[8] However, while the program delivered benefits to the intended population, it was discontinued in 1991 because the associated high default rates were too onerous for the banks. All in all, the program was not desirable from a cost-benefit analysis standpoint.

As Morduch (1999) suggests, governments and practitioners around the world now view microfinance as a valid alternative to past failed initiatives to deliver sustainable, low-cost credit to the poor. Yaron, Benjamin, and Charitonenko (1998) suggests that microfinance programs like the Bank Rakyat Indonesia should address specific market failures cost effectively through well-designed and self-sustaining interventions.

Several studies attempt to assess the impact of microfinance on the welfare of clients, but most neglect self-selection issues and endogenous program placement and thus obtain biased estimates of the impact. Microfinance programs usually target certain groups of clients, such as women in poor neighborhoods. Such endogenous program placement effectively makes borrowers and nonborrowers different in some set of characteristics (for example, borrowers have lower incomes than nonborrowers, on average). When participation is voluntary, the fact that clients select themselves into the program indicates differences (observable or unobservable) between borrowers and nonborrowers. For instance, borrowers in

---

8. A differences-in-differences technique compares the change in outcomes over a given period of time in treatment areas with the change in outcomes in control areas. The difference in outcomes from $t = 0$ to $t = 1$ in the control areas is subtracted from the difference in outcomes from $t = 0$ to $t = 1$ in the treatment areas to obtain the estimated impact of the policy.

microfinance programs designed to promote household businesses may be intrinsically more entrepreneurial than nonborrowers.

Because of endogenous program placement and endogenous program participation, those who are not borrowing often are not a good group to compare with those who are borrowing because the observed differences in the outcomes have to be attributed to both the program's impact and the preexisting differences between the two groups.

One of the most thorough attempts to correct for self-selection and nonrandom program placement is Pitt and Khandker (1998), which uses data from three programs in Bangladesh. They exploit a set of exogenous eligibility criteria to measure impact by comparing outcomes of households with and without program choice, conditioning on village fixed effects to control for endogenous placement. They find positive and significant impacts of the program and larger effects for women than for men. Although the eligibility criteria prevented households with more than 0.5 acres of land from borrowing, the rule was not strictly followed in practice. Morduch (1998) notes that in Pitt and Khandker (1998), households that in principle should have been excluded received credit in program villages but that the eligibility criteria were strictly followed in non-program villages; hence, he argues, the treatment group did not conform to the control group and the result is potential overestimation of the program's impact.

Coleman (1999) is possibly the cleanest impact assessment to date. The author uses data from a quasi-experiment in northeast Thailand, where several NGOs were expanding their coverage to several new villages. He selected six villages where the program would begin the following year and asked villagers whether they would become members once the program was in place. Over the year he surveyed the "control" members, who were not yet receiving credit; the "treatment" members, who already were receiving credit in eight older program villages; and nonmembers in both types of villages. The results indicate that program loans had little impact, although interestingly enough, "naïve" estimates of the impact that fail to correct for self-selection and endogenous program placement tend to overestimate the impact significantly. Coleman argues that the lack of impact could be due to relatively small loan sizes. Average household wealth was $21,000, and the size of the loans ranged from $60 to $300. Thus they may have been used for consumption rather than for (lumpy) investments. In another paper, Coleman (2001), the author uses the same data to assess the impact on village committee members and rank-and-file members separately. While the results continue to be insignificant for the rank and file, committee members experienced positive and significant impacts. Indeed, some of the committee members used their influence to avoid the loan size limits by using different family names.

There are several ongoing studies—see Gine and Karlan (2006)—and other projects from the Poverty Action Lab and the Centre for Microfinance in Chennai that use experimental methods to assess the impact of microfinance on welfare. The key in experimental methods is random assignment, which removes any systematic correlation between treatment status and both observed and unobserved characteristics of clients. Clients (or groups of clients) are randomly assigned to a treatment group (which will be given a chance to borrow) and a control group (which will not be allowed to borrow). The randomization procedure ensures that the two groups are identical at the outset. Individuals in the groups live through the same external events throughout the same period of time and thus encounter the same external intervening factors.

The only difference between the two groups is that those in the treatment group are allowed to borrow and those in the control group are not; therefore, any difference in the outcomes between the two groups at the end of the study must be attributable to the ability to borrow. Random assignment ensures the direction of causality: the ability to borrow causes an improvement for the client (or the institution).

Despite the positive (albeit small) effects found in the current literature, many unresolved issues still exist regarding who should be in the client base as well as what specific features microfinance contracts should have. Both topics are covered in the following discussion.

Type of Institution

Currently some disagreement exists among donors, practitioners, and academics on what microfinance priorities should be. At the heart of the issue is the potential trade-off between outreach and sustainability. Outreach refers to the effort by microfinance institutions to extend financial services to an ever-wider audience (breadth of outreach) and especially toward the poorest of the poor (depth of outreach). Sustainability sometimes is taken to be operational sustainability—that is, the ability of the institution to generate enough revenue to cover operating costs but not necessarily the full cost of capital. Other times it is taken to be financial sustainability—that is, whether the institution requires subsidies to operate.

Subsidies or donor funds originally were perceived as temporary aids to help programs overcome start-up costs; however, for some institutions subsidies are an ongoing reality. Ironically, the availability of donor funds has acted in some instances as a disincentive to increase the scale of operations and become innovative.[9]

The Consultative Group to Assist the Poor (CGAP) and the donor community at large exhort microfinance providers to pursue sustainability aggressively by raising interest rates and lowering costs. In their view, ongoing dependence on subsidized funds is plagued with problems. First, donors may cease to provide funds in the future, forcing the institution to shut down. Second, as mentioned before, donor budgets are limited, restricting the scale of operations to the size of the subsidy. Third, subsidized programs run the risk of becoming inefficient and losing any incentive to innovate and reduce costs. By reducing donor dependence and achieving sustainability, microfinance lenders may attract commercial lenders and should achieve much better leverage on their equity than their subsidized counterparts, allowing them to greatly increase the scale of outreach. Thus, sustainability and outreach go hand in hand, without an apparent trade-off.

However, an alternative approach argues that the focus should be on *targeted* outreach rather than on scale or sustainability. Proponents of this view claim that a narrow focus on cost recovery and elimination of subsidies would force microfinance institutions (MFIs) to drop the poorest borrowers from their portfolios because they are the most difficult and costly to serve. In essence, the literature has outlined a basic trade-off between outreach and sustainability, with advocates in one side emphasizing social motives and those on the other emphasizing financial motives.

Unfortunately, rigorous empirical studies that might explain the nature of the trade-offs and whether they have any practical relevance are lacking. Christen (2000) uses several case studies from Latin America to conclude that as some microfinance institutions achieved sustainability, the industry experienced greater commercialization and competition. Some institutions applied for a banking license and so became subject to supervision. But more important, those institutions even increased their portfolio of clients, staying true to their initial mission of serving poorer clients.

Zeller and Johannsen (2006), the second paper of the session, examines whether the trade-offs between financial sustainability and outreach vary by the type of financial institution providing microfinance services. Using a nationally representative sample of 800 households in Bangladesh and in Peru, the authors examined differences in outreach among different types of financial institution: semiformal institutions (NGO-MFIs); member-based institutions such as credit unions and village banks (supported by NGOs); microbanks using individual

9. Morduch (1999).

and group lending or a linkage model (with preexisting self-help groups); and finally, other institutions such as public banks (sectoral, agricultural, and rural) and private commercial banks with microfinance operations. In both countries the authors employed a multistage cluster sampling design to ensure adequate representation across geographic regions and rural and urban areas. In Peru, eight of the twenty-four regions were randomly selected and probability proportionate to size sampling (PPS) was used to select 100 households in each of the departments, with equal population shares at every subsequent stage of the sampling. In Bangladesh, ten *thanas* (the lowest administrative level in Bangladesh) were randomly selected from among five divisions and eighty households were selected by PPS in each *thana*.

The Microenterprise Results and Accountability Act of 2004 defines the very poor as those in the bottom half of the population living in poverty, according to the national poverty line, as well as all those living on less than a dollar a day in purchasing power parity terms, an amount often referred to as the international poverty line. The 2000 National Living Standard Measurement Survey of Peru found that according to the government's official poverty line, 54 percent of Peruvians were poor. The poorer half of that population (or 27 percent) would be considered "very poor" according to the U.S. definition. In Bangladesh, which is a very poor country, more clients count as "very poor" under the dollar-a-day definition. The Household Income and Expenditure Survey (HIES) of 2000 found that 50 percent of Bangladeshis lived below the poverty line. Thus, only 25 percent of Bangladeshis would be classified as very poor under the U.S. definition, while 36 percent of the population lives on less than a dollar a day. The authors therefore use the dollar-a-day benchmark to classify "very poor" households in Bangladesh. For each country the authors converted $1 into the local currency according to the purchasing power parity rate and adjusted the poverty line by the loss in purchasing power due to inflation up to the survey date.

Table 3-1 reveals some interesting patterns among clients of Bangladeshi financial institutions. While clients of NGOs are overwhelmingly women (and those of public banks overwhelmingly men), the clients of public banks and government institutions are predominantly rural (84 and 92 percent respectively). Of the clients served by NGOs, 67 percent are rural.

Table 3-2, however, reveals that NGOs serve a greater proportion of poor clients (32 percent) than do public banks (17 percent) or government institutions (8 percent). Still, at less than one-third for all three institution types, the figure may be lower than many people have assumed. Unfortunately, it is impossible to discern from the data whether it represents a problem (substantial leakage to the non-poor) or a success (impact on clients). Because of the limited sample size the

Table 3-1. *Gender and Residence of Clients and Non-Clients in Bangladesh, by Financial Institution*

Percent

Sample	Does client live in rural area?		Sex of client		Share of total clients
	No	Yes	Female	Male	
Clients by institution					
NGO providing microfinance	33	67	91	10	64
Public bank	16	84	8	92	29
Other government institution providing microfinance	8	92	54	46	5
Other (private bank, cooperative, etc.)	69	31	54	46	3
Non-clients	20	80	50	50	0
Total	22	78	53	47	100

Source: Zeller and Johannsen (2006).

Table 3-2. *Poverty Status of Clients and Non-Clients, by Financial Institution*

Sample	Daily expenditures per capita (takas)	Percent below the median poverty line[a]	Percent below the national poverty line[a]	Percent below the international poverty line[b]
Clients by institution				
NGO providing microfinance (N = 328)	34.6	21	38.7	32.3
Public bank (N = 144)	42.2	7.6	25	16.7
Other government institution providing microfinance (N = 24)	52.7	8.3	8.3	8.3
Other (private bank, cooperative, etc.) (N = 13)	39.2	30.8	30.8	30.8
Non-clients (N = 1,700)	37.1	16.5	35.7	28.1
Total (N = 2,209)	37.2	16.6	35.1	27.8

Source: Zeller and Johannsen (2006).
a. Adjusted by region.
b. Dollars in purchasing power parity = $1.08 at 1993 prices.

authors were unable to limit their comparisons of outreach to only those clients who had recently joined their respective programs. It is unclear therefore whether the presence of non-poor clients implies that programs are targeting wealthier households or that formerly poor clients moved out of poverty. In the latter case, the presence of wealthy clients in the sample is, of course, a good thing. The authors show that clients who have been in a program the longest (more than five years) have the lowest rate of poverty, although that is not a real indication of impact; it could reflect changes over time in targeting by programs or it could be simply because older clients have had more years to improve their income and accumulate assets. Nonetheless, the lower poverty rate among older clients squares with the impact analysis in Khandker (2005) and other studies that show a positive impact on microfinance clients in Bangladesh.

These findings make it especially difficult to interpret the comparison of outreach between Grameen Bank and BRAC (Bangladesh Rural Advancement Committee) reported in Zeller and Johannsen (2006). While the authors find that BRAC serves a considerably poorer clientele (48 percent of BRAC clients but only 35 percent of Grameen clients are within the bottom tercile of per capita expenditures), they note that, on average, Grameen clients have been members for much longer. Assuming that membership has a positive effect, it is difficult to say whether BRAC's targeting or Grameen's impact is driving the relationship.

The results from Peru show a different mix of clients across institution types, although the overall (potential) level of leakage to the non-poor is similar. Here NGOs, municipal savings and loans (CMACs), and private banks serve a similarly high proportion of women. The lowest percentage of women served, by public banks, is still more than 50 percent. Households in the Peruvian survey are far more urban than the Bangladeshi households, as the breakdowns in Table 3-2 and Table 3-3 reflect. Public banks, however, serve substantially more poor clients than do private banks (24 percent and 4 percent respectively). CMACs serve the fewest poor clients, at 3 percent, while NGOs serve 20 percent. A comparison of six MFIs reveals a substantial range in the percentage of poor clients served, from 16 percent to 44 percent. Unsurprisingly, households with formal savings accounts were less poor than those without (11 percent and 35 percent respectively).

A comparison of Bangladesh and Peru reveals that twice as many households are members of financial institutions in Bangladesh (46 percent) as in Peru (19 percent). In both countries clients use the institutions mainly for credit services and less for savings and insurance (29 percent of Bangladeshi households and 9 percent of Peruvian households use savings and insurance services). The higher breadth of outreach in Bangladesh may be related to the earlier start of the

Table 3-3. *Gender and Residence of Clients and Non-Clients in Peru,*
by Financial Institution
Percent

Sample	Does client live in rural area?		Sex of client		Share of total clients
	No	*Yes*	*Female*	*Male*	
Clients by institution					
Public bank (Banco de la Nacion)	88.2	11.8	58.8	41.2	22.5
Private bank (including micro-banks such as MiBanco)	93.0	7.0	75.4	25.7	37.7
Municipal savings and loan banks (CMACs)	74.3	25.7	77.1	22.9	23.2
Other (NGO, rural savings bank, cooperative, etc.)	72.0	28.0	72.0	28.0	16.6
Non-clients	70.1	29.9	47.0	53.0	
Total	71.0	29.0	48.6	51.4	100.0

Source: Zeller and Johannsen (2006).

microfinance movement, which began in the 1970s. In contrast, because many households lost savings during the hyperinflation and economic instability of the 1980s, Peru suffers from public distrust of formal financial institutions. Furthermore, MFIs in Bangladesh benefit from high population density and low administrative costs, while Peru must contend with heterogeneous geography, including the Andes and the rainforest.

The authors conclude that while outreach to the poor appears to differ by type of microfinance institution, the data analyzed here do not provide conclusive evidence on whether the legal status of the MFI really matters for outreach. In the meantime, they argue that outreach depends on the MFI's mission, management, and targeting strategy. They also cite group lending for its ability to use social capital to exploit cost advantages for banking with the poor. As shown in the following discussion, however, the case for group lending may not be so clear cut.

Type of Liability

Group-liability lending, in which group members are responsible for the repayment of their fellow members' loans, has been associated with the success of the Grameen Bank and its many replications around the world. In a comprehensive survey, Ghatak and Guinnane (1999), the authors suggest four ways in which joint liability can help overcome problems commonly faced by lenders: ascertaining how risky a borrower is (*adverse selection*); ensuring that funds will be used properly (*moral hazard*); ensuring that the borrower tells the truth about his or her inability to repay in case of default (*auditing*); and enforcing the repayment agreement (*enforcement*). The authors claim that joint liability contracts perform well because borrowers can better monitor each other's investment, borrowers have information about each other's creditworthiness, and neighbors may be able to impose powerful nonpecuniary sanctions on each other at low cost to the lender. Thus, group lending provides a mechanism for overcoming some of the informational disadvantages faced by commercial lenders.

Most empirical research to date has focused on explaining whether joint liability lending contributes to its high observed repayment rates. Wydick (1999), using data from Guatemala, validates the claim that improvements in repayment rates are associated with variables related to the ability to monitor and enforce group relationships. Wenner (1995) finds evidence from Costa Rica of screening of prospective members before they are admitted into the program. In addition, Wenner (1995) and Sharma and Zeller (1996), using data from Bangladesh, find that repayment rates are higher in remote towns, although other studies find the opposite. Karlan (2005) takes advantage of a natural experiment in Peru in which groups did not self-select and were not neighborhood based, as is typical. The quasi-random group formation studied provided sufficient variation to test the influence of the initial social connections of the group members, and the author found that groups with stronger social capital were more likely to repay their loans and to save more.

But, as noted above, the Grameen Bank no longer uses joint liability, and both Grameen and its competitor, the Association for Social Advancement, have achieved remarkably high repayment rates with individual-liability loans. Other MFIs have followed in their footsteps, switching to individual-liability lending. The shift raises the questions of whether group liability was responsible for Grameen's success or whether the poor simply are good credit risks, even in the absence of group liability.

There are reasons why both clients and MFIs might favor individual liability. Clients may dislike paying for their fellow group members and they may dislike the tension that it creates among them. As groups age and loan sizes among group members diverge, such problems may be exacerbated. MFIs may be concerned that defaulting group members will cause good clients to drop out of the program. The best way to determine the relative merits of group- versus individual-liability lending is to design a real-world experiment in which all aspects of a microfinance program are kept the same but the liability contracts are varied.[10] While it is simple enough to offer both group- and individual-liability loans, it would not be useful to compare the performance of clients who self-selected one or the other option. It is easy to imagine that certain types of clients might be more likely to prefer one type of liability option: clients with risky enterprises, for example, might feel more comfortable with group liability, knowing that their fellow group members would cover their payments in bad weeks, while clients who keep emergency savings might resent that arrangement and prefer individual liability. Random assignment is the only way to be sure that clients receiving individual liability are the same, on average, as those receiving group liability.

Working with the Green Bank of Caraga, a rural bank in the Philippines engaged in microlending, Gine and Karlan (2006) took 169 group-lending centers of approximately twenty-five clients each (divided in groups of five) from Leyte Province and randomly selected half of the centers to be converted to individual liability; the others were to serve as the control group. All other aspects of the program remained the same: clients still met in groups each week and made the same weekly payments. Group and center savings were dissolved in favor of personalized savings, but there was no change to clients' total deposits. That ensured that the only difference between the treatment (individual-liability) centers and the control (group-liability) centers was the change in liability and therefore that any differences between the two groups at the end of the study period could be confidently attributed to the change in the program.

After tracking both the group-lending and the converted individual-lending centers, the authors found that in the converted centers the default rate did not rise, client retention increased, and more new clients took out loans. That finding provides empirical evidence that clients preferred individual liability. In fact, new entrants in individual-liability centers had closer ties to previous members than did new entrants in the group-liability centers, suggesting that under group liability, clients' fear of the peer pressure that they might feel if a person that they recommended later defaulted kept them from bringing new people into the program. While the repayment rate did not decrease overall, those with weaker social networks were more likely to have default problems under individual liability than under group liability. That outcome may be related to the authors' finding that individual liability led to less monitoring of each other's loan performance— clients in converted centers remembered less about other members' defaults and new clients in converted centers were less likely to predict defaults of other members correctly.

10. Armendariz de Aghion and Morduch (2005).

The results suggest that individual-liability lending can work, but they do not by themselves indicate that individual-liability lending is profitable for the lender. Repayment is only one aspect of profitability. Group lending shifts the burden of screening clients and enforcing repayment from the lender to clients and creates an element of insurance whereby clients can rely on their peers during difficult weeks, reducing their chance of default. If repayment had been maintained in the converted centers only through the intense efforts of loan officers, the cost of individual lending would be prohibitive. The authors examined that possibility by conducting an activity-based costing exercise in which each credit officer kept a detailed diary of his or her activities. They found no significant differences in the way that credit officers allocated their time, and although the results were not statistically significant, credit officers spent *less* time on loan enforcement, though they spent more time on approving new loans.

Observers might note that however interesting the findings may be, they have only limited applicability to other settings because the subjects are a very particular group: clients who joined a group-lending program thinking that they would stay in a group-lending program. It would not be possible to continually surprise clients by changing the liability rules once they had joined the program. To extend the generalizability of the findings, the authors are conducting related research with the same program, in a new area. The procedure to start operations in new areas is novel and consists of two parts, identification of eligible villages and of potential clients through a marketing meeting. The identification of the villages is first done by gathering basic information about the villages from the municipality office (equivalent to a U.S. county's administrative office). That information is used mainly to exclude villages with low population density as it is deemed too costly to start operations in those villages.

The credit officer visits the selected *barangays* to conduct a survey to verify several criteria, including the number of microentreprises, residents' main sources of income, village accessibility and security, and perceived demand by the residents for microcredit services. Once the villages are selected, a census is conducted of all the businesses in them to assess which are interested in obtaining credit and may eventually become clients. The census records basic information regarding the size of the businesses and their credit history. While it is being conducted, microentrepreneurs are told about the marketing meeting. The sample villages are randomly assigned to one of four groups: BULAK, where Green Bank will offer the group-liability loan program; BULAK to BULAK II, where Green Bank will offer a group-liability program and remove the program after the first loan cycle; BULAK II, where Green Bank will offer an individual-liability loan program; and a control group.

Note that the sample of business women is not made up of actual borrowers but of "potential clients." Propensity score matching and weighting uses the baseline characteristics of potential clients to statistically identify those most likely to participate in the program. The key in this sample formation is to identify those who would receive a loan from Green Bank if Green Bank were to operate in the village. The impact of the program on each client can be measured by comparing the outcomes of participants to the outcomes of those in the control group with a similar propensity to participate. Because the sample selection in the four groups is consistent, sample bias in subsets from the groups is consistent and the impacts on any of the four groups can be compared.

Microfinance Mechanisms

Although microfinance institutions use different mechanisms to overcome informational asymmetries and to elicit repayment from their low-income clients, the most common are *joint liability* (also known as group lending); *dynamic incentives,* such as offering loans with frequent installments at increased amounts and threatening to cut off any future lending in the case of default; *regular repayment,* which takes place in public group meetings; and *collateral substitutes,* such as forced savings. However, those mechanisms are not well suited for farmers, whose highly seasonal income conflicts with the regular repayment obligation. For that reason, most microfinance clients are self-employed individuals or microentrepreneurs.

Rutherford (2006), the fourth paper in the session, addresses a concern expressed by some that the rapid growth in delivering organized financial services to the world's poor may in fact do damage by displacing valuable informal services. To examine whether that is the case, Rutherford used a research technique called *financial diaries* to explore what happened to the rural poor when the Grameen Bank in Bangladesh radically revised its products in 2001 with the rollout of Grameen II. Under Grameen II the bank greatly increased the variety of loan terms, repayment schedules, and loan amounts and allowed borrowers to top up their loan midway through the term. The bank entirely changed its approach to deposits, doing away with forced saving in favor of an open passbook account and an optional long-term pension savings plan. In addition, Grameen eliminated joint-liability loans, though borrowers still form groups. Since Grameen has formed the template for much of the microfinance industry worldwide, its high-profile overhaul is of considerable interest to the microfinance industry.

Financial diaries record in as much detail as possible the financial behavior of a small sample of households, which are interviewed at two-week intervals for at least a full year. With the first financial diaries, recorded in Bangladesh in 1999–2000, households were interviewed every other week for a year to gather details on every cash flow to come in or out of the household—including income and expenditures; changes in physical assets; and the opening, closing, or servicing of financial instruments—as well as to determine whether any person joined or left the household or took or left a job (including casual labor). From an initial level of cash on hand, the household's income, expenditures, deposits, and withdrawals were tabulated after each interview and cross-checked against the current cash on hand to ensure that no transactions were missed (Collins 2004). Through the diaries Collins found that poor rural and urban households indeed had active financial lives. All had both assets and liabilities, and even the poorest used at least four financial instruments over the course of the year.

The analysis in Rutherford (2006) is based on a sample of fifty-three households from various areas served by Grameen Bank over three years (2002–05). Rutherford found that Grameen Bank's revamped services related to informal finance in four principal ways:

—Grameen II products are *incorporated* into existing practices. While it is well known that female microfinance clients often channel their loans to their husbands, it is surprising that of the 239 loans tracked through the financial diaries, twenty-seven (11 percent) were wholly lent by the borrowers to other villagers outside of the household. Microfinance clients have thus become moneylenders. Whereas in the 1999–2000 financial diaries this practice typically was undertaken using traditional loan terms, such as a given amount of rice per *taka* borrowed, it seems that clients have adopted MFI practices; they now charge a fixed repayment per week to cover principal and interest.

—Grameen II products *complement* existing practices. Ten percent of loans tracked were wholly used and another 30 percent were used in part to pay down other debt. While some observers have worried that such borrowers could end up in an expensive cycle of debt, Rutherford argues that debt levels among the fifty-three households remained modest relative to their income over the three years that they were tracked.

—Grameen II products *extend* existing practices. The majority of members in the sample opened a Grameen pension savings account, which is a ten-year commitment savings plan, and many made monthly deposits greater than the minimum required. With this type of long-term savings plan, Grameen Bank is providing a service unavailable in the informal market at a higher interest rate than commercial banks offer. Without ways to save over the long term, the poor traditionally have locked their savings into livestock, buildings, gold, and land. Rutherford offers the example of a longtime Grameen client who left the bank after she could no longer repay loans regularly yet retained her pension account, which will be worth $3,400 when it matures in 2010. She makes the $15 monthly payment with the help of her sons.

—Grameen II products are beginning to *replace* existing practices. The flexibility of deposit and loan products under Grameen II is leading a small but growing number of households to use Grameen Bank as their sole financial service provider. For the first time, the range of products offered by Grameen gives the poor access to banking services that are the same as those the non-poor take for granted. Grameen staff were initially nervous about allowing members unfettered access to their savings, but they now see that allowing members to make withdrawals to make loan payments in difficult weeks helps borrowers manage their loans.

Conclusion

Each of the four papers presented in the second conference session brings a key piece of information to the case for expanding financial access to the poor. To merit the considerable attention and resources required of the public and private sectors, increasing financial access must be beneficial and it must be achievable. The first paper, Beck, Demirgüç-Kunt, and Levine (2006), makes a strong case for the benefits of deepening financial access, showing that with private credit comes economic growth that is shared by the poor. That finding provides a mandate to expand financial access, but not a roadmap. The level of private credit in a country cannot simply "grow"; it must be put somewhere. No doubt financial deepening should be occuring among the types of financial institution that serve and benefit the poor. Zeller and Johannsen (2006), the second paper, shows that the type of institution matters for poverty outreach, although popular notions of which types of institutions serve the poor may not hold.

Even among institutions that focus exclusively on serving the poor there are many potential variations in products and services offered to clients. The third paper, Gine and Karlan (2006), offers one example of a way to cleanly evaluate the importance of a single mechanism central to the methodology of thousands of microfinance programs worldwide: group liability. Its findings indicate that at least in certain settings the poor can be good credit risks, even in the absence of group liability. Perhaps more important, they demonstrate the feasibility of using randomized controlled trials to evaluate the impact of a microfinance product or mechanism.

As already discussed, randomized trials have been used to evaluate a variety of key aspects of microfinance and many more are currently under way. Ashraf, Karlan, and Yin (2006) evaluated the impact—on clients and the program—of offering a specialized commitment savings product and found that clients randomly selected to be offered the product increased their savings substantially more than the control group. Bertrand and others (2005) compared the effects of various marketing techniques with those of changes in interest rates, finding that while clients are sensitive to rate changes, they are much more sensitive to marketing, such as the description of the loan. De Janvry, McIntosh, and Sadoulet (2006) offered training to randomly selected clients about the importance of credit bureaus for their future credit opportunities. Clients who were informed about the benefits and pitfalls of credit reporting (that is, that paying late harms their access to credit elsewhere while paying on time gives them access to credit elsewhere at potentially lower rates) had higher repayment rates and also borrowed elsewhere after establishing a good credit record.

But randomized controlled trials also have limitations. Despite providing a cleaner method for establishing causality, they tend to be localized and small scale. Generalizations that stem from these evaluations have to be taken with a grain of salt, because the institutions, context, and population elsewhere may be very different. A solution to that problem is to replicate the same experiment in a variety of different contexts.

The final paper of the session, Rutherford (2006), uses detailed financial diaries to offer a glimpse of the future of expanded financial access in perhaps the best-known financial institution for the poor, the Grameen Bank. The author finds that Grameen's financial products complement and extend the existing informal financial options available to the poor. Only after increasing the flexibility of its services and offering a range of products unavailable in the informal market did Grameen start to replace existing financial sources, becoming the sole financial service provider for a small but growing number of clients.

In sum, the papers presented in the session show that there is no uniform approach to improving access to financial services among the poor. Thus the relevant constraints need to be measured and identified and incentive-compatible programs designed to alleviate them.

References

Adams, Dale W., Douglas Graham, and J. D. von Pischke, eds. 1984. *Undermining Rural Development with Cheap Credit.* Boulder, Colo.: Westview Press.

Armendariz de Aghion, B., and J. Morduch. 2005. *The Economics of Microfinance.* MIT Press.

Ashraf, N., D. Karlan, and W. Yin. 2006. "Tying Odysseus to the Mast: Evidence from a Commitment Savings Product in the Philippines." *Quarterly Journal of Economics* 121, no. 2: 673–97.

Banerjee, A., and A. Newman. 1993. "Occupational Choice and the Process of Development." *Journal of Political Economy* 101: 274–98.

Beck, T., and A. de la Torre. 2006. "The Basic Analytics of Access to Financial Services." World Bank Policy Research Working Paper 4026. Washington: World Bank.

Beck, T., A. Demirgüç-Kunt, and R. Levine. 2006. "Finance, Inequality, and Poverty Alleviation: Cross-Country Evidence." World Bank Policy Research Working Paper 3338. Washington: World Bank.

———. 2007. "Finance, Inequality, and the Poor," *Journal of Economic Growth* 12: 27–49.

Beck, T., A. Demirgüç-Kunt, and M. Martinez Peria. 2007. "Reaching Out: Access to and Use of Banking Services across Countries." *Journal of Financial Economics*, forthcoming.

Beck, T., R. Levine, and N. Loayza. 2000. "Finance and the Sources of Growth." *Journal of Financial Economics* 58: 261–300.

Bertrand, Marianne, and others. 2005. "What's Psychology Worth? A Field Experiment in the Consumer Credit Market." Yale University Economic Growth Center Discussion Paper 918.

Besley, T. 1994. "How Do Market Failures Justify Interventions in Rural Credit Markets?" *World Bank Research Observer* 9, no. 1: 27–48.

Burgess, R., and R. Pande. 2003. "Do Rural Banks Matter? Evidence from the Indian Social Banking Experiment." *American Economic Review* 95, no. 3: 780–95.

Christen, R. P. 2000. "Commercialization and Mission Drift: The Transformation of Microfinance in Latin America." CGAP Occasional Paper 5. Washington: CGAP.

Coleman, B. 1999. "The Impact of Group Lending in Northeast Thailand." *Journal of Development Economics* 60: 105–42.

———. 2001. "Microfinance in Northeast Thailand: Who Benefits and How Much?" *Asian Development* 2, no. 4: pp. 5–7 (Manila, Philippines).

Collins, D. 2004. "The Financial Diaries." Centre for Social Science Research. South Africa: University of Cape Town (www.financialdiaries.com).

De Janvry, A., C. McIntosh, and E. Sadoulet. 2006. "From Private to Public Reputation in Microfinance Lending: An Experiment in Borrower Response." Department of Agricultural and Resource Economics Working Paper. University of California, Berkeley.

Demirgüç-Kunt, A., and V. Maksimovic. 1998. "Law, Finance, and Firm Growth." *Journal of Finance* 53, no. 6: 2107–31.

Galor, O., and J. Zeira. 1993. "Income Distribution and Macroeconomics." *Review of Economic Studies* 60: 35–52.

Ghatak, M., and T. Guinnane. 1999. "The Economics of Lending with Joint Liability: Theory and Practice." *Journal of Development Economics* 60:195–228.

Gine, X., and D. Karlan. 2006. "Group versus Individual Liability: Evidence from a Field Experiment in the Philippines." World Bank Working Paper Series 4008. Washington: World Bank.

Gine, X., and R. Townsend. 2004. "Evaluation of Financial Liberalization: A General Equilibrium Model with Constrained Occupation Choice." *Journal of Development Economics* 74, no. 2: 269–307.

Karlan, D. 2007. "Social Connections and Group Banking." *Economic Journal* 117: F52–F84.

Khandker, S. R. 2005. "Micro-Finance and Poverty: Evidence Using Panel Data from Bangladesh." *World Bank Economic Review* 19, no. 2: 263–86.

Levine, R. 1997. "Financial Development and Economic Growth: Views and Agenda." *Journal of Economic Literature* 35: 688–726.

———. 2006. "Finance and Growth: Theory and Evidence." In *Handbook of Economic Growth,* edited by Philippe Aghion and Steven Durlauf. Netherlands: Elsevier Science.

Lloyd-Ellis, H., and D. Bernhardt. 2000. "Enterprise, Inequality, and Economic Development." *Review of Economic Studies* 67, no. 1: 147–68.

Microcredit Summit Campaign. 2005. "State of the Microcredit Summit Campaign Report 2005." Washington (www.microcreditsummit.org/pubs/reports/socr/2005/SOCR05.pdf [May 14, 2007]).

Morduch, J. 1998. "Does Microfinance Really Help the Poor? New Evidence from Flagship Programs in Bangladesh." Princeton University (www.princeton.edu/~rpds/downloads/morduch_microfinance_poor.pdf [May 15, 2007]).

———. 1999. "The Microfinance Promise." *Journal of Economic Literature* 37: 1569–614.

North, D. 1990. *Institutions, Institutional Change, and Economic Performance.* Cambridge University Press.

Pitt, M., and S. Khandker. 1998. "The Impact of Group-Based Credit Programs on Poor Households in Bangladesh: Does the Gender of Participants Matter?" *Journal of Political Economy* 106: 958–996.

Rajan, R., and L. Zingales. 1998. "Financial Development and Growth." *American Economic Review* 88: 559–586.

Rutherford, S. 2006. "Adding Value: How Graneen II Complements Informal Finance in Bangladesh." Paper presented at "Access to Finance: Building Inclusive Financial Systems." Brookings Institution and World Bank, Washington, May 30–31.

Sharma, M., and M. Zeller. 1996. "Repayment Performance in Group-Based Credit Programs in Bangladesh: An Empirical Analysis." *World Development* 25, no. 10: 1731–742.

Wenner, M. D. 1995. "Group Credit: A Means to Improve Information Transfer and Loan Repayment Performance." *Journal of Development Studies* 32: 264–281.

Wydick, B. 1999. "Can Social Cohesion Be Harnessed to Repair Market Failures? Evidence from Group Lending in Guatemala." *Economic Journal* 109 (July): 463–75.

Yaron, J., McDonald Benjamin, and S. Charitonenko. 1998. "Promoting Efficient Rural Financial Intermediation." *World Bank Research Observer* 13, no. 2: 147–70.

Zeller, M., and J. Johannsen. 2006. "Is There a Difference in Poverty Outreach by Type of Microfinance Institution? The Case of Peru and Bangladesh." Paper presented at "Access to Finance: Building Inclusive Financial Systems." Brookings Institution and the World Bank, Washington, May 30–31.

STEPHEN PEACHEY

4

Microfinance Institutions and Financial Access: The Double Bottom Line

T HIS CHAPTER GIVES an overview of the financial institutions that provide the bulk of accessible finance in developing and transition economies. Evocatively named *double bottom line institutions* by Richard Rosenberg, one of the contributors to the conference session that this chapter summarizes, in an earlier paper with colleagues at the Consultative Group to Assist the Poor (CGAP), these institutions serve in total some 1.5 billion accessible account relationships across the developing and transition world.[1] The chapter starts by broadening the concept of accessible finance from a narrow focus on microfinance to include access provided by all institutions that combine a financial bottom line (making

This chapter was produced with the support of the World Savings Banks Institute, a sponsor of the World Bank and Brookings Institution global conference entitled "Access to Finance: Building Inclusive Financial Systems," which was held in Washington May 30–31, 2006. An early draft was produced for the conference, but it was significantly rewritten in the light of especially helpful comments from Marguerite Robinson, the commentator on the session that the chapter summarizes. I also received considerable assistance in preparing this chapter from the staff of the Joint Office of the World Savings Banks Institute and the European Savings Bank Group in Brussels, particularly Angela Arevalo, Mark Bienstman, and Catherine Goislot. I would like to express my thanks to Adrian Gonzalez and Richard Rosenberg and to Robert Cull, Asli Demirgüç-Kunt, and Jonathan Morduch, my fellow presenters at the conference session. The chapter also has benefited from discussions with Anjali Kumar and Patrick Honohan. Finally, my thanks go to colleagues at Oxford Policy Management for their ongoing support, particularly Alan Roe and Robert Stone of the Economics Program.

1. Christen, Rosenberg, and Jayadeva (2004).

a profit) with a social bottom line: bringing access to finance to individuals and businesses that often find themselves excluded from commercial banking services. The double bottom line group includes a range of microfinance entities, such as nongovernmental organizations, nonbank financial institutions, and specialist schemes run by commercial banks. But this chapter defines such double bottom line institutions even more broadly, to include other institutions with a long tradition of fostering access. Among them are community banks and credit unions and cooperatives as well as some government-run policy lending institutions and various types of savings bank around the world.

Providing access is part of the fabric of the operations of double bottom line institutions. They work in close proximity to the mass market, either as locally constituted entities or through a widespread national distribution network. Their product design and pricing facilitate access even for those with small-scale needs. They may have accessibility written into their operating mandate, either in legal form in their founding statutes if they are public or philanthropic institutions or in their guiding mission and business strategy if they are private organizations. Some of these institutions, including many microfinance schemes, explicitly target the poor with their services; others aim to provide universal access for all. Some commercial banks may consider that a down-market focus, but they are mistaken. The focus is universal, and many a double bottom line institution has built a formidable universal retail banking franchise based on that focus.

After introducing the wider group of institutions that have a mandate to provide access, this chapter looks at what each type of institution brings to the accessible finance market. The chapter examines the scale and scope of activity against the World Bank's four dimensions of access, reworked from the perspective of those who supply financial services. The chapter then seeks to answer the question that lies at the heart of the conference session that it summarizes: can access be provided at prices that at least cover the proportionately higher costs of doing what often can be a small-scale and irregular business? What lessons do different types of access-oriented institution offer about the trade-off, if any, between providing access and staying profitable?

The double bottom line—a social bottom line as well as a financial bottom line—is a concept that can be communicated quite well to those who need services as well as those who deliver them. It is a way of saying that a reasonable profit is necessary to support the continuous investment needed to sustain and improve any services offered. The consensus is now predominantly in favor of sustainability and against subsidy. The biggest argument is one of potential volume of supply—a subsidized program eventually will be limited by the availability of the subsidy, whereas a sustainable program, especially one that mobilizes savings as well as provides credit, tends to be limited only by its clients' needs.[2]

In any case, there is ample evidence that subsidized lending tends to get diverted from target groups, particularly in the field of rural finance, and becomes concentrated on a few privileged borrowers.[3] Indeed, there seems to be an almost perverse inevitability that a subsidy will end up disproportionately supporting nonperforming borrowers. Nonetheless, the three papers presented at the conference session examined the evidence from microfinance and savings banking to determine whether access can be delivered profitably and found that it can, for all institutions other than most government-run microcredit schemes.[4] The route to profitability differs, however, depending on whether an institution focuses primarily on the provision of credit or the mobilization of savings and the provision of affordable payment services.

The focus of this chapter is how institutional form and product focus affect the ability of a range of double bottom line institutions to function without subsidy. The chapter first analyzes the other two papers presented at the conference session and then turns to my work on savings banks. Next it broadens the concept of institutions providing affordable financial access to include more than microfinance institutions and discusses key questions about accessibility and the supply of access. It then summarizes a commentary on the three papers by Marguerite Robinson, who identifies in her contribution to the conference session three cross-cutting findings on profitability and access. First, providing access to the poor need not be an unprofitable activity, and indeed, access is provided more often when the process is kept profitable. Second, reaching scale in outreach to poor clients improves profitability. Third, while accessible finance is provided by many thousands of institutions worldwide, the vast bulk of customers are served by a few market leaders. The chapter concludes with thoughts on the structure and performance of the accessible finance industry and what in particular determines the chances of achieving breakthrough on the path toward full access.

The State of Microfinance: Outreach, Profitability, and Poverty

Working with a large dataset drawn from the three main sources on microfinance, CGAP's MicroBanking Bulletin (MBB) and Microfinance Information eXchange (MIX) and the Microcredit Summit (MCS), Gonzalez and Rosenberg put

2. For an example, see the description in Robinson (2001) of Bank Rakyat Indonesia's leveraging up of its welfare impact when it moved to a sustainable model.
3. See Adams, Graham, and von Pischke (1984).
4. Gonzales and Rosenberg (2006); Cull, Demirgüç-Kunt, and Morduch (2006); Peachey (2006).

together a single database on some 2,600 organizations that declared themselves to be in the microfinance market and that provided a total of 94 million microloans.[5] In effect, their paper is a partial version of the earlier work done by Rosenberg and colleagues for the CGAP study on double bottom line institutions.[6] It includes microfinance nongovernmental organizations (NGOs) and nonbank financial institutions (NBFIs), plus microfinance schemes run by commercial banks or policy lending institutions and some credit unions and cooperatives. It excludes most savings bank activity, most agricultural and development bank lending, and credit unions that do not see themselves as microfinance institutions.

The dataset contains a mix of information about institutional type, number of borrowers, loan size, and mix of borrowers (including management estimates of the number of borrowers in the "poorest" category), plus a measure of financial performance. The data are not of the quality used in the next paper by Robert Cull, Asli Demirgüç-Kunt, and Jonathan Morduch, but they cover far more institutions.[7] The main gaps are that there is no independent verification of inputs, the criteria for declaring nonperforming loans are not standardized, and the definition of sustainability makes no adjustment for differences in funding structure or level of subsidy received.

Despite those shortfalls, a number of interesting results emerge about who supplies microcredit. Typical microcredit penetration rates are still very low when measured as a percentage of a whole population—on the order of 2.5 percent in Asia and 1 percent elsewhere. Bangladesh remains the most penetrated country (18 percent of the whole population), followed by El Salvador (7 percent), Nicaragua (6 percent), and Bolivia (5 percent). Public sector programs and the self-help groups that they support account for about 60 percent of microcredit supply. NGOs, which are commonly perceived as the core of microfinance, in fact supply only 24 percent of total microloans, and licensed private microfinance institutions supply only 17 percent of the total. Supply of microcredit is growing at about 12 percent annually. At that rate, supply doubles every five to six years. Like many other industries, microcredit tends to be concentrated. The typical share of the largest microfinance institution (MFI) in a country is one-third of the entire market. The median share is 81 percent for the top five MFIs and 95 percent for the top ten. Microcredit also is concentrated on the global level, with the largest 10 percent of institutions supplying 75 percent of all microcredit covered

5. Gonzalez and Rosenberg (2006.)

6. Christen, Rosenberg, and Jayadeva (2004).

7. Cull, Demirgüç-Kunt, and Morduch (2006)

by the dataset. Given that the dataset misses a lot of very small institutions with tiny loan volumes, the concentration would be even more acute if all microcredit institutions could be captured.

Gonzalez and Rosenberg also examine sustainability. Defined as whether institutions cover their operating costs with operating revenue, operational sustainability appears difficult to achieve. Overall, more microloans (55 percent of the total) are supplied by unsustainable (loss-making) institutions than by sustainable ones, but there are significant differences by institutional type. Roughly 60 percent of microloans from NGOs and licensed private microfinance institutions are made by sustainable institutions. In contrast, public sector microcredit is rarely sustainable; more than 80 percent of public sector microloans are supplied by loss-making institutions—and that is after any subsidies. Moreover, the proportion of NGO microloans coming from sustainable institutions is trending upward quite strongly, from 53 percent in 2001 to 64 percent in 2004. Loss-making microfinance institutions dominate small-scale supply, but sustainable institutions are taking over among institutions that have more than about 10,000 customers. That may reflect early loss making in the start-up phase, when microfinance institutions necessarily have small numbers of borrowers.

The authors' regression work suggests that good managers can sustain both growth and profitability. Interestingly, there are few signs of economies of scale beyond 5,000 to 10,000 borrowers, and an institution that has failed to become sustainable by that point is unlikely to become profitable through further growth. Moreover, there are signs that institutions that are going to become profitable are reaching breakeven sooner and that overall, half of what are now sustainable institutions reached breakeven in three years or less.

The final issue addressed by Gonzalez and Rosenberg is whether reaching out to the poorest people affects profitability. That is not an easy question to answer because there are no really firm estimates of outreach. Loan size is assumed to be a proxy (smaller average loan size implies more outreach to the poorest people), but that needs testing. Institutions may offer management estimates of their outreach to the poorest people (defined as those living on less than one dollar a day or those in the bottom half of the group of people living below a nation's poverty line), but only very rarely are they independently verified. What Gonzalez and Rosenberg do find is that average loan size and self-estimates of outreach to the poorest people are negatively correlated, with an almost one-for-one trade-off, but that there is a lot of variation around the relationship, which overall is weak. In addition, the relationship between average loan size and profitability is weak, confirming the findings of the second paper, Cull, Demirgüç-Kunt, and Morduch, which uses a smaller sample of better-quality data. Gonzalez and Rosenberg's estimates of the trade-off show a very slightly negative correlation between return on assets and average loan size and very large variation around the estimate, particularly at the smallest average loan sizes.

Overall, therefore, Gonzalez and Rosenberg show that small loan size is a proxy, albeit a crude one, for outreach to the poorest people; that sustainability is not related to either loan size or the share of poor borrowers; and that the MFI market already is very concentrated and indeed is now concentrating around institutions that already are profitable. If that is the case, one might ask whether it is a good use of donor funds to let, as the authors put it, "a thousand flowers bloom." However, their data also show that current new entrants to the market are getting profitable more quickly than previous entrants. Moreover, economies of scale, in terms of customer numbers, are limited and apply only in the early stages, when an institution begins to build its client base.

Financial Performance and Outreach:
A Global Analysis of Leading Microbanks

Cull, Demirgüç-Kunt, and Morduch worked on a much smaller but higher-quality dataset for their paper, which takes as its starting point the challenge of realizing the full promise of microfinance: to reduce poverty without ongoing subsidies. Doing that requires translating high repayment rates into profits, a challenge for most microbanks and one that requires looking at more than repayment performance alone. This issue is addressed econometrically by using MicroBanking Bulletin data on 124 institutions in forty-nine countries—unusually high-quality data from institutions that are united in claiming a strong commitment to achieving financial self-sufficiency and willing to open their accounts to scrutiny. Cull, Demirgüç-Kunt, and Morduch feel that those institutions represent some of the best hopes for combining poverty reduction with profitmaking or, at least, for achieving a profit without an ongoing subsidy. Having wide-ranging cross-country data provides substantial variation in contractual types, prices, institutional sizes and locations, and target markets; that variation in turn provides a means to describe the nature and trade-offs implicit in different lending relationships. The dataset therefore allows the authors to examine for the first time several important questions in a large comparative survey:

—Does raising interest rates exacerbate agency problems, indicated by lower loan repayment rates and less profitability?

—Is there evidence of a trade-off between the depth of outreach to the poor and the pursuit of profitability?

—Has "mission drift" occurred—that is, have microbanks moved away from serving their poorer clients in pursuit of commercial viability?

The results of the study bring some good news for microfinance advocates. While the average return on assets was negative overall, more than half of the institutions in the survey already were profitable (even after accounting adjustments were made) and others were approaching profitability or at least financial self-sufficiency. Moreover, simple correlations on the whole set of institutions show little evidence of agency problems or trade-offs between outreach and profits. Nor is mission drift necessarily a consequence of striving to achieve profitability. That is, it may be possible to stay true to an initial social mission even while aggressively pursuing commercial goals.

Disaggregating institutions by lending type, however, uncovers trade-offs and tensions that are not apparent when no differentiation is made. The patterns of profitability and the nature of customers revealed by the dataset vary considerably with the design of the institutions, particularly in regard to the contracts that they sign with their clients. The Cull, Demirgüç-Kunt, and Morduch paper focuses on three main types of lending:

—The best-known approach is *group lending*, made popular by Grameen Bank and BancoSol. This method uses self-formed groups of customers who assume joint liability for the repayment of loans given to group members. This sort of joint liability contract can, in principle, mitigate moral hazard and adverse selection by harnessing internal group information and enforcement possibilities and putting them to use for the bank.

—Another method is *village banking*, which is based on larger groups than group lending but on a similar notion of joint liability, with a view to bringing the same potential benefits to the lender.

—The third main method is *individual-based lending*, which involves a conventional bilateral relationship between lender and borrower. Individual-based lending lacks the internal information and enforcement possibilities of joint liability lending. This type of microcredit is most vulnerable to the information problems in dealing with informally organized customers who have a limited track record and no collateral to offer as a way of improving contract compliance.

The dataset contains institutions representative of each approach—including twenty institutions based on village banks, fifty-six individual-based lenders, and forty-eight group-based lenders—enough to give generally robust findings for at least the two larger sets of institutions. Consistent with predictions from the economics of information, direct evidence on loan repayments shows that the fraction of a lender's portfolio that is at risk rises with interest rates for most of the institutions using the individual-based lending model. Moreover, raising interest rates beyond a certain point (60 percent is the estimate given) is counterproductive in terms of profit. That is absolutely consistent with adverse selection—only the worst borrowers who know that they carry a high risk of failure will rationally borrow at excessive rates. In contrast, raising interest rates in order to invest relatively more in training the institutional workforce is associated with greater profit for individual-based lenders because the extra employees can do more of the screening and monitoring that group- or village-based lenders get from their customers. To confirm that these relationships really are related to the lending method, the equations tested were structured to see whether the same effects applied to the two forms of joint liability lending. With one exception, they did not.

The Cull, Demirgüç-Kunt, and Morduch paper then addresses the question of why an institution would ever favor the individual-based approach over either of the joint liability methods. It shows that individual-based lenders mitigate the cost of individual screening by providing substantially larger loans (five times as large, on average). That way they can exploit a U-shaped cost curve for lending that the authors suggest bottoms out at roughly 2.5 times per capita gross domestic product (GDP)—interestingly, the upper limit of what the MBB calls high-end microfinance. Few institutions in the sample operate beyond that level.

Loan size typically is taken as a proxy for a customer's poverty level. The evidence suggests that for customers who are less poor and who are willing and able to invest in larger businesses, joint liability methods become cumbersome. Working with relatively few customers who take out larger loans can be a path to financial self-sufficiency for lenders, but they must develop the capacity to do individual-based lending. That path veers from the traditional focus of microfinance, with its emphasis on making smaller loans on as wide a scale as possible. However, Cull, Demirgüç-Kunt, and Morduch point out that the shift could still improve overall welfare—it is not just the poorest people who demand and can take advantage of better access to finance. Nevertheless, the authors note that larger institutions, particularly the older and more established ones, have on average lower measures of outreach and that there appears to be a trade-off between breadth of outreach (number of customers served) and depth of outreach (size of loan).

While that finding is not, strictly speaking, evidence of mission drift (that is, by pursuing improved financial performance, institutions reduce their focus on the poor), the results for larger and older institutions are consistent with the idea that as institutions mature and grow, they might focus increasingly on clients who can absorb larger loans. That said, the paper's results also suggest that financially self-sustaining individual-based lenders (as opposed to all lenders) tend to have a smaller average loan size and lend more to women, suggesting that pursuit of profit and outreach to the poor can go hand in hand. The question of whether larger institutions serve an absolutely greater number of the very poor remains open, and it can be answered only with disaggregated data.

Overall, the paper concludes that there are agency problems in microfinance that are overcome by joint liability lending or by spending more to screen individual customers. It also concludes that there are cost economies from increasing loan size that end only at the upper ceiling of the microfinance target market. Interestingly, however, cost efficiency itself is not a predictor of profitability, because of the net profitability to individual-based lenders of spending more on staff to improve credit screening. Moreover, just raising interest rates does not in itself raise profitability because it is accompanied by more bad debts and because beyond a certain threshold (estimated here at 60 percent), it actually becomes counterproductive. Finally, while older, larger institutions have worse outreach indicators, financial self-sustainability can go hand in hand with greater outreach, at least for individual-based lenders.

The authors find that institutional design and orientation have a substantial effect on patterns of profitability, loan repayment, and cost reduction. They find in particular that lenders who do not use group-based methods experience weaker portfolio quality and lower profit rates when they just raise interest rates substantially. For individual-based lenders, the key to achieving profitability is to invest more heavily in staff costs, a finding consistent with the economics of information. The authors go on to demonstrate that economies of scale are limited in terms of loan size, undermining the view that microfinance is by definition expensive because of its small loan sizes.

Savings Banks and the Double Bottom Line

My contribution to the conference tests three propositions: Do the 1.1 billion account relationships at savings banks worldwide truly count as accessible? Do different types of savings bank have different levels of outreach? If a microfinance business is accessible, has it been built at the expense of profitability?[8] The paper shows how outreach can be assessed by using the World Bank's identified dimensions of access and gives savings banks a relatively good score on how usable they are for even low-value and irregular financial needs; their openness to all levels of society and household members; their balance of formality and approachability; and the capacity of many of them to meet the full spectrum of customers' functional needs.

Although savings banks generally are accessible on all four dimensions, there are differences among types. The paper identifies three distinct types of savings bank

8. Peachey (2006).

in terms of operational focus: payments and savings institutions that do not do credit business with customers; payments, savings, and (micro) credit institutions that do at least some small-scale crediting; other payments, savings, and credit institutions for which the World Savings Banks Institute (WSBI) has no information on credit mix. Savings banks are first ranked by a composite indicator of likely outreach that balances account numbers against average balances relative to per capita income; next they are split into the groups outlined above. They then can be plotted in terms of their operational focus, country income band, probable outreach, and assessed level of access in the countries within which they operate. No absolute case can be made that one particular operational focus is guaranteed to be superior to another in terms of outreach. That said, there are more examples of broad-outreach payments, savings, and credit banks doing at least some low average value lending than there are examples of broad-outreach payments and savings only banks. Moreover, having a demonstrable capacity to do small-scale lending reinforces outreach more than having just a generalized credit capacity. The paper concludes that combining savings and payment services with small-scale credit provision offers the best chance of broadening outreach.

The paper also establishes that it is difficult to increase access without having a strong savings bank movement, although occasionally a retail-focused agricultural bank may partially fill any gap left by an underdeveloped savings bank. That is illustrated in figure 4-1. The grey area represents accounts per adult at savings and other policy lending banks. The dark line represents all accounts at double bottom line institutions, expressed per adult. The white spaces under the line represent supply by microfinance NGOs and NBFIs, plus credit unions and cooperatives and microbanks, plus specialist microcredit schemes run by commercial banks. The figure suggests that much microfinance may substitute for savings banking only in countries with repressed access (less than one accessible account at a double bottom line institution for one in five adults).

The paper then looks at savings bank profitability (see figure 4-2a). Two striking conclusions emerge. Despite a high degree of social ownership, savings banks are a predominantly profitable group of institutions; only six of the seventy WSBI members reporting profit data made a loss in 2003. That suggests that for those that do lending, where that credit goes is less significant than it historically has been in policy lending institutions such as agricultural or development banks. Moreover, profitability does not vary systematically with relative outreach—that is, as savings banks broaden their outreach, there is no reason why their profitability should fall. The exception might be at the very top end of the spectrum, where the very large broad-outreach savings banks in stable, advanced economies are able to operate at finer net profit margins.

Figure 4-1. *Double Bottom Line Accounts, by Type of Supplier*

Number of accessible accounts per adult

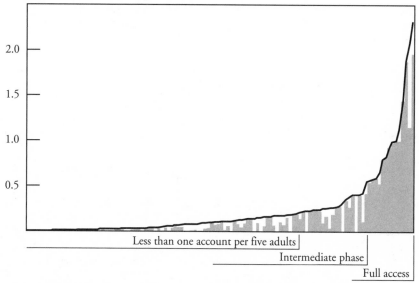

Source: WSBI (2006).

Underpinning the ability to sustain profitability as outreach broadens is the ability to keep cost ratios under control (see figure 4-2b). For the savings banks with the broadest outreach, all but three have cost-to-asset ratios below 5 percent. That said, there are some narrow-outreach savings banks that also have cost-to-asset ratios below 5 percent, but far more of them have ratios above 5 percent. The paper suggests that underpinning generally good cost ratios is the very high productivity of the staff of savings banks, which typically have around 1,000 accounts per employee (see figure 4-2c). A microfinance NGO or NBFI, in contrast, typically has around 150 loans per employee. There are differences between loan and savings businesses, but even with lending, the savings bank model seems to work best when it delivers a high volume of simple operations efficiently. The relationship between productivity and outreach is complex. As outreach broadens, it tends to require a broader range of products, thereby increasing complexity and limiting productivity. But to achieve really broad outreach, savings banks must keep costs under control and therefore productivity high. The overall conclusion of the paper is that savings banks can broaden their outreach without compromising profitability and therefore can justifiably be called double bottom line institutions, balancing as they do the twin objectives of providing access and making a necessary profit.

Figure 4-2. *Distribution of Savings Bank Profitability and Cost Efficiency*

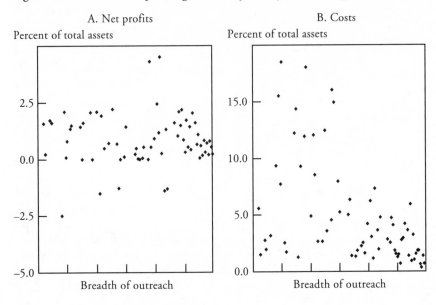

A. Net profits
Percent of total assets

B. Costs
Percent of total assets

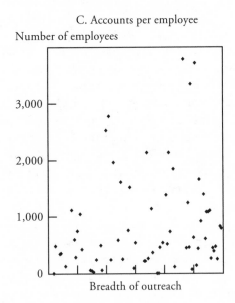

C. Accounts per employee
Number of employees

Source: WSBI (2006).

Double Bottom Line Institutions and the Supply of Access

In recent years, the conception of the range of institutions involved in providing access to affordable financial services has been expanded beyond microfinance institutions to include other kinds of financial institution that have a similar commitment to providing access. That expansion has brought in a range of policy lending institutions, particularly agricultural and rural finance institutions, which operate at loan sizes within the CGAP definition of microfinance, albeit toward the top end. A few of them would classify themselves as microfinance institutions—for example, Bank Rakyat Indonesia (BRI)—but many would not. It also has brought in credit unions and credit cooperatives that operate at loan sizes very similar to those of explicitly microfinance-oriented institutions but that have a clearer commitment to mobilizing savings. And finally, it has brought in the savings bank movement, with its billion-plus accessible savings accounts around the developing world and a hitherto unrecognized number of small-scale loan accounts as well.

This conceptual expansion does not follow any unidirectional, chronological sequence. The microfinance idea has not spread out from the established microfinance industry to other institutions taking up the same model; rather, recognition has expanded that there is more than one tradition that shares a fundamental concern about access to finance. Savings banks and credit unions and cooperatives have been operating in this field for centuries, and not just in the industrialized world; the model was taken up wholesale in many newly independent developing countries and often was implanted even during colonial times. Agricultural banks and rural finance institutions have an equally long history of trying to expand finance outside the major urban centers, although there might be legitimate doubts as to their success in regard to delivery.

That is not to say that learning cannot take place. Some commercial banks have opened units that focus specifically on microfinance, having seen the profit that can be made from small-scale lending. Further, some agricultural and rural finance institutions have moved themselves almost entirely over to an explicitly microfinance footing. Many savings banks in developing countries around the world run major microfinance programs either as one of their standard services or as special schemes.

Double bottom line finance has operated in similar ways in advanced industrial economies. The term "double bottom line" emerged from the Johnson administration's Great Society program in the United States in the late 1960s, which led to the creation of a number of community development financial institutions (CDFIs), which have made in total several billion dollars of investment in underbanked communities. Banks followed with similar approaches, providing several more billions of dollars of finance. But those amounts are dwarfed by the trillion dollars or so of commercial bank finance provided to poorer communities under the Community Reinvestment Act—an amount that in turn is barely half the funds managed by ethical investment vehicles in the United States, some of which are now beginning to target the communities served by CDFIs. Even these very large numbers are smaller than the deposits mobilized and loans advanced by savings banks across the industrialized economies of the world. These banks all share a commitment to retail banking—that is, serving the mass household and enterprise markets—and maintain a deep regional presence, not just a presence in major money centers. They are operating in a socially responsible way and often remain or even strengthen their presence in communities and market segments that have been abandoned by other, purely commercial, banks.

The definition of microfinance can be expanded, first, beyond microcredit provided by the self-declared microfinance industry—the sort of institutions that submit data to CGAP's MIX-MBB or Microcredit Summit or both—estimated at some 94 million loans in number, or 162 million account relationships. When one adds similar double bottom line institutions that do not explicitly define themselves as MFIs, the numbers of account relationships expand to some 1.5 billion. These figures broaden the quantitative measure of access to cover not just loans but also savings, deposits, and membership contributions.

Such broader measures offer a new way to measure the potential supply of accessible finance, based on account relationships. Account relationships are calculated as the larger of loan numbers, savings/deposit account numbers, or membership numbers.[9] The presumption is that deposit-taking or membership-based institutions would lend primarily to depositors or members, so in those cases the number of savings/deposit accounts or the number of members would be a good representation of the potential loan market for these institutions. For MFIs that require only compulsory savings contributions from borrowers and take no voluntary savings or deposits, counting savings and deposit accounts reveals nothing new about the potential loan market. Only the number of loans is counted, and indeed it often is the only number supplied. For some microlenders, there are no savings accounts at all, and, again, the number of loans is the only measure of the potential for accessible finance.

Broadening the universe of institutions doubles the measure of the supply of credit. But it is the combination of broadening institutional coverage and expanding the definition of the potential loan market to include account relationships that dramatically expands the measure of potential supply (see table 4-1).

9. Christen, Rosenberg, and Jayadeva (2004).

Table 4-1. *Supply of Accessible Finance*

Item	Self-declared microfinance institutions	Other institutions with a mandate to provide access to finance	Total platform for the supply of potentially accessible finance
Loans only	94 million	143 million	237 million
Total account relationships	162 million	1,336 million	1,498 million

Source: WSBI (2006).

All the quantitative analysis leaves two major questions to be answered:

—Are the institutions with a mandate to provide access really accessible?

—With so many potentially accessible accounts across the developing world—enough for nearly every second adult to have one—is there really a problem with access to finance?

The answers to those questions—a qualified yes to the first question and an emphatic yes to the second—are explored next.

Are Double Bottom Line Institutions Accessible?

The World Bank and others have developed a coherent framework for measuring access.[10] Kumar and Ellis lay out four dimensions of access from the demand side:

—Does access exist? Is it used? Is it usable?

—Is access available at the individual level or household level?

—Are the institutions that offer access predominantly formal or informal?

—What functional products and services must customers be able to use to qualify as having access?

Interestingly, geographical accessibility is not featured as a prime dimension of access in this framework, only as an explanatory variable. Affordability, another traditional aspect of access, also is not an independent measure but a factor regarding usability.

These demand-driven dimensions of access can be reframed in terms of the supply of access; by reframing, one can avoid holding a debate over access entirely in terms of what the customer wants. Instead, these measures can help to bridge the gap between consumer demand and the needs and conceptual frameworks of financial services firms. The supply side counterparts to the four demand-driven dimensions described above might include:

10. See Kumar and Ellis (2005).

—Usability. Are users able to open accounts with small balances and maintain low-value and generally irregular flows without paying charges that make the account a value-destroyer?

—Openness. Do account opening and operating procedures discriminate against family members other than heads of household? Is the customer interface approachable by both?

—Formality/informality. Where on the spectrum, from fully regulated deposit money banks to unregulated informal institutions, does a supplier lie? Is regulation sufficient to protect customers' money without compromising usability and openness?

—Functional capacity. Does the supplier have the capacity to meet some or all of the four core product needs (payments, savings, credit, and insurance)?

The five main double bottom line institutional groups covered in this chapter can, building out from the self-declared microfinance community, be characterized as shown in table 4-2.

Overall, the double bottom line institutions discussed here can be described as reasonably but not always fully accessible. Organizational form and entrepreneurial constraints seem to hold back the more grassroots organizations, such as NGOs, credit unions and cooperatives, and community microbanks. There are, of course, exceptions, but the data suggest that the problem must be widespread. As formality increases, so does product range. Formality, however, often is accompanied by less openness to the poor, whether because of government regulation or business strategy. Moreover, many policy lending institutions have serious legal and governance constraints and suffer from political interference, which leads them to lend to the wealthy or well-connected even when they offer subsidized credit, which is supposed to target the poor and financially excluded.

The issue remains of why access cannot be left to mainstream depositary banks. Here a recent World Bank study presented at the conference gives some clear pointers.[11] At first glance the results are surprising—deposit money banks (that is, mostly commercial banks) service large numbers of loans and deposits. Even in the poorest countries, they still probably represent the biggest suppliers of financial services, in terms of numbers as well as value. They typically run twice as many deposit accounts as savings banks do and 1.5 times as many loan accounts as microfinance NGOs and NBFIs. But in terms of accessibility, they are out of the range of even the high-end microfinance target market, with average loan sizes and savings balances equivalent to more than 1,000 percent and 500 percent respectively of per capita GDP in the poorest countries. In middle-income and particularly

11. Beck, Demirgüç-Kunt, and Martinez Peria (2005).

Table 4-2. *Characteristics of the Five Main Double Bottom Line Institutional Groups*

Type	Description	Size
Microfinance NGOs and unregulated non-bank institutions	These institutions operate mainly in poorer countries, providing low average value credits but overall accessibility. They are held back by limited savings services and almost a nonexistent payment capacity. That often is a reflection of their less formal structure and seems to be a significant constraint on building scale.	43 million accounts 50 million total account relationships
Commercial bank microcredit and regulated non-bank institutions	A more formal operating framework gives these institutions more scope to offer credit plus savings and payment services. They operate, however, upward from the top end of the broad target market for microfinance, suggesting some trade-off between usability/openness and increased formality.	
Credit unions and cooperatives and community microbanks	These organizations have stronger self-regulation and a fuller product range than most microfinance NGOs. They appear to be able to scale their business to country income levels, but they are not significant players in the poorest countries.	25–30 million loan accounts 50–55 million total account relationships
Savings banks	These banks are capable of scaling core savings and payments business to country income level and are not insignificant providers of small-scale credits. Although balancing of functional capacity, openness, and formality can be achieved under special regulatory regimes that usually apply to savings banks, it is not always done.	30–40 million small-scale loan accounts 1.15 billion total account relationshps
Policy lending institutions and government-backed self-help groups	These institutions manage significant volumes of lending and savings business and have the capacity to process payments as well. However, apart from a few notable exceptions, this group is known for its vulnerability to political influence, which perversely reduces the openness and usability even of subsidized credit.	Around 125 million loan accounts 245 million total account relationships

Source: WSBI (2006).

upper-income countries, the gap in average loan and deposit sizes narrows markedly and deposit money banks clearly become a much greater part of the fabric of access.

Improving access in the poorer and poorest developing and transition economies is therefore, at least in part, an issue of creating the right conditions for a full range of double bottom line institutions to function effectively, not just an issue of proliferating institutions and providing finance.

Do Double Bottom Line Institutions Deliver Access?

Another question arises: if there are approximately 1.5 billion predominantly accessible account relationships spread across double bottom line institutions in developing countries and even more commercial bank accounts, why is there a problem with access? At first glance, enough account relationships exist to allow one for almost every second adult and at least every household in developing countries, but field experience indicates that access remains a very real problem across much of the developing world. The answer has two parts: First, figure 4-3 shows the marked disconnect between who does accessible lending and who provides the bulk of accessible savings mobilization. Barriers are beginning to break down, but the heterogeneity of double bottom line institutions may impede the crossover of business models and make collaborating on business opportunities rather difficult. Second, the country coverage of double bottom line account relationships is skewed toward a few large countries (China, India, Indonesia, Russia, and so forth) and a penetration level of less than one account relationship for every two households is indicated for some 60 percent of the developing and transition economies in figure 4-4.

What then can be said about how access might be built in developing countries? One way of exploring this question would be to examine the progression of access in countries at different levels of income. Table 4-3 shows, for each institutional type, the median number of loans supplied and the median number of deposit accounts serviced per thousand households, for each country income quintile from the poorest fifth of developing countries to the richest fifth. The first striking feature of table 4-3 is that it confirms the point made above—that even in the poorest fifth of countries, commercial banks on average serve significant numbers of loan and deposit accounts (and have even higher lending and savings balances). But that cannot be taken as constituting access because overall account provision is still low (with just twenty-eight loan accounts and 254 deposit accounts per thousand households) and because the average value outstanding per account is high relative to per capita GDP. Who fills the gap left by commercial bank loan and deposit activity, which is so far out of reach of the mass market? First come savings banks,

Figure 4-3. *Mix of Loans and Deposits at Double Bottom Line Institutions*

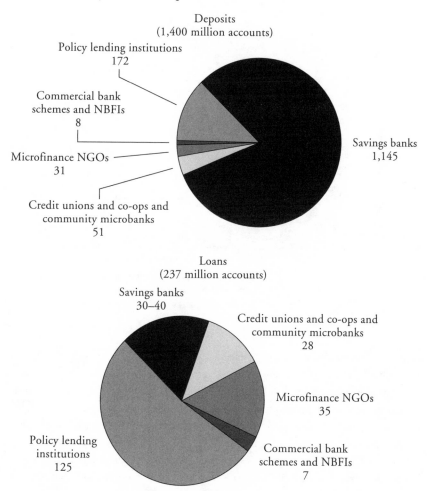

Source: WSBI (2006).

which provide significant volumes of deposit accounts at average balances and are much more within the reach of the mass middle market. Unfortunately, within the typical poorest country, savings banks provide only one account for every tenth household. Moreover, all of the other double bottom line institutions taken together do not quite match the deposit penetration of savings banks on their own. When all double bottom line institutions are taken as a group, there is barely one deposit account for every fifth household in the poorest fifth of countries. Taking into

Figure 4-4. *Household Penetration of Double Bottom Line Institutions*

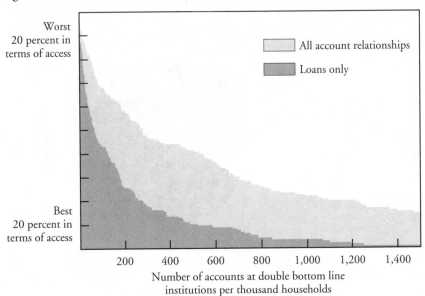

Source: WSBI (2006).

account the households that are rich enough to have multiple commercial bank accounts, the resulting estimate would suggest that up to two-thirds of households in the poorest fifth of developing countries use informal, often high-cost finance.

The picture is even starker when it comes to the supply of credit. The half of total loan accounts provided by commercial banks are at such a high multiple of per capita GDP that they must pertain mostly to large-scale enterprises and high net worth individuals. That leaves slightly less than thirty loans per thousand households from double bottom line institutions at average sizes that are any-where near affordable for the mass market.

Interestingly, deposit provision rises quite fast as countries progress up the income scale. Typical savings bank provision of both deposit and loan accounts jumps sixfold as one moves up from the poorest fifth of countries to the next fifth, which are still poor. Provision by policy lending institutions and credit unions and cooperatives also jumps sharply, but total provision by microfinance NGOs, NBFIs, and private commercial bank microfinance schemes falls slightly. Overall the net effect is still strongly positive, with deposit account supply by double bottom line institutions almost up to one account for every 1.5 households in poor (but not the poorest) countries. Even loan account provision from these institutions rises to

Table 4-3. *Loan and Savings Penetration, by Institutional Type and Country Income Band*

Institution and country income quintile	Loan accounts per 1,000 households	Average loan size (percent of per capita GDP)	Deposit accounts per 1,000 households	Average deposit (percent of per capita GDP)
Commercial banks				
5 richest	1,257	235	5,183	44
4	829	275	2,788	56
3	276	502	1,948	55
2	187	719	687	256
1 poorest	28	1,074	254	510
Savings banks				
5 richest	169	23	1541	31
4	244	17	1,637	5
3	80	31	462	9
2	10	55	580	30
1 poorest	1	274	94	33
Policy lending institutions				
5 richest				
4	6	239	521	
3	42	245	198	
2	22	112	85	
1 poorest	5	279	20	
Credit unions/cooperatives and community microbanks				
5 richest	66	50	205	20
4	105	28	272	14
3	22	44	51	17
2	11	26	31	13
1 poorest	3	46	10	13
Microfinance NGOs				
5 richest				
4	3	12	1	0
3	24	17	3	2
2	10	9	6	2
1 poorest	13	20	12	6

(continued)

Table 4-3. *Loan and Savings Penetration, by Institutional Type and Country Income Band* (continued)

Institution and country income quintile	Loan accounts per 1,000 households	Average loan size (percent of per capita GDP)	Deposit accounts per 1,000 households	Average deposit (percent of per capita GDP)
Microfinance NBFIs				
5 richest				
4	4	8	0	5
3	3	46	17	16
2	3	58	2	6
1 poorest	6	78	12	21
Private commercial bank microfinance				
5 richest				
4	1	19	42	3
3	3	201	4	47
2	2	96	6	38
1 poorest	1	118	3	45

Source: WSBI (2006).

nearly sixty loans per thousand households, still very low but improving. In sum, at least half of all households have some sort of account at a double bottom line institution. Thus, the typical country in the poor (but not poorest) income band already has a platform for providing access to the majority of households, as measured by account relationships.

By the time the middle fifth of countries is reached, there is a dramatic change in commercial bank provision, with twice as many deposit accounts as there are households. The number of deposit accounts at double bottom line institutions barely changes (750 per thousand households), but lending surges to 175 loans per thousand households. By this stage, therefore, commercial banks must be penetrating down into the mass middle market. But double bottom line institutions also are holding their own in the same market and are capable of reaching further through it because they can still operate at significantly lower average deposit balances and loan sizes. The data would suggest that what the World Bank defines as the "access strand" (see Kumar and Ellis 2005) is fully covered by banks and near banks in middle-income countries. Moreover, the role of microfinance institutions is to provide financial services to the 10 or 20 percent of adults who are left after commercial and savings banks have provided mass access.

Above the middle-income bands, accounts proliferate at both commercial and double bottom line institutions (apart from specialist microfinance institutions) and average balances fall. At that level, there remains a small but persistent core of excluded adults, and issues of sex, race, and literacy (both basic and financial) require focused interventions to help them bridge the seemingly impenetrable barriers thrown up by product design, operating procedures, and required documentation.[12]

Summarizing Double Bottom Line Institutions' Supply of Access

The analysis presented here leads to three main conclusions. First, accessible finance is much more than microfinance. Bringing in parallel traditions of providing access—some of them centuries old—increases the potential platform for access enormously. Moving from microfinance to accessible finance doubles the measurable supply of small-scale loans and increases by a factor of fifteen the overall platform for access by bringing in more than a billion small-scale savings accounts, plus much more access to payment services. Second, expanding the range of institutions to include all those with a mandate to provide access moves the balance of provision toward more formal institutions. As more formal institutions are included, one can consider new possibilities in the range of services supplied, particularly in regard to voluntary savings and payment services. But relying on formal institutions can work against actual accessibility. Third, poor supply of access now seems to be more of a problem in the poorest fifth of developing countries. Moving from the bottom to the next-to-the-bottom income quintile suggests that access is increasing through double bottom line institutions and that the majority of households now have an account. For middle-quintile countries, commercial banks penetrate the mass market and the special role of double bottom line institutions is to ensure that the less advantaged do not miss out on the general expansion of access.

Cross-Cutting Issues

As Marguerite Robinson pointed out during the conference, the three papers discussed here are rich in thought—and in data, analysis, and findings.[13] And they are much needed at this particular time in the development of the accessible

---

12. For an overview of the difference between lack of access and exclusion, see my work with Alan Roe (WSBI 2004) and Kempson, Atkinson, and Pilley (2004). These measures of penetration are all per thousand households, rather than population. I am grateful to Marguerite Robinson for making such a strong case for using households as a single financial unit for measuring penetration and to John Bongaarts of the Population Council for his fascinating paper on household size and composition in the developing world (Bongaarts 2001).

13. This section reproduces edited comments presented at the conference by Marguerite Robinson. I am grateful to Robinson for permission to reproduce them in this chapter.

finance industry. None of the papers could have been written ten years ago—or even five years ago—at anything like the level of quality that their authors have now achieved. And so it seems appropriate to recognize the underlying databases for the papers and all those who have contributed to building them. The databases—by the Consultative Group to Assist the Poor, the MicroBanking Bulletin, Microfinance Information eXchange, World Savings Banks Institute, the Microcredit Summit, and others—are among the industry's most crucial resources.

Each of the papers discussed has a global perspective and provides findings of multiple kinds. The focus here is on some of the junctures at which the major findings of the papers converge—and on what that convergence says about the provision of accessible financial services today and as it may develop in the coming decades. Each paper brings to the table different expertise, interests, and perspectives. Each has as a result a different set of questions, data, and conclusions. And yet some of the most important findings are common to all the papers. In their varied ways, the papers show how profitability and outreach can go together. As the Cull, Demirgüç-Kunt, and Morduch paper puts it, "pursuing higher profits and focusing on poorer customers can go hand in hand."

Providing Access Can Be Profitable

Most of the institutions in the microfinance databases used for the three papers, excluding most government-directed lending schemes, are profitable. Moreover, many currently unprofitable MFIs are coming close to reaching profitability. Of the savings banks reported on, more than 90 percent are profitable. Of particular interest is the finding from the Gonzalez and Rosenberg paper that profitable MFIs grow faster than nonprofitable ones. That is not an especially surprising finding, but it is very useful to have it documented on this scale—with data from 2,600 MFIs from around the world.

What then do the papers say about how institutions committed to providing mass access become profitable? Competent management is critical for any financial institution that hopes to reach profitability and to grow. That finding is entirely consistent with field experience with MFIs in many parts of the world, and it is borne out by both the Gonzalez and Rosenberg and the Cull, Demirgüç-Kunt, and Morduch papers:

—Gonzalez and Rosenberg show that with the exception of government-directed lending schemes, the majority of institutions serve their customers profitably. Moreover, apart from the very smallest NGOs, profitable MFIs grow faster than unprofitable ones, and they are steadily taking over the market. Their data suggest that the trend should be sustainable, because today MFIs reach profitability more quickly (half of them have done so in three years or less).

—The Cull, Demirgüç-Kunt, and Morduch paper makes the important, although not so widely understood, point that higher labor costs associated with learning the market and training staff actually pay off and improve profitability. Investing in learning and training is exactly what Bank Rakyat Indonesia's micro-banking system did twenty years ago in Indonesia and what it still does today. Moreover, BRI's microbanking was profitable in 1986 and has been profitable every year since, even throughout the East Asian crisis of the late 1990s, when Indonesia's banking system collapsed. BRI's focus on market knowledge and staff training has, of course, been a necessary but not sufficient condition for its performance over the years. Management has been a key factor, and other factors also have played a role.

It is, however, interesting that the Gonzalez and Rosenberg paper on MFIs and my paper on savings banks report opposite findings from their respective data-bases on how different institutions reach profitability. Profitability is reported to be driven mainly by interest rates and spreads in MFIs and by low costs and high productivity in savings banks. As competition in the microfinance sector in-creases, MFI interest rates and spreads will be driven down, and the MFIs that succeed will be those that learn to decrease costs and increase productivity. More-over, as savings banks increase their microcredit activities, they may see higher costs and lower productivity, at least for some time. All institutions that focus on providing access will need to plan and manage their profitability and growth as the industry moves forward.

Outreach to Poor Clients and Profitability Can Go Together

All three papers agree that there need not be a trade-off between profitability and outreach; with a little variation in caveats, the authors all conclude that outreach to poor clients and commercial profitability can go together. And there is consid-erable evidence to that effect:

—Gonzalez and Rosenberg show there is absolutely no significant statistical relationship between the proportion of all borrowers who are classified as very poor and operational self-sufficiency for the more than 2,000 MFIs in the Micro-credit Summit database. Admittedly, the data have their weaknesses in that the proportion classified as very poor is a self-estimate by MFI managers and the def-inition of self-sufficiency is not as full as it could be.

—The Cull, Demirgüç-Kunt, and Morduch paper shows, if anything, some evidence of reverse mission drift for MFIs following the individual lending model once all other factors are adjusted for. In other words, pursuing higher profits and focusing on poor clients can go hand in hand.

—I find that, apart from the largest savings banks in advanced economies, broad-outreach savings banks operate at exactly the same rates of return on assets (up to 2.5 percent) as narrow-outreach savings banks. Moreover, I find that explicitly providing a microfinance facility is a major determinant of whether a savings bank achieves broad outreach, suggesting that savings banks can push into the less well-off segments of society without compromising their profitability.

Scale and Market Share

Accessible finance is provided by thousands of institutions worldwide, but the bulk of customers are served by the market leaders. Gonzalez and Rosenberg find that worldwide, just 9 percent of MFIs attract 75 percent of all microcredit borrowers. Looking at median shares across individual country microcredit markets, they find that the single largest MFI typically accounts for one-third of an entire country market, the top five MFIs typically account for just over 80 percent of a market, and the top ten MFIs account for 95 percent.

If the platform for this analysis is expanded to include savings banks and policy lending institutions, as in my paper, and to include savers as well as borrowers, then the concentration would be even starker. Just 182 institutions in the combined savings bank and policy lending group together have some 1.4 billion account relationships, while there are 94 million total microcredit borrowers in the Gonzalez and Rosenberg database.

The data do need to be interpreted with care, however. There are a great many countries with five or fewer double bottom line institutions; in such countries, concentration may be a sign of immaturity, not maturity. But figures 4-5a and 4-5b show still high median five-firm concentration ratios in countries with more than fifty institutions. That suggests a mature industry. Figure 4-5c reinforces the dichotomy. Household penetration can be as high or as low in a country that has between one and five double bottom line institutions as it is in a country that has between five and ten institutions—or indeed between ten and one hundred. If anything, having a large number of institutions often seems to increase penetration only to every second household and rarely any further.

On balance, the evidence suggests that commercial microfinance is becoming an industry, much like other industries. In this context, Marguerite Robinson points out that a recent development in microfinance is instructive. In April 2006, the Harvard Business School held its first-ever executive education course for microfinance industry leaders from around the world. Conducted with ACCION International, the course, entitled "Strategic Leadership for Microfinance," exposed CEOs and other MFI managers to a variety of experiences of corporate leaders in different industries. Course participants seemed to find the faculty discussions on strategic leadership in other industries—which covered organizational structure, strategic planning, market positioning, decisionmaking

Figure 4-5. *Indicators of Industry Structure*

A. Market share held by largest institutions[a]

Percent market share of top group

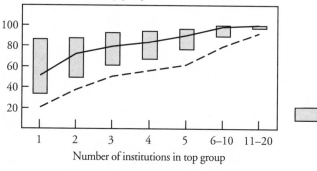

Number of institutions in top group

B. Market share held by largest institutions[b]

Percent market share of top group

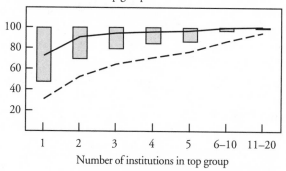

Number of institutions in top group

C. Household penetration versus number of institutions[c]

Number of institutions (log scale)

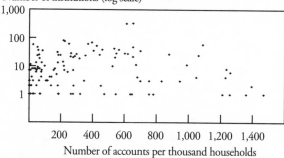

Number of accounts per thousand households

	Middle range of all country experience (between upper and lower quartiles)
— — —	Median value all countries
——	Median value for countries with over fifty institutions

Source: WSBI (2006).
a. Self-declared MFI loans only.
b. All double bottom line account relationships.
c. All accounts at double bottom line institutions.

processes, hiring practices, and the like—to be quite directly relevant to their MFIs. In many cases, the MFIs are now expanding, very rapidly in some institutions. Some institutions have changed their legal status, and some are currently in the process of doing so. Many face changes in ownership, governance, or management or any combination of the three. And all appeared well aware of the transitions, additions, and metamorphoses taking place in the emerging microfinance industry—including new kinds of competition, mergers and acquisitions, strategic alliances, technology-driven competitive advantages, and so on.

Accessible Finance: What Do We Know Now?

Together, the three papers presented at the conference session suggest the extent to which accessible finance already is well established within the financial sector or is rapidly moving into it. With the exception of most government microfinance lenders, most of the MFIs discussed already are profitable and providing substantial access to poor clients. Other MFIs are getting close. Industry leaders are dominating their country's markets, and microfinance is developing in ways that are similar to those in other industries. And it is the clients of MFIs, most of all their poor clients, who are benefiting. Savings banks, with their 1.1 billion savings accounts—little recognized in microfinance literature until recently—have a long history of combining profitability with wide access, and many provide other products and services, including small-scale loans, in addition to the savings accounts for which they are better known.

Now that it is becoming known that specifically "micro" finance can be profitable and that there is a very large unmet demand for it, many new kinds of organizations are entering the commercial microfinance market, playing a variety of roles. They include some existing institutions, such as savings and agricultural banks, that have a mandate to provide accessible financial services and that are broadening their outreach, but they also include players that traditionally have not been interested in the bottom of the pyramid (BoP) market, such as multinational banks, domestic banks, large retailers with wide branch networks, and service companies. Sometimes such institutions expand access to the poor directly or set up their own specialist financial institutions; sometimes they form alliances with MFIs or commercial banks already operating in the low-income market.

In the twenty-first century, for the first time in history, the financial sector will become largely inclusive. Its transformation is now in progress. And given that accessible finance can be profitable, that such a range of businesses—for example, the world's largest cement producer, India's largest private bank, and Mexico's largest retailer—are becoming interested in BoP markets, and that large unmet demand for financial services exists, the trend is probably irreversible. But the industry leaders of today will not necessarily be those of tomorrow.

In their own ways, all these papers and others signal that in its coming of age, accessible yet commercial finance may be reaching the end of what might be called the "Versus Decades"—the years of endless debates on MFI profitability versus service to the poor, subsidies versus sustainability, for-profits versus not-for-profits, group versus individual lending, savings versus credit, and the like. By documenting and analyzing a crucial transitional stage in the development of the commercial microfinance industry, these papers help to shift the industry's mind-set from the past to the present and on to the future.

Conclusion: Structure, Performance, and Breakthrough

What is needed now, for policymakers and practitioners alike, is a more useful way to evaluate suppliers of accessible finance than just by using institutional form. If the data could capture a recurring theme of the conference—namely that microfinance is a functional capacity, not an institutional form—then it would be easier to understand how a breakthrough in the provision of accessible finance has occurred in some countries and what has stopped it from happening in others. For example, is any failure in supplying access the result of a shortfall in provision by commercial banks or double bottom line institutions? Is it because the mobilizers of microsavings have not lived up to the potential clearly demonstrated in breakthrough countries? Is it because savings mobilization and credit creation are too disconnected? Or is it because the credit side of the business is too fragmented, with lots of small-scale, high-cost NGOs where, despite all good intentions, the market that has been created works no better in economic terms to deliver affordable finance than does the imperfect competition typical of informal money lending?[14]

This last point is a controversial one in an industry in which all the players are essentially on the "good" side. But it has to be faced. In some countries the development of the machinery of microfinance—either through new institutions or the reinvigoration of older double bottom line traditions—has brought greater access, deeper financial systems, and demonstrable reductions in poverty. By contrast, in many other countries the proliferation of microfinance institutions may have led to worthwhile microlevel poverty alleviation—the evidence is mixed[15]—but it has not delivered widespread access, nor has it delivered deeper financial

14. See Robinson (2001).
15. See Morduch and Hayley (2002).

systems. Those countries have missed out on the extra growth and generalized reduction in poverty that comes from financial deepening.

One point that will have to be addressed in future work on the supply of accessible finance is the one made by Marguerite Robinson regarding the evolving financial pressures on institutions achieving breakthrough. For credit-based institutions, reaching scale means making a profit without relying so much on very high spread and fee yields—that is, somehow achieving economies of scale on costs. For savings-based institutions, however, the pressures may work in the opposite direction, with profitability best maintained by spending a bit more to develop a good-quality, small-scale lending service and opening it to the classic microfinance target market. Table 4-4 shows the current gap in the way that the two different ends of the double bottom line spectrum make their profit. Savings banks operate at cost/income ratios that are much closer to those of commercial banks than even the more financially sustainable MFIs, let alone all MFIs.

The dichotomy on costs, in particular, is an important issue for the supply of access. Finance is, despite its special place in the economy, an industry like any other; it has a cost of production, an equilibrium price (maybe free, maybe distorted), and a return on capital. If some supply side factor means that the provision of banking services to everyone is necessarily expensive, there are two ways that access will be denied to the poor. If the higher cost is passed on in prices, the service will be priced out of the reach of the poor. All finance is the dematerialization of spending power and its transmission between places or over time or both. If the cost of that dematerialization is more than the insecurity cost of cash or the inefficiency cost of barter, the poor will not waste scarce resources paying for it. Alternatively, if higher costs are not passed on, the return on capital will be depressed and eventually supply will be repressed, because the activity will not be profitable and cannot attract capital.

But the data behind table 4-4 do not yet allow any answers regarding what makes the difference between continued lack of access and the process of institutional breakthrough that ultimately moves a country toward full access. To go back to a point made earlier, if this analysis is to be of any use to policymakers and practitioners alike, a more useful assessment is needed of suppliers—by their accessibility, not just their institutional form. That means merging the currently disparate databases, getting more comparable financial performance indicators, and then grading institutions by how accessible they are and how much financing they offer. Only when that is done can useful questions be answered with any confidence about the substitutability or complementarity of different institutional forms along the path to full access. Moreover, only then can international organizations really assist local policymakers in identifying gaps in the infrastructure of access that need to be filled before there is any chance of moving closer toward full access.

Table 4-4. *Cost Ratios, Income Ratios, and Return on Assets, by Institutional Type*[a]
Percent

Item	Sustainable MFIs				Savings banks				Commercial banks			
	ECA	Asia	LA+C	ME+A	ECA	Asia	LA+C	ME+A	ECA	Asia	LA+C	ME+A
Costs as percent of assets	26.4	13.5	22.2	24.2	4.1	1.0	3.2	6.0	4.0	2.1	4.1	3.0
Income as percent of assets	28.7	20.5	27.5	28.1	6.0	2.0	6.9	4.7	6.5	3.6	6.3	10.3
Net return on assets	2.0	6.1	4.8	3.9	1.2	0.1	1.1	0.4	1.2	0.9	1.2	1.4

Source: WSBI (2006).

a. ECA = Europe and Central Asia; Asia = South and East Asia, excluding Central Asian CIS and Mongolia; LA+C = Latin America and Caribbean; ME+A = Middle East and Africa. Sustainable MFIs as reported in MicroBanking Bulletin (2002). Commercial bank data taken from Thompson Bankwatch (Bankscope 2004).

Finally, there is a real need for case studies of cases of successful breakthroughs—and failures—by individual organizations drawn from across the double bottom line spectrum.

References

Adams, Dale W., Douglas Graham, and J. D. von Pischke, eds. 1984. *Undermining Rural Development with Cheap Credit*. Boulder, Colo.: Westview Press.

Bankscope. 2004. Bureau van Dijk Electronic Publishing (www.bvdep.com/en/bankscope. html).

Beck, T., A Demirgüç-Kunt, and M. S. Martinez Peria. 2005. "Reaching Out: Access to and Use of Banking Services across Countries." World Bank Policy Research Paper 3754. Washington: World Bank.

Bongaarts, John. 2001. "Household Size and Composition in the Developing World." Working Paper 144. Washington: Population Council.

Christen, Robert Peck, Richard Rosenberg and Veena Jayadeva. 2004. "Financial Institutions with a 'Double Bottom Line': Implications for the Future of Microfinance." CGAP Occasional Paper 8. Washington: CGAP.

Cull, Robert, Asli Demirgüç-Kunt, and Jonathan Murdoch. 2006. "Financial Performance and Outreach: A Global Analysis of Leading Microbanks." Paper presented at "Access to Finance: Building Inclusive Financial Systems." Washington, Brookings Institution and World Bank, May 30–31, 2006.

Gonzalez, Adrian, and Richard Rosenberg. 2006. "The State of Microfinance: Outreach, Profitability, and Poverty." Paper presented at "Access to Finance: Building Inclusive Financial Systems." Washington, Brookings Institution and World Bank, May 30–31, 2006.

Kempson, Elaine, A. Atkinson, and O. Pilley. 2004. "Policy-Level Response to Financial Exclusion in Developed Economies: Lessons for Developing Countries." University of Bristol (U.K.), Personal Finance Research Centre.

Kumar, Anjali, and Karen Ellis. 2005. "Indicators of Financial Access." Washington: World Bank.

MicroBanking Bulletin. 2002. *MicroBanking Bulletin: Focus on Standardization* (November). Washington: MicroFinance Information Exchange.

Morduch, Jonathan, and B. Hayley. 2002. "Analysis of the Effects of Microfinance on Poverty Reduction." NYU Wagner Working Paper 1014. New York University.

Peachey, Stephen. 2006. "Savings Banks and the Double Bottom Line." Paper presented at "Access to Finance: Building Inclusive Financial Systems." Washington, Brookings Institution and World Bank, May 30–31, 2006.

Robinson, Marguerite S. 2001. *The Microfinance Revolution: Sustainable Finance for the Poor*. Washington: International Bank for Reconstruction and Development and World Bank.

WSBI. 2004. "Access to Finance: A Study for the WSBI by Stephen Peachey and Alan Roe." Brussels: WSBI Research.

———. 2006. "Access to Finance: What Does It Mean and How Do Savings Banks Foster Access?" World Savings Banks Institute Perspective Series No. 49 (January 2006). Brussels: WSBI.

AJAI NAIR

J. D. VON PISCHKE

5

Commercial Banks and Financial Access

I N RECENT YEARS, there has been a paradigm shift in the concept and practice of providing financial services to traditionally underserved segments of the population such as low-income individuals, microenterprises, and small enterprises. Once the exclusive domain of development banks, special programs, and nonprofit organizations, accessible finance increasingly is becoming the domain of private commercial banks and for-profit financial institutions. First, several nonprofit microfinance institutions (MFIs) have converted to banks and nonbank finance companies; more than thirty-nine such MFIs had converted to banks by 2003. Second, many commercial banks have started providing services that take the character of microfinance. By mid-2006, for example, ICICI Bank in India had a microfinance portfolio of US$321 million.[1] Third, apart from direct engagement in microlending, some banks are lending to or taking equity stakes in microfinance institutions. In 2005 nine international banks reported providing wholesale loans to microfinance institutions and three reported having

The primary materials for this chapter come from presentations and papers for two sessions on commercial banks and financial access held during the Brookings–World Bank conference "Access to Finance: Building Inclusive Financial Systems," held May 30–31, 2006. Materials for the two sessions were prepared by Carolyn Blacklock, Suvalaxmi Chakraborty, Annie Duflo, Enrique Errázuriz, Martin Hagen, Jeff Liew, Jose Antonio Meade, Jose Mena, Herman Mulder, Elizabeth Rhyne, Moumita Sensarma, Khalid Sheikh, Flavio Weizenmann, and Bing Xiao (see the references to this chapter). Loraine Ronchi led the preparation of case studies. Khalid Siraj and Anjali Kumar provided input in the preparation of this chapter.

1. Chakraborty and Duflo (2006).

equity stakes in MFIs.[2] Private investment funds increasingly are investing in microfinance; the global portfolio of such funds was reported to be nearly US$1 billion in 2005.[3]

The Old Paradigm

Traditionally, until around a decade ago, private commercial institutions believed that providing credit to low-income individuals and to micro- and small enterprises, particularly those located in rural areas, was too costly and too risky. Furthermore, it was believed that those groups could not afford credit at market interest rates and that therefore they had to be directly subsidized by the state. If commercial institutions were to serve them, they would have to do so through special state programs and policies. Essentially, the argument was that there was market failure in those financial markets and that direct state intervention was required to address that failure.[4]

In response, governments created a range of specialized banking institutions—agricultural development banks, rural banks, and industrial development banks—generally referred to as development finance institutions. Second-tier institutions and lines of credit to provide wholesale financing to finance retail institutions were established and targeted policies were devised to support that objective. Policies included requiring commercial banks to open rural branches and establishing sector-specific credit quotas and caps on interest rates for small loans or underserved borrowers such as small farmers. Donors and international financial institutions financed the creation of such institutions and special programs. The World Bank alone provided US$16.5 billion for agricultural credit between 1948 and 1992 through stand-alone projects or components of other projects.[5] During 1980–93, the World Bank lent US$11.5 billion to ninety-one development finance institutions.[6]

However, for the most part those initiatives failed to have the expected impact. Access to financial services among the targeted groups did not significantly im-

---

2. Crijns and others (2006).

3. Matthäus-Maier and von Pischke (2006); Abrams and Stauffenberg (2007).

4. The market failure argument also applied to other financial markets, such as housing finance, long-term finance, and export financing. Development banks to address such market failures were established in many countries across the world. Addressing market failures, however, was only one among the justifications for creating development banks and public commercial banks. Others included countering the economic and political power of large private banks, government ownership of strategic sectors of the economy as part of a planned model of economic development, and government takeover of weak banks (Caprio and others 2004).

5. World Bank (1993). The report was prepared by the World Bank's independent evaluation department.

6. Murgatroyd (2004).

prove. Interest rate subsidies that effectively converted credit into capital transfers distorted credit allocation.[7] Lending by government banks was found to be associated with higher borrowing by politically connected firms that subsequently had higher default rates.[8] And in terms of final impact, a recent multicountry study found government ownership of banks to be associated with slower subsequent financial development and economic growth.[9]

The most striking result of the government initiatives, however, was a high level of failure of the development finance institutions themselves, along with their special programs. A review of five Kenyan institutions found 93 percent of their portfolio to be in nonperforming loans. Another review of three such institutions each in Pakistan and Bangladesh found that all six had negative net worth. A 1994 World Bank review of ninety-one development finance institutions concluded that only 13 percent could be considered successful; 30 percent were considered failures, and the status of those remaining was inconclusive.[10] Many failed institutions were closed, although some have been successfully restructured through the use of devices such as private management contracts.[11]

The immediate causes of institutional failure were extremely high levels of loan losses, which often wiped out the net worth of the institutions, and excessive costs. The fundamental causes were political and agency problems. Political problems included pressures to lend to favored individuals and firms and to hire more employees than required, difficulties in collecting loans and enforcing collateral agreements, and failure to curb corruption. Agency problems included pursuing multiple objectives, which made it difficult to set up appropriate incentives for management and staff, and the conflict between government ownership of an institution and the government's regulatory and supervisory role.[12] In essence,

---

7. Adams, Graham, and von Pischke (1984); Yaron, Benjamin, and Piprek (1997).

8. Khwaja and Mian (2005) found that government banks in Pakistan gave preferential treatment to politically connected firms, which borrowed 45 percent more and had 50 percent higher default rates than firms that had no such connections. The economywide costs of the rents identified were estimated to be 0.3 to 1.9 percent of GDP every year.

9. Using bank-ownership data from ninety-two countries across the world, La Porta, López-de-Silanes, and Shleifer (2002) found that "higher government ownership of banks is associated with slower subsequent development of the financial system, lower economic growth, and, in particular, lower growth of productivity." A study that notes a positive final impact of mandated programs is Burgess and Pande (2005), which found that the Indian rural bank branch expansion program between 1977 and 1990 significantly lowered rural poverty.

10. Murgatroyd (2004).

11. Pearce, Goodland, and Mulder (2004) reports the cases of the Agricultural Bank of Mongolia and the National Microfinance Bank of Tanzania, which have been restructured using management contracts financed by donor financing from USAID and the World Bank respectively.

12. Caprio and others (2004).

the failures were the result of the intrinsic inability of government institutions and programs to adopt the commercial approach critical to long-term sustainability of financial institutions and programs.

The performance of government-owned commercial banks, while generally better than that of development finance institutions and programs, still lagged behind that of their private counterparts. In China, the share of nonperforming loans in state-owned commercial banks was estimated to be 24 percent before the Asian crisis and 29 percent afterward.[13] In India in 2000, 14 percent of public commercial bank loans were nonperforming loans, a rate that was about 25 percent higher than that of private banks that had a similar clientele. Those banks also lent 40 percent of their deposits to government and public sector enterprises.[14]

The New Paradigm

Today a new paradigm is emerging that maintains that banks do have a legitimate and even commercially profitable role to play in providing financial services to low-income individuals and micro- and small enterprises. This paradigm is based on a sound and competitive financial system that expands financial access though commercial and privately owned banks and nonbank financial institutions, supported by an incentive-compatible framework of regulations. It reflects a departure from the use of dedicated-purpose public institutions or directed credit for underserved segments. It advocates efficient management of public finances, financial liberalization, and public sector reform. It argues for creation of an appropriate legal and regulatory infrastructure to enable the functioning of a wide range of financial institutions and their effective supervision when required. It supports narrowly targeted use of public funds for creating institutions such as well-functioning asset registries and credit bureaus, for financing innovations, and for providing limited start-up subsidies to establish sustainable financial institutions.[15] The increased acceptance of the new paradigm has led to several results. Several old programs and policies were discontinued; many development banks were either closed or privatized; and lending from international financial institutions for such programs and institutions was reduced dramatically.[16] In addition, donors started shifting their resources to support the emerging microfinance sector.

13. Bonin and Huang (2001).

14. Hanson (2004).

15. Adams, Graham, and von Pischke (1984); von Pischke (1991); Yaron, Benjamin, and Piprek (1997); Ledgerwood (1998); and Zeller (2003).

16. Nevertheless, government-owned banks continue to hold a significant share of bank assets in many countries. Caprio and others (2004) lists eighteen countries where the share was more than 60 percent and twenty-three countries where it was 25 to 59 percent.

The emergence of microfinance as a specialized form of lending to targeted clients using unique lending techniques was pioneered around the world by a combination of not-for-profit organizations such as BRAC and the Grameen Bank in Bangladesh, PRODEM in Bolivia, and K-Rep in Kenya. Some state-owned banks—Bank Rakyat Indonesia and Banco do Nordeste in Brazil, with its CrediAmigo program—also ventured successfully into microfinance. Initially, some of the programs depended on grants and soft loans to start and expand their programs. Soon, many demonstrated a reduced need for subsidies and were able to charge market or near-market interest rates and exhibited extraordinarily low rates of loan losses. As microfinance began to be seen as a sustainable way to address poverty, the movement accelerated. The Microcredit Summit, a global microfinance forum, reported that at the end of 2005 more than 3,100 microfinance institutions were providing services to 113 million clients.[17] At the end of 2006, Grameen Bank reported nearly 7 million borrowers and an outstanding loan portfolio of US$481 million.[18]

But the rapidly expanding microfinance sector also began to exhibit constraints that could limit further growth. Microfinance institutions that were not-for-profit nonfinancial organizations could provide only a restricted menu of products because of regulatory restrictions stemming from their lack of official oversight, limited access to commercial funds such as deposits and equity, and lack of the operational systems needed to efficiently serve large numbers of people. Several of the most progressive microfinance institutions responded by converting into regulated financial institutions. The advantages of operating as regulated financial institutions included better access to depositor and commercial funds and the ability to provide a broader range of financial products.

By 2003, thirty-nine MFIs in fifteen countries had been transformed into regulated financial institutions; while most became nonbank finance companies, five were converted into banks.[19] The increasing commercialization of the microfinance sector was also supported by the growth of rating agencies such as Micro-Rate, M-CRIL, CRISIL, and Planet Rating, which made rating services available

17. Daley-Haris (2006).

18. Figures from the MFI database at the MIX Market (www.mixmarket.org), an online portal serving the microfinance sector.

19. Fernando (2004). The MIX Market (www.mixmarket.org) currently lists more than sixty banks that provide retail microfinance services. Apart from Grameen Bank, some major ones include Comparatamos in Mexico, Mibanco in Peru, and Equity Bank in Kenya. At the end of 2006, Compartamos reported more than 616,000 active borrowers and a US$275 million loan portfolio; Mibanco reported more than 223,000 borrowers and a US$320 million loan portfolio; and Equity Bank reported more than 252,000 borrowers and loans of US$164 million.

to microfinance organizations. By 2005, private investments in microfinance, both as debt and equity, amounted to nearly US$1 billion.[20]

Institutions such as ACCION promoted the commercialization of microfinance. ACCION supported the first transformation of a nongovernmental organization (PRODEM) into a bank (BancoSol) and also pioneered the concept of equity funds that invest in microfinance institutions (ProFund, Gateway Fund).[21] At the end of 2006, ACCION's partners had 2.46 million active clients and a loan portfolio of US$2 billion. Three of its partners (Banco Solidario of Ecuador, Compartamos of Mexico, and Mibanco of Peru) each reach more than 100,000 low-income microentrepreneurs.[22]

The changing conceptual paradigm regarding financial access and the evolution of the microfinance sector set the stage for commercial banks to focus on microfinance. Their sustained ability to move in this direction, discussed below, depends on several factors, both external and internal. Public policy toward financial access, competitive pressures, the potential for partnerships, corporate citizenship imperatives, and the availability and cost of technology are among the external factors affecting banks' decisions to undertake microfinance. Internal factors include the willingness of banks to invest in market development, their aptitude for handling the risks inherent in developing new business lines, and their ability to innovate.

Details of the microfinance operations of a number of commercial banks, based on conference presentations, are discussed below. They illustrate the role of external and internal factors in shaping bank decisions as well as the success of banks' ventures into microfinance and the likelihood of sustainability. Also discussed are key public policies and programs to facilitate commercial banks' role in enhancing financial access and innovations adopted by commercial banks themselves to provide services to low-income individuals and small businesses. Finally, lessons are drawn for major stakeholders.

Commercial Banks and Financial Access: Examples of Providers

Several commercial banks across the world, public and private, domestic and international, have demonstrated that it is possible to provide financial services prof-

---

20. Abrams and Stauffenberg (2007). In 2005, five bond issues raised more than US$100 million and four debt issues nearly US$150 million. In 2006, commercial investors purchased US$72 million of a US$99 million issue by Blue Orchard, a microfinance investment vehicle, with Morgan Stanley. Equity Bank in Kenya made an initial public offering for US$28 million.

21. Rhyne (2006).

22. Statistics for 2006 for ACCION partners are available at www.accion.org.

itably to low-income individuals and microenterprises.[23] The menu of micro-finance services offered by such institutions includes both retail and wholesale products (table 5-1). Major private commercial banks offering microfinance services include ICICI Bank in India, Banco Wiese Sudameris in Peru, Stanbic Bank in Uganda, and Capitec Bank in South Africa. ICICI Bank has a loan portfolio of more than US$321 million in microfinance. Khan Bank of Mongolia, a public development bank that was privatized, reports nearly 235,000 active borrowers and a loan portfolio of nearly US$201 million; 50 to 60 percent of that amount is reported to be in microfinance.[24]

Public commercial banks with large microfinance programs include Bank Rakyat Indonesia, Banco do Nordeste in Brazil, Banque du Caire in Egypt, and a large number of banks in India, including the State Bank of India, which has the largest branch network in the world. At the end of 2003, Bank Rakyat Indonesia had nearly 29 million microfinance depositors, US$3.5 billion in deposits, and more than 3 billion borrowers with nearly US$1.7 billion in outstanding loans.[25]

The entry of international banks into microfinance is more recent. A recent survey identified twelve international banks involved in microfinance, of which most offered wholesale products, both financial and nonfinancial.[26] Nine banks provided wholesale loans and three had equity stakes in MFIs; Société Générale Bank and HSBC Bank had the largest wholesale loan portfolios. Six banks provided technical assistance to MFIs, and four provided grants. Five banks had retail loan products; two offered savings and remittance products. Spain's Grupo Santander reported the largest retail microloan portfolio, US$96.7 million, which included loans to some 63,000 microentrepreneurs. ING reported a retail microloan portfolio of US$3.4 million and microdeposits of more than US$2.6 million.

The service delivery models used by the banks vary. Frequently banks have undertaken microfinance delivery, especially for the provision of retail financial services, by creating a separate cost and profit center within the institution or by creating a subsidiary that may take the form of a separate but regulated financial institution or a nonfinancial service company.[27] Citigroup and ING offer their services through domestic commercial banks that are subsidiaries. Citigroup offers its remittance products in Mexico through Banamex, a domestic commercial bank that it acquired in 2001. ING offers savings and loan products through ING

23. Harper and Arora (2005).
24. MFI database at the MIX Market (www.mixmarket.org); DFID (2005).
25. Harper and Arora (2005); Kumar (2005).
26. Crijns and others (2006).
27. Isern and Porteus (2005).

Table 5-1. *Microfinance Products offered by Commercial Banks*

Business	Financial products	Nonfinancial products
Wholesale	Loans to MFIs	Technical assistance
	Guarantees	Credit, risk management, and
	Securitization	IT systems
	Equity stakes	Entry to banking networks and
	Bank accounts	platforms
Retail	Bank accounts	Business services for SMEs
	Individual or group loans	
	Savings	
	Insurance	
	Remittances	

Source: Crijns and others (2006).

Vysya, the domestic bank that is its subsidiary in India. Spain's Grupo Santander offers products through its specialized Chilean subsidiary, Banefe.

The presentations made by banks engaged in microfinance at the Brookings–World Bank conference provide a closer look at the spectrum of innovations adopted by a number of such institutions that have facilitated the provision of microfinance services. The experiences of individual banks with low-income individuals and small businesses, as presented at the conference, are summarized in table 5-2. A brief description of each institution and its role in the area of microfinance also is given. All but two of the banks are privately owned.

ICICI Bank

ICICI Bank, India's second-largest bank, had total assets of about US$38.5 billion as of March 2005. It has a network of about 610 branches and more than 2,000 ATMs. ICICI Bank originally was created by ICICI, a development bank, as a fully owned subsidiary in 1994. It was privatized through successive public stock offerings in India and the United States, and through secondary-market sales to institutional investors between 1998 and 2002. ICICI and ICICI Bank were merged in 2002.

ICICI Bank's foray into microfinance came through the acquisition of Bank of Madura, a small private bank that does significant rural outreach and lending to microfinance groups. ICICI continued to lend to microfinance groups, then shifted to lending through microfinance institutions as service agents. Figure 5-1 shows the phenomenal growth of ICICI Bank's microfinance portfolio from 2001 to 2006.

In addition to lending through microfinance institutions serving as service agents, ICICI Bank provides long-term subordinated debt (quasi-equity) and life and non–life insurance products (through its subsidiaries). It facilitates venture capital investment in microfinance institutions through partnerships with local venture capital firms. In addition to financial services, the bank offers nonfinancial services in areas such as business process engineering, internal control and audit systems, cash flow management, and automation. The bank also has set up six microfinance resource centers in partnership with other institutions and the Center for Microfinance, which is involved in impact assessment, product development, and financial training.

ABN AMRO

ABN AMRO is a multinational bank operating with more than 3,500 branches in seventy countries. In Brazil, Banco ABN AMRO Real, a subsidiary, is present in every state; in 2002 it served 6 million clients through 600 branches. In partnership with ACCION, Banco ABN AMRO Real established Real Microcredito in 2002. Since then, Real Microcredito has made 18,400 loans totaling more than US$13.5 million. Forty percent of its loans are for less than US$500. As of early 2006, it had more than 8,000 clients and outstanding loans amounting to about US$5.4 million.

In India, ABN AMRO has twenty-three branches and operates in sixteen cities. It started its microfinance operations in India in 2003 by making wholesale loans to MFIs. By April 2006, it had a loan portfolio of about US$20.5 million that included eighteen MFIs, which in turn retailed the loans to 190,000 clients. In addition to providing loans, ABN AMRO provides advisory services to MFIs on information technology, credit management, and governance.[28]

ANZ

ANZ, with assets of US$319 billion, is the leading bank in the Pacific. ANZ launched its microfinance program in Fiji in 2004 in collaboration with the United Nations Development Program (UNDP). UNDP assisted ANZ with the feasibility study, served as liaison with the central bank and the government, and designed a financial literacy program for people in the villages to be targeted by ANZ; it also is involved in the program's impact monitoring. Initial market research revealed that more than 400,000 people in Fiji had no access to banking.

ANZ's microfinance program in Fiji is a mobile banking service that has a fleet of six mobile banks that travel on a regular schedule to 250 villages. The service

---

28. Mulder and Sheikh (2006); Sensarma (2006); and Weizenmann (2006).

Table 5-2. *Commercial Banks in Microfinance, Select Examples*

Name	Country	Organizational type	Primary Underserved Client Group	Outreach
ICICI Bank	India	Domestic commercial bank	Low-income individuals/households	US$321 million
ABN AMRO	India Brazil	International commercial bank	Low-income individuals/households	190,000 borrowers; US$20.5 million (India) 8,000 borrowers; US$5.3 million (March 2006) (Brazil)
ANZ	Fiji	International commercial bank	Rural households	54,000 savers (98% first time); US$2 million savings (April 2006)
BancoEstado	Chile	Domestic commercial bank	Microbusinesses	170,000 borrowers; US$272 million loan portfolio
ProCredit Bank	Kosovo	Domestic commercial bank	Low- and middle-income individuals and small businesses	189,000 deposits less than €1,000 (88.3% of total); 38,700 loans less than €10,000 (2005)
Wells Fargo	United States	Domestic commercial bank	Small businesses	450,000 borrowers; US$8 billion loan portfolio

Source: Authors' compilation, based on presentations at the Brookings–World Bank conference "Access to Finance," Washington, May 30–31, 2006.

Figure 5-1. *ICICI Bank Microfinance Business*

Loan portfolio (US$ millions)

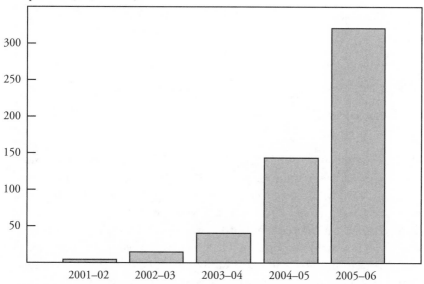

Source: Chakraborty and Duflo (2006).

offers two savings products—a long-term savings account and a transaction account—and a microloan product. Within a year of its launch at the end of April 2006, the program had opened 54,000 rural accounts with total deposits of more than US$2 million and 400 loan accounts with an outstanding portfolio of US$200,000. Clients who have been regular savers for six months are eligible for loans, which do not require any physical collateral; instead, support is required from a community leader—a chief, priest, or provincial council manager. The loan portfolio has arrears of less than 2 percent. The current cost of the program is US$12 per client per year; ANZ expects to bring that down to US$10 and to break even by mid-2007.[29]

ProCredit Bank

ProCredit Bank, previously known as the Microfinance Bank of Kosovo, is the largest bank in Kosovo. The bank was created in the UN-administered territory

29. Blacklock (2006); Liew (2006).

Table 5-3. *ProCredit Bank, Kosovo*[a]

Particulars	2000	2003	2005
Deposit accounts	26,000	124,241	196,794
Deposits	89	263	343
Loans	3.3	72	171
Money transfers	488	583	483
Profits	3.2	3.9	3.8

Source: Hagen and Koehn (2006).
a. Financial data in € millions.

of Kosovo after the civil war in Yugoslavia by Frankfurt-based IPC (Internationale Projekt Consult) with equity funding from several international financial institutions. In 2000, the year it was created, the economy was devastated: unemployment and poverty rates were more than 50 percent, infrastructure was severely damaged, and the financial sector had ceased to exist. A market survey revealed that only 6 percent of the population had a savings or a current account and that only 2 percent had access to credit during the three years prior to the survey. Table 5-3 shows ProCredit's growth in operations and profits since 2000.

By May 2006, ProCredit Bank had over 214,000 deposit accounts with savings of more than €340 million and over 43,000 outstanding loans in a loan portfolio of €140 million. Its market share is 40 percent for deposits and 30 percent for loans. ProCredit's core business is microfinance. Approximately 88.3 percent of its deposit accounts held less than €1,000, and approximately 89.5 percent of its loan accounts were for less than €10,000. The bank offers current, savings, and time deposits and micro loans, loans for small and medium-size enterprises, housing loans, and agricultural loans. Agricultural loans are available from €100, with a maximum tenure of thirty-six months; flexible repayments are permitted. No collateral is required for loans up to €5,000. The bank, which has more than 82,000 active debit cards, operates thirty-four ATMs and 256 point-of-service (PoS) terminals. It is a member of the Maestro Card network.[30]

BancoEstado

BancoEstado is a public commercial bank in Chile formed in 1953 by the merger of four development banks. Operating 312 branches and 1,050 ATMs, it has the largest outreach in the country. One of every two Chileans is a customer, and it

30. Hagen and Koehn (2006).

Figure 5-2. *BancoEstado Microfinance Business*

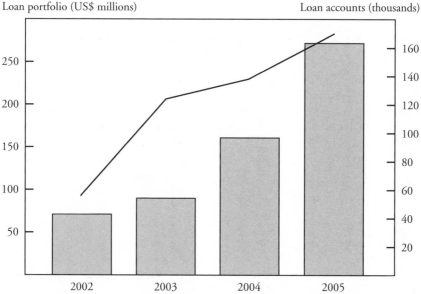

Source: Mena and Errázuriz (2006).

is the only bank in nearly 41 percent of localities in Chile. BancoEstado has assets of US$20.5 billion, 8 million savings accounts, and more than 500,000 mortgages and credit cards. It has 80 percent of the savings accounts in Chile, 13 percent of the credit market, and 65 percent of the mortgage market. Its insurance subsidiary serves 1.3 million customers. Nearly 70 percent of the bank's transactions have been automated. BancoEstado has consistently been profitable, with a return on equity that has exceeded the average for the banking system in Chile over the past twenty years.

BancoEstado started its microfinance subsidiary in 1996. Special branches serve its micro- and small clients, and mobile vans are used in remote places. By 2005, the subsidiary had 170,000 clients and a US$272 million loan portfolio. The bank does not require collateral on its microfinance loans; it uses credit scoring instead. Figure 5-2 shows the growth of BancoEstado's microfinance business from 2002 to 2005.[31]

31. Mena and Errázuriz (2006).

Wells Fargo

Wells Fargo Bank, which has more than 23 million customers, is part of the Wells Fargo Company, which had assets of US$482 billion at the end of 2006. Founded in 1852, it is the fifth-largest bank in the United States and the only U.S. bank with an AAA rating from Moody's.

In 1995, it started making direct loans of up to US$100,000 to small businesses—firms with sales of less than US$2 million. It became the largest U.S. lender in that segment in 2001, with a market share of 15 percent. By 2005, it had 450,000 small business customers in the United States and Canada; the businesses, 70 percent of which had five or fewer employees, had median sales of US$325,000. The bank's average credit line loan balance was US$15,000 and the median deposit was US$7,000. Outstanding loans totaled US$8 billion, of which 91 percent was unsecured.[32]

Scaling up Microfinance Services

How did these banks succeed in scaling up their microfinance services? While there is no direct evidence, the institutions described above maintain that their new lines of business are able to cover costs and, in some cases, to make substantial profits. Two broad groups of factors appear to have helped to shape their successes. The first are internal factors related to the banks' ability to come up with innovative responses to the challenges posed by their provision of microfinance services. The second are the external factors that provided an appropriate enabling environment for the institutions' operations.

Private Innovations: Converting Opportunities into Businesses

Commercial banks' strengths include access to adequate resources, existing outreach, capacity to provide multiple services, and well-developed risk management systems. Their challenges are their limited knowledge of the microfinance or small business finance markets and their relatively high cost structures. Many commercial banks address the challenge of profitably providing relatively low-value financial services by creating innovative service delivery models, which effectively delegates provision of retail microfinance services to MFIs or service companies. Those involved in direct provision of financial services have developed business process innovations that reduce the costs of financial transactions. Clearly, direct provision

32. Xiao (2006).

of microfinance services is a larger challenge for commercial banks.[33] Table 5-4 lists the innovations and their benefits.

PROVIDING WHOLESALE LENDING. Wholesale lending is one of the most common models of commercial bank involvement in microfinance.[34] In this model, banks lend to a microfinance institution, which then undertakes the retail lending. Lending to microfinance institutions is innovative because, unlike typical clients of commercial banks, they do not have strong balance sheets or assets to serve as collateral. Lending decisions are based on the bank's assessment of the microfinance institution's quality of governance and management, the transparency of its systems, and its capacity to do retail lending. Often commercial banks providing wholesale loans also provide technical assistance to the borrowers.

USING RISK-SHARING SERVICE AGENTS. While several banks provide wholesale loans, microfinance institutions' weak financials constrain the scaling up of that model of lending. The service agent innovation attempts to overcome that constraint. Under this innovation, which is used by ICICI, microfinance institutions originate, monitor, and collect loans on behalf of ICICI; the loans remain on ICICI's books. The microfinance institution shares risk through a first loss deficiency guarantee, which requires it to be responsible for a pre-agreed initial share of loan losses based on expected losses in the loan portfolio. This innovation achieves three benefits. One, it ensures that the microfinance institution has a financial interest in minimizing loan losses. Two, it restricts the microfinance institution's contingent risk to the maximum value of the guarantee, thereby limiting its capital requirements. Three, the first loss deficiency guarantee serves as a credit enhancement if the portfolio is securitized.

In other variations on the service agent model, the agents are not microfinance institutions but commercial entities or mobile phone operators. The most well-known example of the former is found in Brazil, where a range of entities such as supermarkets, drug stores, and lottery houses are engaged as "banking correspondents" to provide savings, credit (to a limited extent), and payment services on behalf of the bank. The advantage of using correspondents as agents instead of microfinance institutions is their larger number and local knowledge. The provision

33. Isern and Porteus (2005) identifies the following factors as necessary for banks interested in providing retail microfinance services: commitment from board and management, strong internal champions, and alignment with the bank's core commercial strategy; knowledge of microfinance best practices and how to serve microclientele; conveniently located infrastructure to serve clients; products especially adapted for low-income and informal markets; systems and procedures adapted to microfinance operations, for example, systems that support immediate follow-up on missed payments; and appropriate staff training and incentives.

34. Isern and Porteus (2005).

Table 5-4. *Key Innovations in Commercial Bank Lending to Microfinance*

Innovation	Institution	Benefits
Undertaking wholesale lending	ABN AMRO (India)	Allows lending to MFIs with weak balance sheets but strong outreach capacities
Risk sharing with service agents	ICICI (India)	Permits higher leverage for agent Reduces credit-risk to lender Aligns agent's incentives with the lender's
Delivering financial services through a separate service company	ABN AMRO (Brazil)	Allows operation under a low-cost structure Enables equity stakes to be taken by the technical assistance provider
Establishing new greenfield banks	ProCredit Bank (Kosovo)	Brings together social investors' higher risk appetite and management skills of the private sector
Introducing business process innovations, such as simplifying eligibility requirements and application process	Wells Fargo (U.S.) ANZ (Fiji)	Increases demand for service Reduces client-transaction cost
Using credit scoring	Wells Fargo (U.S.) BancoEstado (Chile) ABN AMRO (India)	Reduces lender-transaction costs Accelerates loan processing
Automating credit decisions	Wells Fargo (U.S.)	Reduces lender-transaction costs Accelerates loan processing
Introducing risk-based pricing	Wells Fargo (U.S.)	Permits lending to larger number of clients

Source: Authors' compilation, based on presentations at Brookings–World Bank conference "Access to Finance," Washington, May 30–31, 2006.

of financial services through mobile phones is being pioneered by mobile phone operators and banks in the Philippines, Kenya, and South Africa.[35]

USING SERVICE COMPANIES. Microfinance is a low-margin, high-volume business that requires special skills and systems. A service company is a nonfinancial subsidiary often created in partnership with a service provider. Real Microcredito in Brazil is a service company in which a 97 percent stake is held by Banco ABN AMRO Real and a 3 percent stake by ACCION. Banco ABN AMRO Real funds and carries the loans on its books and provides the management team, managerial support (human resources, legal, accounting, and marketing services), infrastructure support, and access to its branch network. Real Microcredito defines the microfinance strategy, hires the commercial and operational teams, identifies clients, makes loan decisions, and coordinates the credit process from approval to collection. ACCION transfers the methodology and manages portfolio growth.

Apart from ABN AMRO, other banks that have used this model include Banco de Pichincha, the largest bank in Ecuador, to start Credife in 1999, and Sogebank, the largest bank in Haiti, to start Sogesol (both in partnership with ACCION). In a variation on the service company model, the subsidiary itself is a regulated financial institution. Institutions that have used that approach include Teba Bank in South Africa and the National Bank in Jordan. Yet another variation is seen with Unit Desas of Bank Rakyat Indonesia and CrediAmigo of Banco do Nordeste in Brazil, in which the microfinance operation is a profit center within the bank.[36]

ESTABLISHING GREENFIELD MICROFINANCE BANKS. Unlike the other innovations discussed here, which allow existing commercial banks to increase their financial access, ProCredit Bank in Kosovo represents the creation of a private commercial bank. ProCredit Bank was created by the company Internationale Projekt Consult; majority equity was provided by the international financial institutions FMO, EBRD, KfW, and IFC.[37] Other investors include Commerzbank, a German commercial bank, and ProCredit Holding, an affiliate of Internationale Projekt Consult.

---

35. Frederik (2006); Ivatury (2006); Lyman, Ivatury, and Staschen (2006); and Kumar and others (2006).

36. Isern and Porteus (2005).

37. The latter three invested indirectly through the FEFAD Foundation in Albania and the Micro Enterprise Bank of Bosnia (IFC: International Finance Corporation, a member of the World Bank Group; EBRD: European Bank for Reconstruction and Development; FMO: an official development bank of the Netherlands government; KfW: an official development bank of the German government).

The example of ProCredit Bank suggests the potential of creating commercial banks that focus on providing microfinance and small enterprise finance where private commercial banks do not exist or have no interest in providing those services. Post-conflict Kosovo was a good example. With this model, international financial institutions can facilitate creation of a new bank by taking the major share of risk and having an interested private minority shareholder take a smaller risk, provide know-how, and retain management responsibility.

The ProCredit family includes nineteen banks in eastern Europe, Africa, and Latin America. While some were new banks, others were formed from existing banks that were taken over and restructured. At the end of 2006, the banks together reported €2.1 billion in outstanding loans and an average loan amount of €2,800. More than 85 percent of the portfolio is financed through local deposits, and the consolidated return on equity was 15.3 percent in 2005.[38]

INTRODUCING BUSINESS PROCESS INNOVATIONS. Business process innovations simplify service requirements and improve operating processes, thereby allowing a firm to reach new clients, retain existing clients, reduce the cost of providing services, and ultimately increase profits. Table 5-5 summarizes the changes in business processes that Wells Fargo introduced as it started to focus on small business lending. Its strategic innovation was to adopt standard consumer lending practices and adapt them for small business lending:

—*Simplifying eligibility requirements and the application process*: Individuals from low-income households and small businesses often do not apply for bank services because of the cumbersome procedures involved. These individuals and businesses can least afford the time and resources required to obtain the different documents that banks often demand; hence they opt for more easily accessible but costlier service providers. Also, they often do not have assets that can be used as collateral.

Wells Fargo and ANZ recognized that it is critical to simplify bank processes to attract and retain good clients. Wells Fargo changed its loan application process to permit consumers to apply by mail and telephone, did away with requiring copies of tax returns, and stopped requiring collateral for most loans. The loan application was made short and simple so that it usually can be completed within five minutes. Wells Fargo also uses data-driven, targeted marketing to attract low-risk small businesses. ANZ decided to accept, instead of a letter from an employer, a letter from a village head or district commissioner plus a birth or baptism certificate or inclusion on a school roll as proof of an applicant's identity.

---

38. ProCredit Institutions section at www.procredit-holding.com.

Table 5-5. *Wells Fargo Business Process Innovations*

Traditional process	New process
Applications are submitted in a branch with a loan officer	Applications are taken by mail or phone, or service outlets
Tax returns and financial statements required	No tax return or financial statements needed
Application reviewed in detail by lender	Most decisions made automatically based on scorecard
Annual review required	No review, lines of credit are "evergreen"
Collateral often required	Unsecured
Booked on commercial loan system	Booked on consumer loan system
Focus on very low losses	Higher losses acceptable with risk based pricing

Source: Xiao (2006).

Wells Fargo and BancoEstado do not require any collateral for their microfinance loans.

—Using credit scoring and automating loan decisions: ABN AMRO, BancoEstado, and Wells Fargo use credit scoring to make their loan decisions; only Wells Fargo uses it to significantly automate credit decisionmaking. That is not surprising given that the quality of client data available in Chile, Brazil, and India does not match that in the United States. Approximately two-thirds of Wells Fargo's small business applications are approved or declined automatically; only a third are reviewed by a loan officer. Automated credit decisions are based on statistical credit-scoring models that employ rules and models for small business lending and use information on businesses and their owners available from both public and private sources.

In the Wells Fargo small business model, the estimated credit score reflects the credit risk of a business, but that score alone does not determine the lending decision. Rules described as limits or parameters determine lending decisions, with scores as inputs. For example, rules forbid lending to bankrupt individuals or businesses, gambling casinos, and so forth. A client's other relationships with Wells Fargo, such as use of business deposits and payment services, also may be considered in defining rules. In microfinance lending in most countries, however, credit scoring is likely to continue to be more useful as a way to help loan officers make a credit decision than as a substitute for them.[39]

39. Schreiner (2006).

—*Risk-based pricing*. Risk-based pricing allows Wells Fargo to lend to riskier clients but to offset the risk of higher losses by charging a higher interest rate. Wells Fargo believes that this approach has allowed it to reach a large number of clients whom it would have rejected under an approach that uses fixed pricing and aims to minimize loan losses.

Public Policies and Programs: Creating Opportunities

Even innovative financial institutions would find it difficult to succeed without a supportive environment for developing private financial markets, and the government plays a critical role in creating that environment. As is now recognized, however, the most effective approach does not lie in devising policies and programs that aim to increase access directly. The government role encompasses a number of other approaches, such as strengthening the overall business environment by supporting appropriate legal, physical, and financial infrastructure; undertaking efficient macroeconomic management; and adopting specific policies that facilitate the market functioning of financial institutions through financial liberalization.

EFFICIENT MACROECONOMIC MANAGEMENT. A stable, low-inflationary macroeconomic environment facilitates financial sector development. Low inflation protects the capital base of financial institutions and encourages individuals and firms to hold financial assets, thereby making it possible for financial institutions to mobilize deposits and provide long-term financial products such as mortgages, annuities, and insurance products. Stable exchange and interest rates facilitate financial institutions' access to funds in foreign currencies and to long-term funds.[40]

Reduced public borrowing increases credit to the private sector, drives down interest rates, and forces banks to find new investments. In contrast, high public borrowing crowds out private credit. When the less risky option of investing their funds in Treasury bills is available, banks do not need to take the risk of making and collecting loans; they have even less incentive to find new markets such as microfinance and small enterprise finance.[41]

India and Brazil have had relatively stable and low to moderate inflationary environments in the past decade. Both countries had only one year of double-

---

40. Using a dataset of eighty-six developing countries, Detragiache, Gupta, and Tressel (2005) finds that high inflation is negatively correlated with private sector credit.

41. Hanson (2003) finds evidence of crowding out of private sector credit in an analysis of data for twenty-five large developing and transition countries from 1990 to 2000. During that period, bank credit to governments in these countries, on average, more than doubled as a percentage of GDP, from 3.6 percent to 8.4 percent. Banking system deposits in these countries accounted for 84 percent of banking system deposits in all developing countries in 2000.

digit inflation in the period 1996–2006.[42] However, public borrowing continues to be high in both countries, potentially crowding out private credit.

LEGAL, PHYSICAL, AND FINANCIAL INFRASTRUCTURE. A system of laws that create property rights and contracts is a prerequisite for economic development, including that of the financial sector. Laws that permit easy creation and enforcement of collateral agreements and provide for adequate protection of creditors' rights reduce the transaction cost of lending. Legislation that creates a legal framework for specialized financing instruments, such as leasing, that increase financial access for small firms also are important. The legal framework also needs to evolve to clarify contracts arising out of new technological developments, such as online and mobile phone banking. However, laws are useful only when they are effectively and efficiently enforced. A well-functioning system of courts is therefore critical in translating the potential benefits of a good legal system into real benefits.

The availability of good physical infrastructure (especially for transportation, communications, and power) reduces the transaction cost of providing financial services. Well-functioning asset registries and efficient credit bureaus facilitate financial transactions by reducing the information costs associated with providing credit. Asset registries reduce the cost of creating liens, and credit bureaus help consumers build a credit history that can reduce the need for physical collateral to secure lending.[43]

FINANCIAL LIBERALIZATION. Financial reforms facilitate competition and thereby improve services. Measures that strengthen the financial sector in general include permitting easier and orderly entry and exit of commercial banks, leveling the playing field for different types and categories of financial institutions, requiring low levels of reserves, establishing nondistortionary and reasonable tax rates, and, perhaps the most critical, permitting the market to determine interest rates. Freedom to set interest rates that cover all costs and provide a reasonable return is critical because the cost of providing microfinance services typically is higher than that of other bank services because of the small size of the transactions.

India and Brazil have undertaken significant financial reforms in the past decade, although both countries still impose a large number of mandates that act as taxes, and they maintain a ceiling on interest rates on small loans by commercial banks.

---

42. World Bank (2006).

43. In Beck, Demirgüç-Kunt, and Martinez Peria (2006), a cross-country analysis of factors associated with barriers to banking access, the authors find that in countries that have better contractual and informational frameworks, banks impose lower barriers to access. They also find that physical infrastructure is one of the most robust predictors of level of access.

Reforms in India allowed the creation of ICICI Bank by public financial institutions and its eventual privatization by permitting it to raise equity from the domestic and international markets. Reforms also allowed ICICI Bank to enter into innovative arrangements with microfinance institutions and to price its loans flexibly. India also stopped its obligatory branch licensing program for commercial banks. Reforms in Brazil in the 1990s increased financial stability and transparency. A number of government financial institutions were closed, and the proportion of credit subject to administered interest rates was decreased.

ENABLING INTERVENTIONS. Major steps have been taken to reorient the provision of financial services by restructuring development banks into banks or development agencies with a limited mandate. Financiera Rural, created by restructuring BanRural, a large loss-making development bank in Mexico, is a good example. The restructured entity is a development agency whose incentives have been designed to address the key incentive problems of traditional development banks. Key features of the new institution include a narrow service mandate, hard budget constraints, and a legal mandate to maintain the value of its initial endowment.[44]

Financiera Rural is legally barred from raising additional funds through deposits or any other type of market funding. Its initial capital was provided by the government, financed in part by a US$500 million loan from the World Bank. Its mandate is to provide credit to individuals and community-based financial organizations, primarily credit unions, and to provide technical assistance to credit unions. Since its inception in 2003, it has provided more than US$3.5 billion in loans, and at the end of 2005 it had assets of US$1.89 billion. In 2005, its return on equity was 2.1 percent and the ratio of delinquent loans to total loans was only 2.5 percent. Financiera Rural operates through more than 5,600 commercial bank branches. Its long-term success, however, depends on the political will of the government to retain the organization's incentive structure.

A number of smaller innovations also have been attempted in order to foster increased access. Examples include the development of financial literacy programs, increased use of banks to route government payments, and government action to encourage or require banks to offer "basic" bank accounts. The UNDP designed and implemented a financial literacy program along with ANZ's rural banking program in Fiji. ANZ considers the literacy program, which takes four hours to complete and is available in Fijian, Hindi, and English, crucial to the success of its banking program.[45] In the United States, the government's Financial

44. Meade (2006).
45. The topics covered in the program include understanding one's personal financial situation; understanding income and spending patterns; setting goals and priorities; planning household budgets;

Literacy and Education Commission develops educational materials, coordinates activities related to financial literacy with various government agencies, maintains a financial literacy website (www.mymoney.gov), and operates a toll-free hotline. Nongovernmental organizations, academic institutions, and banks also have shown interest in financial literacy.[46]

Lessons

The stories of successful commercial bank engagement in microfinance discussed in this chapter suggest that the new paradigm on financial access can work. Provision of financial services to low-income individuals and small businesses by commercial banks appears to be a growing trend rather than a rare occurrence. While disaggregated data on the profitability of this business segment are not available, the involvement of an increasingly large number of private commercial banks suggests its commercial feasibility.

The stories discussed here also offer some important lessons for key stakeholders such as governments, commercial banks, and donors that are interested in enhancing access to finance. Moreover, there is significant potential for collaboration among these stakeholders, an example being the collaboration between UNDP, ANZ, and the government of Fiji.

Lessons for Governments

Low-income individuals and micro- and small enterprises demand a broad range of financial services besides credit. Commercial banks are better placed to provide those services because they are regulated and they are part of the national payment system. Publicly funded financial literacy programs are a potentially useful instrument for educating low-income individuals and small enterprises to make better use of financial services.

Past experience suggests that direct provision of financial services by governments generally does not work. Even when it does work, it entails very high costs, often much higher than initially expected. When a failed development bank is restructured, an option that may work is to convert it into a development agency

---

rationale for and means of saving; information on microfinance and service providers; and preparing a savings plan.

46. Citibank and INSEAD have jointly organized three annual conferences (in 2004, 2005, and 2006) on financial education that have brought together various stakeholders and have contributed to improving understanding of the benefits of improved financial literacy (http://financialeducationsummit.org). Microfinance Opportunities and Freedom from Hunger have jointly published a set of training guides on financial literacy (Cohen, Sebstad, and Stack 2006).

with a narrow mandate, support it through transparent subsidies from the budget, and create an incentive structure that encourages sustainable operations.

Key government actions to encourage commercial banks to provide services to underserved segments include maintaining a stable, low-inflationary macroeconomic environment, keeping public borrowing low, creating an effective legal framework for property rights and contracts, and developing good physical infrastructure. Financial liberalization to create a competitive and level playing field for different financial institutions also provides incentives for commercial banks to increase their outreach to underserved segments. Among the different measures of financial liberalization, particularly important is permitting financial institutions to charge market prices for their services.

Lessons for Commercial Banks

Improving macroeconomic environments and increasing financial liberalization are improving the business environment in many countries, thereby creating an opportunity for domestic and international commercial banks to expand their business. The examples of India and Brazil discussed in this chapter suggest that that is the case even in countries that continue to retain many policies and programs created under the old paradigm.

Providing financial services to low-income individuals and micro- and small enterprises can be a profitable business if commercial banks can develop innovations or adapt existing practices to reduce transaction costs. In some contexts, that might simply mean lending to existing microfinance institutions. In others it might mean using microfinance institutions as service agents, and in yet other contexts it might mean promoting a financial subsidiary or a service company. Business process innovations are more important for banks aiming to provide retail financial services.

The rapid improvements in technology and its falling costs can help reduce the transaction costs of dealing with a large number of small financial transactions. Commercial banks already are using ATMs, point-of-sale terminals, hand-held computers, the Internet, and geographical information systems to increase their outreach and better manage clients and portfolios. Many business process innovations developed by Wells Fargo, ABN AMRO, and BancoEstado draw on improvements in technology.

Partnerships and alliances with MFIs and commercial entities offer a new opportunity for commercial banks to increase their outreach. Because these partnerships and alliances help both banks and their partners increase their outreach while reducing the overall costs of providing services, they create a win-win situation. The service agent model being used by ICICI in India and the partnership between ABN AMRO and ACCION in Brazil suggest that the potential of such links is tremendous. Other examples include correspondent banking in Brazil and mobile phone banking in the Philippines, South Africa, and Kenya.[47]

Lessons for Donors

As in the case of governments, donors' primary role in increasing commercial banks' provision of financial access is indirect. Donors can help governments carry out financial and public sector reforms and help create and improve their legal, physical, and financial infrastructure. They also can finance service delivery and product innovation, assess the effectiveness of innovations, and disseminate successful innovations and best practices. UNDP's financing of the financial literacy program in Fiji is a good example of financing an innovation.

The case of Financiera Rural suggests a potential role for donors in helping governments restructure failed development banks by facilitating technical assistance and providing financial assistance. The case of National Microfinance Bank of Tanzania is another example. However, there are too few examples to conclude that such restructuring will succeed in the long run.

The example of ProCredit in Kosovo (and that of other banks in the ProCredit family of banks) suggests the potential for donor support in helping to create banks in contexts where private financial institutions themselves are unlikely to make investments. Donors also can support the transformation of well-performing MFIs into banks, as in the case of MFIs such as Mibanco in Peru and K-Rep in Kenya. However, care needs to be taken to ensure that donors do not crowd out private capital.[48]

Conclusion

There are promising new ways in which private commercial banks can step into the provision of financial services for the underserved segments of the population—poor people, microentrepreneurs, and residents of a remote rural area. Commercial banks are recognizing the potential for profits in this area but understand that success depends on thinking "out of the box" and finding new ways to do business, whether through new partnerships, new technologies, or new institutions unencumbered by the mandates of the past. And governments and donors are increasingly recognizing that the new entrepreneurial efforts of commercial banks can be aided by appropriate policies.

---

47. For additional examples, see Gallardo, Goldberg, and Randhawa (2006); Matthäus-Maier and von Pischke (forthcoming).

48. Abrams and Stauffenberg (2007).

References

Abrams, Julie, and Damien von Stauffenberg. 2007. *Role Reversal: Are Public Development Institutions Crowding Out Private Investment in Microfinance?* Washington: MicroRate.

Adams, Dale W., Douglas H. Graham, and J. D. von Pischke. 1984. *Undermining Rural Development with Cheap Credit.* Boulder, Colo.: Westview Press.

Beck, Thorsten, Asli Demirgüç-Kunt, and Maria Soledad Martinez Peria. 2006. "Reaching Out: Access and Use of Banking Services across Countries." World Bank Policy Research Working Paper 4079. Washington: World Bank.

Blacklock, Carolyn. 2006. "ANZ and UNDP: Banking the Un-Banked but Bankable in the Pacific." Paper prepared for "Access to Finance: Building Inclusive Financial Systems." Brookings Institution and World Bank, Washington, May 30–31.

Bonin, John P., and Yiping Huang. 2001. "Dealing with the Bad Loans of the Chinese Banks." *Journal of Asian Economics* 12, no. 2: 197–214.

Burgess, Robin, and Rohini Pande. 2005. "Do Rural Banks Matter? Evidence from the Indian Social Banking Experiment." *American Economic Review* 95, no. 3: 780–95.

Caprio, Gerard, and others. 2004. *The Future of State-Owned Financial Institutions.* Brookings.

Chakraborty, Suvalaxmi, and Annie Duflo. 2006. "ICICI Bank in Microfinance: Breaking the Barriers." Paper prepared for "Access to Finance: Building Inclusive Financial Systems." Brookings Institution and World Bank, Washington, May 30–31.

Cohen, M., J. Sebstad, and K. Stack. *Financial Education for the Poor: 2006.* Washington: Microfinance Opportunities and Freedom from Hunger.

Crijns, Gemma, and others. 2006. *A Billion to Gain? A Study on Global Financial Institutions and Microfinance.* Amsterdam: ING Microfinance Support.

Daley-Harris, Sam. 2006. *The State of the Microcredit Summit Campaign Report 2006.* New York: Microcredit Summit Campaign.

Detragiache, Enrica, Poonam Gupta, and Thierry Tressel. 2005. "Finance in Lower-Income Countries: An Empirical Exploration." IMF Working Paper WP/05/167. Washington: IMF.

DFID. 2005. "Banking the Underserved: New Opportunities for Commercial Banks." Policy Division Working Paper. London.

Fernando, Nimal A. 2004. *Micro Success Story? Transformation of Nongovernment Organizations into Regulated Financial Institutions.* Manila, Philippines: ADB.

Gallardo, Joselito, Michael Goldberg, and Bikki Randhawa, 2006. "Strategic Alliances to Scale Up Financial Services in Rural Areas." World Bank Working Paper 76. Washington: World Bank.

Hagen, Martin, and Doris Koehn. 2006. "Profiling Financial Institutions Operating in Difficult Environments: The Case of MEB, Kosovo." Paper prepared for "Access to Finance: Building Inclusive Financial Systems." Brookings Institution and World Bank, Washington, May 30–31.

Hanson, James. 2003. "Banking in Developing Countries in the 1990s." World Bank Policy Research Working Paper 3168. Washington: World Bank.

———. 2004. "Transformation of State-Owned Banks." In *The Future of State-Owned Financial Institutions,* edited by Gerard Caprio and others, pp. 13–49. Brookings.

Harper, Malcolm, and Sukhwinder Singh Arora. 2005. *Small Customers, Big Market.* Warwickshire, U.K.: ITDG Publishing.

Isern, Jennifer, and David Porteous. 2005. "Commercial Banks and Microfinance: Evolving Models of Success." Focus Note 28. Washington: CGAP.

Ivatury, Gautam. 2006. "Using Technology to Build Inclusive Financial Systems." Focus Note 32. Washington: CGAP.

Khwaja, Asim, and Atif Mian. 2005. "Do Lenders Favor Politically Connected Firms? Rent Provision in an Emerging Financial Market." *Quarterly Journal of Economics* 120, no. 4: 1371–411.

Kumar, Anjali. 2005. *Access to Financial Services in Brazil: A Study.* Washington: World Bank.

Kumar, Anjali, and others. 2006. "Expanding Bank Outreach through Retail Partnerships: Correspondent Banking in Brazil." World Bank Working Paper 85. Washington: World Bank.

La Porta, Rafael, Florencio López-de-Silanes, and Andrei Shleifer. 2002. "Government Ownership of Banks." *Journal of Finance* 57, no.1: 265–301.

Ledgerwood, Joanna. 1998. *Microfinance Handbook : An Institutional and Financial Perspective.* Washington: World Bank.

Liew, Jeff. 2006. "Banking the Unbanked in Fiji: The ANZ Bank and UNDP Partnership Model." Paper prepared for "Access to Finance: Building Inclusive Financial Systems." Brookings Institution and World Bank, Washington, May 30–31.

Lyman, Timothy R., Gautam Ivatury, and Stefan Staschen. 2006. "Use of Agents in Branchless Banking for the Poor: Rewards, Risks, and Regulation." Focus Note 38. Washington: CGAP.

Matthäus-Maier, Ingrid, and J. D. von Pischke. 2006. *Microfinance Investment Funds: Leveraging Private Capital for Economic Growth and Poverty Reduction.* Berlin: Springer Verlag and KfW.

———. Forthcoming. *New Partnerships for Innovation in Finance.* Berlin: Springer Verlag and KfW.

Meade, Jose Antonio. 2006. "The Experience of Financiera Rural in Mexico." Paper prepared for "Access to Finance: Building Inclusive Financial Systems." Brookings Institution and World Bank, Washington, May 30–31.

Mena, Jose, and Enrique Errázuriz. 2006. "Expanding Borders: Inclusive Finance at BancoEstado." Paper prepared for "Access to Finance: Building Inclusive Financial Systems." Brookings Institution and World Bank, Washington, May 30–31.

Mulder, Herman, and Khalid Sheikh. 2006. "ABN-Amro's Innovations for Financial Access." Paper prepared for "Access to Finance: Building Inclusive Financial Systems." Brookings Institution and World Bank, Washington, May 30–31.

Murgatroyd, Paul. 2004. "Development Finance Institutions." World Bank.

Pearce, Douglas, Andrew Goodland, and Annabel Mulder. 2004. "Rural Financial Services through State Banks." Operational Note 3. Washington: CGAP.

Rhyne, Elizabeth. 2006. "Accion International: Experience of a Global Microfinance Institution and the Road Ahead." Paper prepared for "Access to Finance: Building Inclusive Financial Systems." Brookings Institution and World Bank, Washington, May 30–31.

Robinson, Marguerite. 2002. *The Microfinance Revolution.* Vol. 2: *Lessons from Indonesia.* Washington: World Bank.

Schreiner, Mark. 2006 (forthcoming). "Credit Scoring: The Next Microfinance Revolution?" In *New Partnerships for Innovation in Finance*, edited by Ingrid Matthäus-Maier and J. D. von Pischke. Berlin: Springer Verlag and KfW.

Sensarma, Moumita. 2006. "The Microfinance Challenge at ABN AMRO India." Paper prepared for "Access to Finance: Building Inclusive Financial Systems." Brookings Institution and World Bank, Washington, May 30–31.

Von Pischke, J. D. 1991. *Finance at the Frontier: Debt Capacity and the Role of Credit in the Private Economy.* Washington: World Bank.

Weizenmann, Flavio. 2006. "Microfinance in Brazil: A Commercial Bank View." Paper prepared for "Access to Finance: Building Inclusive Financial Systems." Brookings Institution and World Bank, Washington, May 30–31.

World Bank. 1993. "A Review of Bank Lending for Agricultural Credit and Rural Finance: 1948–1992." Report 12143. Washington.

———. 2006. *The Investment Climate in Brazil, India, and South Africa: A Contribution to the IBSA Debate.* Washington.

Xiao, Bing. 2006. "Wells Fargo's Model for Financial Outreach." Paper prepared for "Access to Finance: Building Inclusive Financial Systems." Brookings Institution and World Bank, Washington, May 30–31.

Yaron, Jacob, McDonald P. Benjamin, and Gerda L. Piprek. 1997. "Rural Finance: Issues, Design, and Best Practices." Environmentally and Socially Sustainable Development Studies and Monographs Series 14. Washington: World Bank.

Zeller, Manfred. 2003. "Models of Rural Financial Institutions." Paper presented at "Paving the Way Forward for Rural Finance: An International Conference on Best Practices." USAID, Washington, June 2–4.

DAVID PORTEOUS

6

Financial Infrastructure and Financial Access

I F UNBANKED PEOPLE are to have greater access, two key aspects of the delivery of financial services must be addressed: providers must be able to manage and price for the risk of each product and they must be able to distribute products cost effectively to convenient locations.

Information and communications technology (ICT) has provided the infrastructure that has supported innovation in risk management and in the distribution of products in the financial sector over the past fifty years. ICT applications enable a constant flow both of information, allowing better risk management, and of payment instructions, reducing the cost of transactions and changing the geography of access.

In the field of risk management, two specific applications of ICT have had a major impact on access to credit: credit bureaus have grown in number and coverage across the world in the past twenty years and banks and other lenders have increasingly made use of credit scoring systems to grant and manage retail credit. Those developments have been documented elsewhere.[1] The focus of this chapter is on another aspect of service delivery: the role of the financial infrastructure supporting the wider distribution of financial services. Advances in ICT over the past thirty years have greatly changed the financial infrastructure for payment and banking transactions: at one time, banking transactions were restricted to

1. See, for example, Miller (2003).

bank branches; now, they may take place on widely distributed automated teller machines (ATMs), in even more widespread merchants' premises, and most recently, even by mobile phone.

The papers presented during the third session of the conference, "Infrastructure: How Can It Support Outreach?" all addressed different aspects of the financial infrastructure for the distribution of financial services, focusing especially on the development of electronic payments in a variety of forms. Massimo Cirasino and his colleagues from the World Bank and the Bank of Italy reported on the development of retail payment systems, contrasting the recent experience in Europe of customer adoption of electronic payment instruments with efforts in the Latin America and Caribbean (LAC) region to improve the payment infrastructure.[2] Their central premise is that well-functioning infrastructure that can efficiently and safely process modern e-payment instruments such as credit transfers, direct debits, and card payments is necessary to enhance access to banking. Those instruments are important for providing access to the unbanked, since their cost is usually one-third to one-half that of their paper-based alternatives. Given the high initial costs of setting up e-payment infrastructure, a cost advantage is reached only at large volumes of usage.

Cirasino and his colleagues reported on an empirical study of the factors that have influenced the shift toward electronic payments in Europe. Three possible factors are identified: institutional framework; technology and security; and interoperability; studies show that the latter two factors are more important than the first. That suggests that in advanced countries, regulators may catalyze processes that result in greater security of payment instruments or greater interoperability but that they may not need to intervene directly. The single euro payments area (SEPA) project in Europe provides a case study of the balance between self-regulation and the active involvement of regulators to achieve the objective of an integrated European payment infrastructure. Questions have arisen as to whether the self-regulatory approach to date has been effective.

The authors note that in developing countries, more pervasive market and coordination failures may justify a more activist role by regulators. Citing evidence gathered from twenty-three country assessments conducted by the World Bank as part of the Western Hemisphere Payments and Securities Clearance and Settlement Initiative (WHI), they find that the migration to electronic instruments in most LAC countries has been slow, with low levels of interoperability resulting in inefficient use of infrastructure and often limited involvement by central banks. There also is no equivalent to SEPA, which seeks to develop a

2. Cirasino and others (2006).

regional infrastructure. The authors propose elements of an agenda for developing countries in which central banks in particular play a more active role in promoting an efficient, interoperable payment infrastructure that results in safe, convenient instruments for consumers.

Core banking technology is the back office engine on which all products, services, and information are processed. In his conference paper, Murray Gardiner, from Temenos, one of the top four banking system vendors worldwide, made the case for financial institutions to upgrade their core banking systems as a means of maintaining their competitive advantage.[3] As microfinance becomes more competitive, through commercial banks' downscaling, entrance of new providers, and microfinance institutions' (MFIs) growing to scale, the need for accurate, robust information systems grows. Gardiner suggested, however, that PC-based systems were adequate for smaller entities such as small credit cooperatives and MFIs. In comparing the cost of ownership of in-house and of shared applications, he found that shared applications reduced initial and capped costs. The fees charged depend on the number of transactions.

My conference paper presented an overview of three recent papers that address the potential and risks of emerging distribution systems for the provision of retail financial services, especially cash withdrawal and deposit, to low-income populations.[4] The first is Kumar and others (2006), which reports on the explosive growth of banking correspondent networks in Brazil following the passage of enabling regulations in 1999. The spread of correspondents, which numbered more than 25,000 by 2004, has reduced to zero the number of municipalities in Brazil without a financial presence. Second is Lyman, Ivatury, and Staschen (2006), which considers the regulatory risks involved in the provision of branchless services and how those risks may be addressed. The authors distinguish the functional risks of outsourcing front-end banking roles to agents from the prudential risks of new nonbank players effectively taking deposits through issuing electronic money (e-money). Third is Porteous (2006b), which surveys developments in mobile banking (m-banking), especially in Africa, and assesses the potential for emerging models to be transformational, in the sense of leading to reaching out to unbanked people. While the potential for transformation exists, this study argues that it may not happen spontaneously. To be sure, m-banking as an add-on channel for existing customers will continue to grow as functionality improves, but there are complex, overlapping regulatory or policy factors, often not specific to m-banking models alone, that inhibit transformational models. The

3. Gardiner (2006).
4. Porteous (2006a).

study identifies six key principles that will enable a more certain and more open environment for the emergence of transformational m-banking in low-income countries.

Remittance flows to developing countries are material, and they are growing. Remitters and receivers both are looking for cheaper, faster, more convenient, and more reliable service. In the final paper of this conference session, Bharat Sarpeshkar of Citibank sketches some of the macro issues in the remittance infrastructure that may constrain the ability to address these needs fully:

—Lack of a level regulatory playing field for banks and nonbanks

—National payment systems with limited working hours, no international standards, and no access by smaller institutions

—Lack of a universal instruction format for remittances, including lack of a worldwide account number format and codes for the purpose and method of payment.[5]

Banks can and do play many roles in the remittance value chain at both the retail and the wholesale level. However, Sarpeshkar identifies four areas in which banks can innovate: improving their customer interface, improving their core processing capability, packaging appropriate products around remitters, and, most notably, developing remittance ecosystems through new forms of linkage with nonbank providers.

Drawing on these papers and the discussions that followed, this chapter seeks to answer in turn the following main questions about the deployment of retail financial infrastructure:

—How does the rollout of infrastructure affect access to financial services?

—Can unbanked people use the electronic infrastructure?

—What constrains the rollout or adoption of electronic instruments?

—How are developed and developing world different or similar?

First, the chapter places the development of retail financial infrastructure in historical perspective.

Waves of Development in Financial Infrastructure

Retail financial infrastructure has developed in successive waves over the past fifty years (figure 6-1). The first wave started in the 1950s, following the development of mainframe computing. In the early days, banks—at least large banks—implemented their own information technology (IT) systems, which Murray Gardiner

5. Sarpeshkar (2006).

Figure 6-1. *Waves of Development of Financial Infrastructure*

Number of new adopters

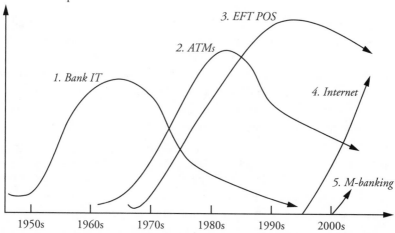

Source: Author's illustration.

calls "core banking systems." By eliminating the need for manual record keeping, computing reduced the cost of processing transactions substantially. Communications networks then extended computers' processing power across branch networks to the point of contact with the customer. Subsequent waves of infrastructure built on the platform provided by bank IT systems, allowing remote devices to interface electronically with the core system, where clients' account details were stored. Today, most banks around the world have deployed core banking solutions of some sort. Because of developments in electronic communications technologies, such systems no longer need to be located on a bank's own computers; they can be accessed from a service provider as needed on a fee-for-service basis.

The second wave brought the deployment of ATMs. First invented in the late 1960s, ATMs were widely used in developed countries in the late 1970s and 1980s.[6] Human tellers were no longer required for basic banking services such as balance inquiries, cash withdrawals, or even deposits. By automating the processes involved, ATMs changed the geography and convenience of basic banking: since it costs less to install an ATM than to open a bank branch, banks could now offer basic services in more areas and outside of regular banking hours. Today, there are

---

6. Reportedly the ATM machine was developed in the 1960s but patented in the United States only in 1973. See "The ATM Is 30 Years Old," CNN, September 20, 1995 (http://cgi.cnn.com/TECH/9509/atm [May 22, 2007]).

more than 1.2 million ATMs in the world, twice as many as there are bank branches,[7] and ATM deployment continues apace in larger emerging economies like Brazil.[8]

The third wave involved the widespread deployment of electronic fund transfer point-of-sale (EFT POS) machines. These devices replaced the mechanical "zip-zap" machines that merchants used previously to obtain a customer's credit card imprint on a signed authorization slip, telephoning for authorization from the bank if the size of transaction required it. The EFT POS devices automatically obtain the authorization and print the slip for signature or accept a personal identification number (PIN) instead. An important advantage was that real-time access for authorization at the point of sale enabled the spread of debit cards as another channel to existing bank accounts, alongside checks and proprietary ATM cards. By the 1990s in developed markets, EFT POS devices also offered the convenience of obtaining cash back at checkout, meaning that retailers' checkout clerks served in effect as bank tellers for simple transactions and their tills became "manned ATMs." EFT POS devices initially required dial-up over fixed telephone lines. Their diffusion therefore depended on reliable, cost-effective, and pervasive fixed telephony, which was limited outside of developed countries. Now, POS devices are increasingly available with wireless modems that use global system for mobile communications (GSM) or general packet radio service (GPRS) networks to send messages. As mobile phone infrastructure expands in developing countries, the network of EFT POS devices is able to grow there too.

The rapid spread of Internet access in developed countries in the 1990s generated the fourth wave: Internet banking. Customers could now access their account information and initiate transactions online from their own homes, more conveniently than they could by using phone banking, which was available earlier. Most retail banks in developed countries today offer Internet banking, adding yet another channel of access for their clients. Many developing country banks have followed suit, but widespread use of Internet banking in most developing countries is still restricted by relatively limited Internet access.[9]

Finally, the rapid adoption around the world since the mid-1990s of mobile phones has led to the emergence of a new, fifth wave: banking and making payments by mobile phone (m-banking and m-payments). Today, more than 2 bil-

---

7. See data in figure 6-2.

8. The number of ATMs almost doubled between 2000 and 2004; see figure 6-4.

9. The International Telecommunication Union (ITU) reported that in 2005, 15 percent of people around the world used the Internet, but there was wide variation, from 3.2 percent in Africa to 9.6 percent in Asia and more than 70 percent in European countries, such as Sweden. ICT Statistics Database, "Hosts, Users, and Number of PCs" (www.itu.int/ITU-D/icteye/Indicators/Indicators.aspx [May 22, 2007]).

Figure 6-2. *Banking Touch Points*

Number (thousands)

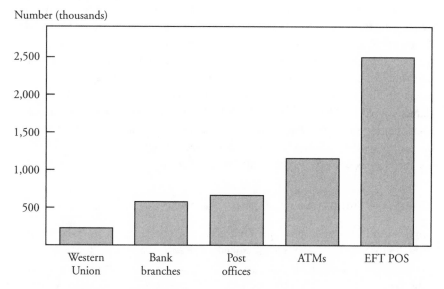

Source: Littlefield, Helms, and Porteous (2006).

lion people use mobile phones, more than half of them in developing countries.[10] Even in low-income countries, over half of the population lives in areas that already have wireless coverage.[11] Many customers already make micropayments using their phone to buy ringtones and other value-added services; however, relatively few outside of a few Asian markets such as Japan, Korea, or the Philippines are using the full line of m-banking services.[12]

Figure 6-2 summarizes the number of touch points created by each wave of development in financial infrastructure. Also included for comparative purposes are the number of offices of the world's largest money transfer operator, Western Union, and the number of postal offices, which are often, although not always, also used by customers of postal banks or other banks to make transactions.

Building on one another, these technologies have changed how people access banking and payment services. Underlying the changes at the retail level have been developments in the wholesale payment infrastructure connecting financial

10. Based on an increase from the most recent figure of 2.2 billion mobile subscribers reported by ITU for 2005. See ICT Statistics Database, "Mobile Cellular Subscribers per 100 People" (www.itu.int/ITU-D/icteye/Indicators/Indicators.aspx# [May 22, 2007]).

11. ICT Statistics Database, "Mobile Cellular Subscribers per 100 People."

12. Porteous (2006b).

intermediaries and financial markets. Great efforts have been made to improve this "bulk" infrastructure—an example in Latin America and the Caribbean is the Western Hemisphere Payment and Securities Clearance and Settlement Initiative, led by the World Bank.[13] However, as Cirasino and his colleagues point out, the development of retail payment systems has often been underplayed in national payment system development. Official guidance on payment system development, such as a report recently released by the Committee on Payment and Settlement Systems (CPSS) at the Bank for International Settlements (BIS), tends to focus mainly on systemically important payment systems.[14] The need for the development of retail systems is increasingly recognized but to date has not been the main focus of most regulators and policymakers.

How Does Infrastructure Improve Access to Financial Services?

Financial infrastructure provides a platform for the execution of the payment transactions that are the core of financial service provision. Good infrastructure improves access by reducing the cost of each transaction, both the cost to the provider of executing the transaction and the cost to the consumer of using the service. The total transaction cost to the consumer should be measured both in financial terms and in terms of the time required to use the service and the convenience of using it, which are approximated by measures of geographic access. Today's new models of financial infrastructure have reduced costs and increased geographic access to banking services, even as they continue to evolve.

Cost

Information from surveys and from econometric estimation of cost functions consistently shows that electronic payment instruments may cost one-third to one-half of the paper-based alternatives.[15] Figure 6-3 graphically depicts cost differences in line with that norm across a range of manual (branch, call center, mail) and electronic channels (ATM, Internet), using data from a survey of developed country banks by Bankers Administration Institute (BAI).[16] Even in a developing country like India, where the relative price of labor to capital is lower, the use of new electronic interfaces has reduced the transaction cost for ICICI Bank.

---

13. Described in Cirasino and others (2006).
14. Bank for International Settlements (2006).
15. Cirasino and others (2006), citing work by Humphrey, Kim, and Vale (2001), Humphrey and others (2003), and Cabo Valverde, Humphrey, and Lopez del Paso (2004).
16. Cited in Ivatury (2006).

Figure 6-3. *Cost per Transaction, by Channel*

U.S. dollars

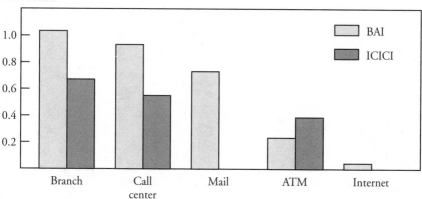

Source: Ivatury (2006).

While cost numbers are not shown for m-banking transactions in figure 6-3, they are likely to be similar to those for Internet transactions on the supplier side; indeed, one of the reasons that these transactions are cheaper for providers is that more of the costs of transacting (the hardware and cost of the connection) are borne by the customer.

Underlying the cost numbers is the reality that electronic payment systems usually require a high initial fixed investment but operate at low marginal cost once implemented; in other words, they are subject to strong economies of scale. Once scale is achieved on a new network, the low average cost of executing a transaction may enable each individual transaction to be priced cheaply. However, as Cirasino and others (2006) points out, uncertainties over the rate and size of take-up may deter private providers from making the large initial investment necessary to create new payment infrastructure.

Third-party providers can help. Banks can avoid the fixed costs of implementing a basic core banking system by instead buying the service from an application service provider on a fee-for-service basis, as Gardiner (2006) illustrates. Third-party providers also create ATM and EFT POS networks—for example, they operate some of the Brazilian correspondent networks on behalf of banks. However, third-party providers are not immune from the underlying cost dynamics; they too must rely on providing specialized services at sufficient scale in order to be profitable.

Figure 6-4. *Brazil: Bank Access Points*

Number (hundreds)

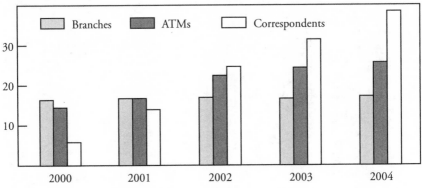

Source: Compiled with data from Kumar and others (2006).

Geography

In Brazil, the deployment of EFT POS devices through correspondent networks has significantly changed the geography of access to financial services. Kumar and others (2006) shows that the percentage of Brazilian municipalities without a single point of financial presence fell from 26 percent in 2000 to 0 percent in 2003. That change in coverage resulted from the large-scale rollout by Brazilian banks of correspondent networks. Starting from scratch in 1999, the number of correspondents reached almost 40,000 in 2004 (figure 6-4). Notwithstanding a rapid increase in ATM deployment over the same period, banking correspondents also increased as a proportion of all bank service points from 12.8 percent to 42 percent over that period.

It is not only in Brazil that the value of electronically linking agents to provide basic financial services is recognized. For example, Firpo reports from a recent technology pilot project in Uganda that "the model which showed the greatest potential and return was the agent model in which merchants were designated as virtual bankers."[17]

Emerging Models for Deploying New Infrastructure

New infrastructure not only changes the cost of financial service provision and the geography of access but also may change the playing field by enabling new entrants to enter the market and new relationships to be formed among them.

17. Firpo (2005, p. 7).

The new relationships formed around correspondents in Brazil can translate into lower cost to the consumer because they harness the capacity of merchants who already are dealing with cash. However, lower cost to the consumer does not follow automatically from lower cost to the provider. Merchants often are happy both because they reduce the cash in their tills and because banking customers often spend more on other goods and services in the store when they conduct their banking business. According to Kumar and colleagues, 88 percent of correspondent business owners in Brazil reported an increase in their sales; as a result, there was strong demand to become bank correspondents.[18] While the correspondent model has come to scale in Brazil, some issues still need to be resolved—for example, the high incidence of fraud experienced by banks and the need to manage liquidity at the agent level so that sufficient cash is available on demand.[19] In addition, Cirasino and others (2006) points out that while plentiful, Brazilian payment networks often are not interoperable. That limits their usability by consumers and their viability to their owners.

Nonetheless, the correspondent networks offer a useful example of what Bharat Sarpeshkar would call an emerging *ecosystem*, meaning that new mutually sustaining relationships are entered into by banks with nonbank partners. Such relationships characterize his vision for the international remittance system as well. Because large banks may not be well equipped to service the "last mile" for the remitter or the receiver in a developing country, he argues for "co-opetition," whereby banks offer at least their wholesale infrastructure and cooperate in new ways with other remittance providers.

Correspondent networks are one way in which banks can effectively outsource the front-end retail process in the financial service value chain while retaining control of the client's account. However, some of the emerging infrastructure models challenge this last redoubt of the banking system as well. Nonbank entities such as telephone companies (telcos) or prepaid card issuers effectively offer basic bank account services to clients, often pooling the aggregated balances of retail clients in one account with the banking system. This "pooling of deposits" approach is common, especially in countries where retail bank systems are obsolete or interfaces for online connections are limited. The pooling of deposits constitutes the issuance of e-money by the telco to its client in exchange for bank money. The issuance may not be intentional, but when prepaid airtime balances at telcos are used to buy non-telco services not supplied to the telephone directly,

18. Kumar and others (2006, p. 16).
19. Ivatury (2006).

Table 6-1. *Categorization of Models*

Account held at deposit-taking entity	Bank	Non-bank	
		Mobile phone company	*Non-bank entity*
Distribution	Merchants	Merchants, including airtime agents	Merchants, including airtime agents
Example	Caixa/Banco Postal (2000, Brazil)	Globe (2004, Philippines)	
Example—Africa	MTN Banking (2005, South Africa)	M-Pesa (2005, Kenya)	SmartMoney (2006, Kenya)

Source: Derived from Lyman, Ivatury, and Staschen (2006); Porteous (2006b).

the telco is effectively providing e-money (from the prepaid balance) for the transaction, as recent regulator guidance in Europe has shown.[20]

The emerging models that use the new payment infrastructure can be most usefully distinguished by:

—which entity is legally responsible for the deposit—whether a bank or nonbank (including a telco)

—the nature of the agency relationships involved.

Table 6-1 cites examples of each type, drawing on Lyman, Ivatury, and Staschen (2006) and Porteous (2006b).

The risks of each of the different models are the main subject of Lyman, Ivatury, and Staschen (2006). Lyman and his colleagues at the Consultative Group to Assist the Poor (CGAP) locate the regulatory risks arising from the new agency relationships in the broader spectrum of risks from outsourcing bank activities. The BIS has issued general guidelines on this subject, although most outsourcing to date has been in the areas of back office systems and functions, rather than front office client interfaces.[21] The main category of risk in agency models arises from the potential for customer abuse, although, from the Brazilian experience and from analysis of the possible risk events, that risk appears to be manageable. There are other risks, however, that are less well understood: for example, how banking correspondents manage the liquidity risk associated with accepting large volumes of cash in payments at particular times of the month or with having insufficient cash available at other times to meet withdrawal requests.

20. See, for example, Financial Services Authority (2003).
21. See BIS, "Outsourcing in Financial Services: 2005" (www.bis.org/publ/joint09.htm [May 9, 2007]).

However, the lack of liquidity at a particular agent does not appear to create the systemic risk of a run on the associated bank or the banking system.

The risks of unregulated e-money issuance are usually less well understood than other risks and often are not addressed in national legislation or regulations. Approaches in developed countries to regulation in this area have differed. The European Union adopted the E-Money Directive, seeking to create a certain enabling environment for a new type of nonbank e-money issuer.[22] A recent review concluded that the legislation had not fully succeeded in enabling innovation and in fact may have limited it.[23] The U.S. approach has been to avoid overarching federal legislation for nonbank prepaid cards, leaving room for innovation but also for uncertainty.[24]

Can and Do Unbanked People Use Electronic Infrastructure?

While the expansion of the electronic payment infrastructure may make banking more accessible in terms of cost and availability, are unbanked people actually able and willing to use electronic payment instruments?

To be sure, by volume if not value, cash remains the most common medium for retail transactions in almost all countries. However, empirical evidence is limited on how or why consumers choose particular payment instruments from the other options that have become available. That is true for consumers in general, even in developed countries, not to mention the unbanked.[25] However, the fact that electronic channels are now visibly displacing traditional paper payment instruments such as checks has prompted an upsurge in scholarly and regulatory interest in the subject. As Stacey Shreft notes: "The question 'What's in your wallet?' is finally interesting."[26]

There are wide differences in the use of electronic payment instruments across Europe. In 2004, the average Finn used non-cash instruments 237 times, whereas the average Italian used only them only forty-five times. Cirasino and others (2006) reports on empirical studies by Banca d'Italia that have sought to explain such cross-country diversity by using macroeconomic variables. Their results suggest that

22. Directive 2000/46/EC (http://europa.eu.int/eur-lex/pri/en/oj/dat/2000/l_275/l_27520001027 en00390043.pdf [May 22, 2007]).
23. Commission Staff Working Document on the Review of the E-Money Directive (2000/46/EC) (http://ec.europa.eu/internal_market/bank/e-money/index_en.htm [May 9, 2007]).
24. See comments made at 2005 Conference on Payment Cards and the Unbanked, "Conference Summary" (www.phil.frb.org/pcc/conferences/2005/PaymentCardsandtheUnbankedSummary.pdf [May 22, 2007].
25. See Shreft (2005).
26. Shreft (2005, p.1)

higher use of electronic channels is related more to the functionality available—for example, having cards with multiple functions and interoperability—than it is to level of central bank oversight and intervention.

This finding accords with intuition: after all, consumers want enhanced functionality from the use of technology, not the technology itself. Fast, reliable, convenient, low-cost service is what both remitters and receivers of remittances look for in providers, as Sarpeshkar (2006) notes, and technology is useful to consumers only to the extent that it delivers that kind of service. In the process, the technology itself fades into the background of the customer experience, as does any infrastructure.

There is limited evidence specifically on the appeal and adoption of electronic instruments by the unbanked in developing countries; what is available comes largely from middle-income countries, such as Brazil and South Africa, where major efforts have been made to understand the profile of unbanked people and to provide banking services to them.

Kumar and others (2006) shows that of clients who used the correspondent banking services of two of the largest retail Brazilian banks, Caixa and Banco Postal/Bradesco, 88 percent and 73 percent respectively earned below R$400 per month, the national poverty line (approximately US$175 at current exchange rates).[27] Caixa in particular has developed a low-cost bank account (Conta Caixa) linked to a debit card that can be used at its correspondent outlets. The convenience of access means that those accounts were widely used, although to date mainly for payment services. There is no evidence that low-income people in Brazil resist the use of bank cards for basic banking services.

In 2004, South African banks launched a basic bank account targeting unbanked people, under the umbrella Mzansi brand. The account has no fixed fees and is accessed using a debit card. Within seven months of launch, more than 1 million new accounts had been opened by first-time users at that bank, although they may have banked at another bank before.[28] Mzansi builds on the success of electronic offerings such as E-Plan, launched by South African banks in the 1990s as a way to provide bank services to unbanked workers of low and of moderate income.[29] Again, from the take-up there, there is no evidence that the use of the electronic instrument was a barrier to adoption by the unbanked.

27. Kumar and others (2006, table 14).
28. See Banking Association press release, "One Million Mzansi Account Holders" (www.banking.org.za/documents/2005/MAY/PresReleaseonemillionaccount.pdf [May 9, 2007]).
29. For history of the development of E-Plan and electronic transaction banking, see chapter 2 of Porteous and Hazelhurst (2004).

FinScope surveys of South African adults nationwide, also presented at the Brookings–World Bank conference, provide a picture not only of financial instrument usage but also of consumers' attitudes toward technology and financial services. Those surveys show little evidence of systematic differences in attitudes toward technology between lower-income and higher-income people: 73 percent of low-income adults, who were mainly unbanked, reported that they were prepared to learn to use new technology, while among adults with higher income, who also were more literate and mainly banked, the proportion, at 83 percent, was not much higher.[30] Among both groups, a majority expressed a preference for face-to-face transactions, and a sizable minority (a fifth and a sixth respectively) showed antipathy toward ATMs. For those people at least, "manned ATMs" like the Brazilian correspondent banks may be a more appealing alternative. Advances in the EFT POS infrastructure allow for such instruments, but they are only now becoming widely available in South Africa.

The case that the deployment of new technology does not systematically discriminate against poorer people is strengthened by the rapid adoption of mobile phones in low-income countries. Even among individuals in Bangladesh and South Africa who qualified for government grants because of their destitute or very-low-income status, 20 percent or more reported that they either had used or had access to a mobile phone.[31]

However, mobile banking (m-banking), which uses the mobile phone to initiate financial transactions, is very recent in most countries. Only in parts of Asia, such as Japan and Korea, has m-banking recently reached anything like critical mass. The Philippines, with 4 million m-banking users, is likely to have the largest number of users among developing countries, but relatively little public information is available there on the client profile.[32] Most clients are likely to be already banked.

Nonetheless, m-banking has at least the potential to reach the close to one-quarter of the 55 percent of South African adults who were unbanked and had cell phones, which offer a ready-made, low-cost channel of access.[33]

Such great potential is not the same as the current reality in actually reaching out to poor people: as Porteous (2006b) points out, it is highly likely that

30. Porteous and Hazelhurst (2004, table 2-3).

31. David Porteous, "Scoping Report on the Payment of Social Transfers through the Financial System," report commissioned by DFID.

32. See Infodev, "Micro-Payment Systems and Their Application to Mobile Networks: An Assessment of Mobile-Enabled Financial Services in the Philippines" (http://www.infodev.org/en/Publication.43.html [May 22, 2007]).

33. From analysis of the FinScope South Africa 2004 database; a summary of the survey results and questionnaire in various years can be downloaded at www.finscope.co.za/southafrica.html [May 22, 2007]).

m-banking will be adopted initially as an add-on channel for existing banked customers. It is still uncertain that m-banking offerings will be "transformational" in the sense of enabling previously unbanked customers to access banking services, as mobile phone access has been for individuals without telephone service. To distinguish additive services from ones that may be transformational, Porteous (2006b) suggests a list of characteristics based on research undertaken by MicroSave, among others, into the characteristics desired by unbanked customers:[34]

—no minimum balance requirement
—low or no fixed maintenance fees
—easy access for depositing or withdrawing small amounts of cash
—ability to make person-to-person payments.

Since the empirical evidence on outreach to the poor is not yet sufficient, these indicators serve as proxies for the potential of the services enabled by new infrastructure to reach the unbanked.

One delegate at the conference suggested that certain electronic channels may increase the potential for consumer abuse: specifically, she referred to the use by creditors of direct debit mechanisms to deduct or "pull" funds from a customer's bank account, often at uncertain times or in uncertain amounts. Such randomness can create great risk for poorer customers. Since there may be penalties for rejecting a debit instrument or for accepting it but placing the account in overdraft, that risk may even discourage low-income people from using electronic accounts at all. "Pull" mechanisms, whereby the customer is not required to authorize every payment, are inherently uncertain compared with "push" mechanisms, whereby the customer specifically authorizes a deduction. Previously, it was too expensive to obtain authorization on deductions that varied from period to period. Now, newer technologies may reduce the risk of surprise by presenting each debit request electronically to the customer through a text message to a mobile phone for confirmation prior to processing.

Constraints on and Accelerators of New Infrastructure Rollout

Technology itself clearly is not a barrier to the rollout of new infrastructure. The communications technology used to maintain widespread EFT POS networks, such as V-SAT in Brazil, is already available and stable. Similarly, the coverage of GSM and GPRS wireless networks is increasing quickly, and the cost of mobile handsets necessary for consumers to access the networks is falling.

34. See Cracknell (2004); Wright and others (2006).

Is it possible or likely therefore that the rollout of later generations of financial infrastructure will occur spontaneously in developing countries? In fact, there are several factors inherent in the nature of the infrastructure that may inhibit rollout. The first has already been pointed out: high initial costs may prevent providers from undertaking the initial investment if they are unsure that they can achieve the volume of transactions needed to recover the investment. If systems with no interoperability compete, the fixed costs of each are spread across lower transaction volumes, making each system less financially viable; as Cirasino and others (2006) points out, that is often the case in Latin America. The economics are further complicated by a two-sided market effect regarding payment networks: the number of users is linked to the number of places at which they can use the instruments and the number of places is in turn linked to the number of users. That effect raises the risk of coordination failure.[35] It is therefore quite possible that while new infrastructure is both technologically and even economically feasible, it may fail to be widely deployed in practice.

Porteous (2006b) finds that the barriers to growth identified by four current m-banking providers in Africa are in fact similar to those found in developed countries. The study groups these into issues related to business model, such as

—The speed and nature of customer adoption. Will customers trust the mechanisms and find them simple and convenient enough to use on scale? That uncertainty is common to all new service offerings, although perhaps the trust issue is heightened for financial services.

—Interoperability. Will different means of making payment transactions be interoperable, so as to achieve greater scale? That, of course, is applicable only in markets in which infrastructure already exists.

However, there also are regulatory and policy obstacles. In particular, the study identifies the need for a policy and regulatory environment that is both sufficiently open to allow for trying out innovative approaches and sufficiently certain (that is, subject to no arbitrary changes) that the initial investment will be made; further investment then will be needed to take successful approaches to scale. While many low-income countries may start from a position that is more open (due to the absence of prohibitive regulations), more certainty may be needed before significant infrastructural investment takes place; equally, middle-income countries may have more certainty but be less open to the full range of experimentation necessary to find appropriate competitive offerings. The contrasting positions are shown in figure 6-5 below.

35. For a recent summary of the academic literature on two-sided markets, such as payment cards, see Jean-Charles Rochet and Jean Tirole, "Two-Sided Markets: A Progress Report," November 29, 2005 (http://idei.fr/doc/wp/2005/2sided_markets.pdf [May 22, 2007]).

Figure 6-5. *Moving toward an Enabling Environment*

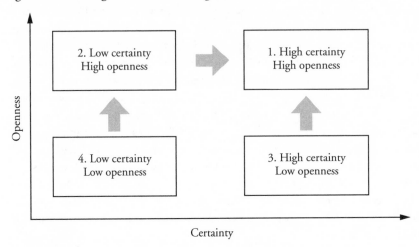

Source: Porteous (2006).

Creating an enabling environment for the deployment of new infrastructure means that regulators must strike an appropriate balance between openness and certainty. That may require regulations to be loosened in some cases and introduced in others. Even then, regulatory change may be a necessary but not sufficient action.

The development of correspondent banks in Brazil provides a useful example. The Brazilian Central Bank passed new regulations in 1999 that allowed the appointment of correspondents, creating the initial openness and certainty necessary for banks to develop correspondent networks, although initially on a limited basis. Since then, the regulatory framework has evolved to become even more open—allowing agency relationships for more classes of institution and for all areas of the country. In Brazil, the passage of enabling regulations was clearly a necessary condition for the take-off of correspondent relationships; however, it may not have been sufficient. Kumar and others (2006) points to other factors that combined to increase the appeal of agency relationships to banks, such as prescriptive labor laws and regulations that imposed high standards and therefore costs on bank branches.

Clearly the role of regulators will differ in different contexts. While Cirasino and others (2006) suggests that institutional arrangements, including direct intervention by the regulator, may be a less significant factor in explaining take-up of electronic instruments in Europe, they take pains to justify a stronger catalytic and facilitative role for regulators in the context of developing country markets such as those in Latin America and the Caribbean, where more market and coordination failures occur. Even in their description of the slow rollout of SEPA in Europe following the hands-off approach of European regulators, they leave open the possibility that a more active role may be required there too in order to meet the agreed-on target: that a critical mass of transactions in Europe will migrate to SEPA instruments, making the process irreversible.

Developed and Developing Countries: Is Leapfrogging Possible?

By contrasting developments in retail payment systems in Europe with those in Latin America and the Caribbean, Cirasino and others (2006) highlights the differences in this area between developed and developing countries. To be sure, they also describe the large differences within the European Union and how the SEPA project has struggled to make progress toward agreed deadlines for a common euro-zone payments area. However, the problems in Latin America and the Caribbean are more deeply ingrained: heavy use of expensive paper instruments like checks is still common, and automated clearing houses (ACH) have only recently been established in some countries for clearing retail electronic payment instruments among banks. Although Brazil has a well-developed banking system, Cirasino and his colleagues note fundamental problems with the retail payment systems there, such as lack of interoperability, which could hinder the viability of correspondent networks going forward or at least increase their cost unnecessarily. The Brazilian Central Bank has focused until recently on the wholesale payment system of the country, including building a real-time gross settlement system, but it is now embarking on a second phase with the explicit purpose of improving the efficiency and extending the coverage of the retail payment system.

Although developing countries start with less financial infrastructure for electronic payments, can they leapfrog some of the waves of development mentioned previously? Leapfrogging in the field of e-finance was identified as a prospect in Claessens, Glaessner, and Klingebiel (2001).

In this context, leapfrogging may carry two meanings, relative or absolute. First, the earlier adoption of later generations of technology may make it unnecessary to deploy older-generation technology. Developing countries therefore may bypass stages on the path traversed by developed countries and move relatively sooner onto lower-cost, more efficient technology platforms. Second, leapfrogging in an absolute sense means that developing countries can bypass the current stage of developed countries by their more rapid adoption of new-generation infrastructure.

The ability to obtain cash back or to pay bills at the point of sale has been available for a while in many developed countries. The rapid growth of the correspondent network in Brazil, which offers similar features, is therefore not leapfrogging in the second or absolute sense. However, it may mean that Brazil is able to deploy fewer ATMs than it would otherwise. In fact, as figure 6-4 shows, ATM rollout has proceeded in parallel with the growth of the correspondent network in Brazil. However, in countries that are less developed than Brazil, where ATMs may be less affordable, it is possible that the rollout of EFT POS networks will have this relative leapfrogging effect.

A stronger candidate for leapfrogging is the rapid deployment of m-banking using the expanding mobile phone infrastructure. That would displace demand for ATMs and EFT POS, since anyone with a mobile phone may in theory offer cash in exchange for a real-time electronic credit transfer. Furthermore, since so far m-banking has been slow to develop in most rich countries because of the alternatives available, developing countries may come to lead in this area. Even here, absolute leapfrogging may not happen because, after all, m-banking is starting to grow fast in certain developed countries, such as Japan and Korea. However, in those countries, most m-banking customers already are banked, so the mobile phone is an add-on channel. Truly transformational models of m-banking targeting the unbanked are more likely to originate in countries with a large unbanked market. They may then be applied to unbanked populations in developed countries.

Porteous (2006b) considers an emerging question within the m-banking wave about an approach that could be transformational and would constitute leapfrogging if widely adopted: Will airtime itself become a virtual currency in developing countries? Mobile operators increasingly offer person-to-person transfers of airtime, which enable one person to top-up the airtime balance of another user on the same network, for a small fee. The transfer of airtime in that way may function as a remittance. So far, only anecdotal evidence exists of such use: in 2005, the *Economist* carried the story of a woman in the Democratic Republic of Congo (DRC) settling a bribe to officials in another part of the country by sending them airtime.[36] In countries like DRC where safe, fast, convenient payment infrastructure is very limited, the attractions of airtime transfers as a substitute are obvious.

In fact, airtime balances share to some extent the underlying features of money: they are denominated in a common unit of account, they are a store of value (within airtime expiry windows at least), and may be a medium of exchange (at least among users on the same network). However, unless and until airtime itself

36. "Africa's Unmended Heart: Special Report on Congo," *Economist,* June 9, 2005.

is accepted widely in place of cash, a major impediment to its usefulness as a medium of exchange may be the cost of redeeming it for cash: because networks pay a substantial commission, often 15 percent to vendors on the sale of "new" airtime, the same vendors will be reluctant to buy or accept "second-hand" airtime at face value. Sales or other taxes on airtime further exacerbate the wedge between cash value and face value. However, a discount of the magnitude of 15 to 20 percent on cashing a small remittance would not be out of line with the costs of remittances on many international corridors today. If airtime were increasingly remaining in circulation longer, rather than being consumed quickly, presumably the holding time on prepaid balances would lengthen. It would be an interesting exercise to monitor the extent to which this is happening, especially in low-income countries where there are few competitive alternatives.

If airtime does indeed become accepted as money in some places, then the issue identified earlier of how to supervise e-money issuers and holders becomes more pressing still.

Conclusion

Developments in information and communications technology have enabled great changes in the infrastructure of retail financial services over the past fifty years. There have been five successive waves of infrastructure development affecting retail distribution:

—First, the implementation of core banking systems from the 1950s onward, which enabled banks to process electronic transactions with consumers, between branches, and with other banks

—Second, the deployment of automated teller machines, which expanded delivery of basic banking services beyond bank branches and regular banking hours

—Third, the rollout of electronic point-of-sale devices, which enabled merchants to accept debit card transactions and to provide cash back

—Fourth, the development of Internet banking from the mid-1990s, which brought convenient at-home access to consumers with Internet service

—Fifth, mobile banking, the most recent deployment, which currently is most advanced in certain Asian markets, such as Japan and the Philippines, although pioneering deployments also are available in Africa.

This chapter has focused especially on how the rollout of electronic retail payment infrastructure enables branchless banking, especially through electronic point-of-sale and mobile banking infrastructure. To integrate the underlying papers, four main questions have been asked and answered.

How does the rollout of infrastructure affect access to financial services?

Because of the economies of scale possible on retail payment infrastructure, the cost to the provider of each transaction is reduced. The lower cost per transaction, together with the availability and reliability of new communications technology, enables providers to offer more points of service, increasing convenient access for customers. In addition, the new infrastructure allows new relationships to be formed—between agents and principals for deposit taking—and new players to enter the arena of basic banking in ways that can reduce the end cost to the customer.

Can unbanked people use new electronic infrastructure?

Although the reasons why consumers choose to use certain payment instruments are not well known in general, there is evidence from Brazil that low-income people, including the previously unbanked, use the correspondent network for payments, deposits, and withdrawals from basic bank accounts. There is no systematic evidence that the technology per se discriminates against poorer people; rather, they, like all consumers, seek the safe, convenient, fast, and cheap financial service offerings that appropriate technology can offer.

What constrains the rollout or adoption of electronic instruments?

Infrastructure requires a high initial fixed investment, which increases the risk of its deployment, especially if future volumes are uncertain or interoperability with existing infrastructure is unlikely. Retail payment systems also are subject to positive network externalities that may slow initial rollout but accelerate it in later phases. In general, an enabling environment is needed in which there is both sufficient openness to innovation and sufficient certainty to encourage providers to invest the necessary capital in a new offering.

How are developed and developing countries different or similar?

Developing countries have the opportunity to accelerate through certain phases in the deployment of infrastructure that already have occurred in developed countries. For example, as cash becomes widely available at the point of sale at a merchant's premises, the need to deploy ATMs may be significantly reduced. Developing countries may even move ahead of developed countries in the use of m-banking because of the demand created by lack of competing earlier-generation alternatives. In some developing countries, it is even possible that electronic money issued by telcos (in the form of prepaid airtime balances) will become widely used as a medium of exchange.

The rollout of new electronic retail payments infrastructure is changing access to financial services in developed and developing countries alike. The new deployments have the potential to significantly improve access, and there is some evidence that some—for example, correspondent banks in Brazil—already are being used by low-income people. Even there, some caution is warranted since the overwhelming usage to date has been for payments only, not wider forms of financial services such as savings or credit, although these too are starting to grow.

In general, there are still large gaps in current understanding of the use of new payment infrastructure, such as the factors influencing the choice of payment instruments by consumers in general and unbanked consumers in particular. Research on these questions has significantly accelerated in developed countries in recent years. The answers in developing countries may be quite different, since the range of choices is less. However, financial products that are "safe, fast, convenient, and cheap," in the words of Sarpeshkar, are likely to be well received everywhere.

In the sense used here, infrastructure has meant the use of ICT to support new models of distribution of financial services. However, the term may be used at a still more basic level. Arguably, basic financial infrastructure today includes the provision of acceptable unique identifiers such as national identity numbers or, failing that, some other form of unique identifier that advances in biometric technology have made possible. Increased demand for unique identification from governments for national security purposes is likely to accelerate the process of adopting national identification systems in countries currently without them and of stabilizing biometric recognition technology so that it will become more reliable for use in financial transactions.

But there is a still deeper possible meaning of infrastructure. As bank accounts become more widespread, they themselves become basic infrastructure: for payments from person to person and even from government to person and certainly for access to enhanced financial services such as savings, insurance, and credit, whether or not from the same provider. For example, the electronic transaction record provided by a basic bank account may be used for credit scoring to assess and price risk when a customer has no collateral for a loan. Such advantages are the basis of the growing debate over whether a special role for the state is justified in mandating or supporting provision of basic banking services.

One should at least raise the question of whether a basic bank account, enabled by ICT, has not itself become a part of the infrastructure of modern society. If so, it is especially important that cost-effective models of deployment of infrastructure be found to enable its rollout on a sustainable basis. To date, governments often have effectively subsidized the provision of basic financial services through the operations of state-owned retail institutions such as post banks. However, even postal infrastructure may be operated privately for financial services, as in the case of Banco Bradesco in Brazil today. The role of the state in the retail financial system has declined in many countries over the past decade. As shown in the paper presented by Kempson at the conference, governments in developed countries have taken other approaches toward the provision of basic bank accounts—imposing universal service obligations, for example, which require banks to open new accounts for all who ask for them.[37]

In developing countries, where the majority of people currently are unbanked, such universal obligations may be too costly for the banking system to bear. But by reducing cost per transaction, the deployment of new generations of ICT technology, including EFT POS and m-banking, makes it more feasible and therefore likely that the functionality of formal financial services will be extended to more people than ever before in the years to come.

References

Note: All papers presented at the Brookings–World Bank conference "Access to Finance" are available at http://web.worldbank.org/WBSITE/EXTERNAL/WBI/WBIPROGRAMS/FSLP/0,,content MDK:20611572~pagePK:64156158~piPK:64152884~theSitePK:461005,00.html [May 22, 2007].

Bank for International Settlements. 2006. "General Guidance for National Payment System Development." CPSS Publication 70 (January) (www.bis.org/publ/cpss70.htm [May 9, 2006]).

Beck, T., A. Demirgüç-Kunt, and M. Soledad Martinez Peria. 2005. "Reaching Out: Access to and Use of Banking Services across Countries." World Bank Policy Research Working Paper 3754. Washington: World Bank.

Cabo Valverde, S., D. Humphrey, and R. Lopez del Paso. 2004. "Electronic Payments and ATMs: Changing Technology and Cost Efficiency in Banking." Paper presented at SUERF Colloquium, Société Universitaire Européenne de Recherches Financières, Madrid, Spain, October 14–16, 2004.

Claessens, S., T. Glaessner, and D. Klingebiel. 2001. "E-Finance in Emerging Markets: Is Leapfrogging Possible?" Financial Sector Discussion Paper 7. Washington: World Bank.

Cirasino, M., and others. 2006. "Retail Payment Systems to Support Financial Access: Infrastructure and Policy." Paper presented at "Access to Finance: Building Inclusive Financial Systems." Brookings Institution and World Bank, Washington, May 30–31, 2006.

Cracknell, D. 2004. "Electronic Banking for the Poor: Panaceas, Potential and Pitfalls" (September). Nairobi, Kenya: MicroSave (www.microsave.org).

Financial Services Authority. 2003. "Electronic Money: Perimeter Guidance." FSA Consultation Paper 172. London (www.fsa.gov.uk/pubs/cp/cp172_newsletter.pdf [May 9, 2007]).

Firpo, J. 2005. "Banking the Unbanked: Technology's Role in Delivering Accessible Financial Services to the Poor." SEMBA Consulting (www.sevaksolutions.org/docs/Banking%20the %20Unbanked.pdf [May 22, 2007]).

37. Kempson (2006).

Gardiner, M. 2006. "The Importance of Back Office, MIS, and Retail Distribution Technology." Paper presented at "Access to Finance: Building Inclusive Financial Systems." Brookings Institution and World Bank, Washington, May 30–31, 2006.

Humphrey, D., M. Kim, and B. Vale. 2001. "Realizing the Gains from Electronic Payments: Costs, Pricing, and Payment Choice." *Journal of Money, Credit, and Banking* 33: 216–34.

Humphrey, D., and others. 2003. "What Does It Cost to Make a Payment?" *Review of Network Economics* 2: 159–74.

Ivatury, G. 2006. "Using Technology to Build Inclusive Financial Systems." CGAP Focus Note 32. Washington: CGAP.

Kempson, E. 2006. "Policy-Level Responses to Financial Exclusion in Developed Economies: Lessons for Developing Economies." Paper presented at "Access to Finance: Building Inclusive Financial Systems." Brookings Institution and World Bank, Washington, May 30–31, 2006.

Kumar, A., and others. 2006. "Expanding Bank Outreach through Retail Partnerships: Correspondent Banking in Brazil." World Bank Working Paper 85. Washington: World Bank.

Littlefield, Elizabeth, Brigit Helms, and David Porteous. 2006. "Financial Inclusion 2015: Four Scenarios for the Future of Microfinance." CGAP Focus Note 39. Washington: CGAP.

Lyman, T., G. Ivatury, and S. Staschen. 2006. "Use of Agents in Branchless Distribution for the Poor." CGAP Focus Note 38. Washington: CGAP.

Miller, M., ed. 2003. *Credit Reporting Systems and the International Economy.* MIT Press.

Porteous, D. 2006a. "Banking and the Last Mile: Technology and the Distribution of Financial Services in Developing Countries." Paper presented at "Access to Finance: Building Inclusive Financial Systems." Brookings Institution and World Bank, Washington, May 30–31, 2006.

———. 2006b. "The Enabling Environment for Mobile Banking in Africa." Report commissioned by DFID. Boston: Bankable Frontier Associates (www.bankablefrontier.com).

Porteous, D., and E. Hazelhurst. 2004. *Banking on Change.* Cape Town, South Africa: Double Storey.

Sarpeshkar, B. 2006. "The Multifaceted Role of Banks in the Remittance Ecosystem." Paper presented at "Access to Finance: Building Inclusive Financial Systems." Brookings Institution and World Bank, Washington, May 30–31, 2006.

Shreft, S. 2005. "How and Why do Consumers Choose Their Payment Methods?" Paper presented at Federal Reserve Bank of Boston Consumer Behavior and Payment Choice Conference, October 2005 (www.bos.frb.org/economic/eprg/index.htm).

Wright, G., and others. 2006. "Mobile Phone–Based E-Banking: The Customer Value Proposition." Microsave Briefing Note 47. Nairobi, Kenya: MicroSave.

MICHAEL S. BARR

7

Government Policies to
Expand Financial Access

THIS CONFERENCE BROUGHT together a wide range of experts on promoting financial access, including through nongovernmental organizations, the for-profit sector, and governments. This chapter provides a systematic framework for understanding government policy. In doing so, it draws in part on presentations from two panels at the conference, made by academic experts, nonprofit practitioners, representatives of international organizations, and government policymakers.[1] Given the breadth of the topic area and the number of presentations, the chapter does not extensively summarize each paper, but it does refer to the presentations in the course of discussing government strategies. The central theme of the chapter, consistent with the themes of the conference, from the opening remarks by Raghu Rajan to the closing remarks by this author, is that a focus on microfinance institutions is not enough.[2] Microfinance is a function, not an institution, and the role of government policy is to develop financial systems that broadly serve society, including the poor.[3]

---

1. See Balkenhol (2006), Barr (2006a and 2006b), Dam (2006a), Isern (2006), Keijzers (2006), Kempson (2006), Kirsten (2006), Knight (2006), Prado (2006), and Sherraden (2006), available at the World Bank website (www.worldbank.org).

2. Rajan (2006).

3. See Barr (2004b).

Domestic financial policies can help to deepen domestic financial markets, thereby contributing broadly to economic growth, which can under some circumstances contribute to poverty alleviation.[4] Credit constraints, for example, affect the poor more deeply than they do the rich, who can rely on relationships and assets in the face of information-poor and legally weak markets. Removal of credit constraints through broad financial and legal reforms, enforcement of creditor rights, and the like could therefore contribute to the ability of all households, including poor households, to access credit. That in turn could help poor households leverage their labor into asset accumulation and other goals; they also might benefit indirectly from economic growth more generally as a result of financial and legal reforms that contribute to financial deepening. World Bank research suggests that financial development does help to reduce income inequality.[5]

Despite the potential for financial development to contribute to poverty alleviation, it does not necessarily do so. As a theoretical matter, financial development can be structured to benefit the rich more than the poor, and as a practical matter that is often the case.[6] Moreover, financial sector growth without the appropriate legal and regulatory structures can lead to financial crises that harm the poor the most.[7] In addition, many financial systems remain closed clubs, in which those with access and assets can obtain financial services and those without cannot. In countries with weak legal and financial infrastructure, it is quite difficult for financial institutions to reach out to serve the general population because it is more difficult to monitor and enforce credit and other financial contracts; at the same time, elites who benefit from the current financial structure in such countries often block reforms that would broaden the financial base.[8] Even where financial reforms are undertaken, poor households are a special challenge because of the difficulty of overcoming the high fixed costs of financial intermediation given small-scale transactions or loans; the difficulty of finding functional substitutes for collateral; and the necessity of finding means of proving creditworthiness besides traditional measures of income, assets, prior loan history, and bank account ownership. How can the financial sector overcome these problems?

Microfinance can be seen as part of the solution.[9] Increasingly, microfinance institutions and other types of institutions are providing the range of financial ser-

---

4. Beck and others (2000); Levine (2004); Beck and others (2004).
5. Beck and others (2000); Clarke and others (2003).
6. Greenwood and Jovanovic (1990); Haber (1991).
7. Stiglitz (1994).
8. Rajan and Zingales (2003).
9. Barr (2004b).

vices that low-income households need. There is increasing recognition that improving access to finance for poor households may provide positive benefits in terms of reduced costs and improved real financial outcomes for low-income households. Better financial services may help households to weather shocks to consumption, for example, or help them to accumulate savings.

Which dimensions of access should be cause for concern? High-cost financial services, barriers to saving, lack of insurance, and credit constraints may contribute to poverty and other socioeconomic problems. Low-income individuals often lack access to financial services from banks and therefore turn to much more expensive, alternative providers of financial services. Lack of access to credit and insurance leaves many low-income individuals vulnerable to emergencies that may endanger their financial stability. The lack of longer-term savings may undermine their ability to invest in human capital, purchase a home, and build assets. More generally, heavy reliance on alternative financial services providers is costly. Taken together, these barriers to financial access contribute to the conditions that keep households in poverty.

Financial services, savings, credit, and insurance are interrelated. Financial services such as bank accounts can provide a gateway to saving or serve as an obstacle to saving, depending on the structure and pricing of products and services. Saving both assists in asset accumulation and operates as a form of self-insurance. Insurance smoothes income and consumption and protects savings and income against catastrophic shocks, but it also acts as a substitute for savings and thus provides incentives not to save. Credit can assist asset accumulation, smooth income and consumption, and provide insurance against income shocks, but imprudent borrowing can destroy asset creation and block access to savings vehicles such as bank accounts.

Financial access problems might arise in a variety of contexts, related to household needs for credit, savings, payments, and insurance. As noted at the World Bank–Brookings conference "Access to Finance: Building Inclusive Financial Systems," many low-income households need access to efficient, low-cost means to receive income, store its value, and make payments; access to a ready mechanism for saving, both as a cushion against short-term emergencies and for longer-term goals, including asset building; access to insurance with respect to life's key risks; and access to credit on reasonable terms. Increasingly, a range of financial service providers are beginning to offer these microfinance functions. As noted in this volume, microfinance is emerging as an effective private sector response to client needs, and it may be able to reach scale and perhaps also achieve self-sustainability, at least in some contexts for some institutions, over the long term.

What, then, is the role of government in financial access? Broadly speaking, one goal of domestic financial reforms can be to help extend the reach of financial markets to include lower-income households. Reforms could encompass both broad-based legal and financial initiatives that serve to create a strong backbone and enabling environment for financial sector development, as, for example, through capital requirements and competent prudential supervision of depository institutions, as well as targeted initiatives designed to increase the likelihood that the financial sector will extend deeper into the income base.[10]

In the past, government policies had focused on directed lending through state-owned banks. Those policies generally failed. (See chapter 5 of this volume.) Government-owned banks usually lacked market discipline and expertise and often sacrificed financial soundness in favor of the short-term political benefits of expansive lending. Many such institutions suffered from cronyism and corruption. Large sums of public resources often were expended, and many countries offered long-running, nontransparent public subsidies. Empirical evidence suggests that government-owned banking in general is associated with weaker financial systems and lower levels of growth.[11] This chapter takes that analysis of development history as a given and argues that the failures of government-owned banking suggest a different approach. Governments do have an important role to play in financial access, but not as direct providers of financial services. Rather, government policy can help enable the private sector to serve the poor.

Consistent with the approaches outlined here, Henriette Keijzer's presentation at the 2006 conference focused on the United Nation's "Blue Book" (entitled *Building Inclusive Financial Sectors for Development*).[12] The Blue Book suggests that countries should develop a "coherent government policy stance fostering a competitive and fair financial sector." She argued that such a policy includes sound macroeconomic policies to promote stability; a regulatory framework that permits all types of institutions to serve low-income households; recognition that the private sector should lead; development of a strong supervisory capacity; and a deepening of a financial infrastructure that "increases risk mitigation, transparency and efficiency, reduces costs, and enhances innovation." The Blue Book suggests, however, that there remains significant debate over interest rate ceilings,

---

10. For a discussion of reforms through capital requirements and competent prudential supervision of depository institutions, see Barr and Miller (2006); for reforms targeted to extend the financial sector into the income base, see Barr (2004a, 2004b, 2005a).

11. Barth, Caprio, and Levine (2001); La Porta, López-de-Silanes, and Shleifer (2002).

12. World Bank 2006 conference on "Access to Finance: Building Inclusive Financial Systems;" for the Blue Book, see United Nations (2006) (www.uncdf.org/bluebook).

subsidized lending, and other matters. Thus the Blue Book suggests a range of options for governments to pursue in different national circumstances. To explore these options, the Blue Book suggests that governments conduct detailed financial sector assessments, including gathering data on household access to finance, an assessment of the legal framework and financial infrastructure requirements, and an honest evaluation of human and institutional capacity and constraints.

This chapter analyzes the role of government policy in financial access, beginning with an analysis of the central problems that government policies ought to address. The chapter then explores different models of government policy:

—Creating a strong legal, financial, and technological backbone and enabling environment for a well-functioning financial system

—Prohibiting conduct among providers of financial services that fosters social and economic exclusion based on certain characteristics, such as race, gender, and ethnicity

—Requiring disclosure of financial sector information to increase market efficiency or to reinforce other legal or social norms

—Affirmatively obligating the financial sector to serve low-income households by offering basic bank accounts or adopting appropriate lending standards

—Regulating prices, products, or services directly

—Providing a range of subsidies—programmatic, risk-sharing, tax, and the like—to encourage the financial sector to serve low-income households

—Promoting positive household financial behaviors, such as saving, through opt-out rules and other institutional mechanisms

—Encouraging changes in bank practices through legislation underpinning voluntary codes, enforced through industry or government monitoring.

The chapter then discusses the trade-offs inherent in these approaches and concludes with directions for both future policy and further research.

Defining the Problem

The determinants of financial development and its role in economic growth and poverty alleviation have beguiled researchers and policymakers for some time. This chapter does not purport to evaluate such research in any depth; it intends only to suggest a typology for understanding the topic and to encapsulate some important lessons. The topic can cover a range of issues, from helping to expand the economy in the developing world in order to promote poverty alleviation to developing initiatives designed specifically to broaden the access of poor households in the developed and developing worlds to financial services. Each of the problems and potential solutions might be arrayed along parameters relating to constraints on supply and demand in financial services.[13]

Legal Infrastructure

Weak legal infrastructure can undermine financial development in a variety of ways. For example, weak contract enforcement and the lack of an independent judiciary or a functioning system of justice drive up the cost of private monitoring and enforcement and make it difficult for parties to enter into any arm's-length transaction. Weak property rights can make it hard for borrowers to offer collateral, thus restricting the supply of credit. Ineffectual creditor rights and secured lending laws or badly designed bankruptcy systems can undermine the willingness of lenders to lend because they will not be able to collect debts at a reasonable cost in the event of nonpayment. In sum, a functioning legal system—not just the right laws—may be essential for broad-based economic growth.

Financial Regulatory Infrastructure

In addition to a functioning legal system, financial development requires the particulars of a functioning financial system. That requirement obligates the government to avoid certain things, such as lowering productivity and economic growth by directly owning and managing the banking system, reinforcing crony capitalism by lending to elites and insiders on preferential terms, imposing excessive interest rate controls that choke off credit unnecessarily, and taking bribes or kickbacks for providing government services, among other actions. Having a sound financial infrastructure also requires governments to do many things right: for example, having a sound domestic system of financial intermediation through depository institutions requires skilled prudential supervision, a system of honest accounting and financial disclosure, enforcement of rules regarding corporate governance, and enforcement of capital adequacy and other essential banking laws. It may require government policies that enforce open competition or, at least, eliminate barriers to it. On occasion, where network or information externalities are strongly present, as in payment systems or credit bureaus, it may also mean government sponsorship or encouragement of the development of such payment system or credit reporting networks.

Market Failures in Credit Markets

Even when countries have well-functioning legal and financial systems, market failures can limit access to finance for portions of society. Information asymme-

---

13. See Beck and de la Torre (2006).

tries, in which lenders lack sufficient information to fully distinguish creditworthy from uncreditworthy borrowers, can result in credit rationing of creditworthy borrowers.[14] Information externalities, which exist when creditors cannot fully recoup the costs of gathering information about creditworthy borrowers because other lenders can use the information generated to lend, can undermine lending incentives and cause credit constraints.[15] That is true particularly in "thin" markets, which have few transactions, because the efficiency of bank lending is in part a function of "market thickness."[16] Incomplete markets can remain stalled, lacking sufficient volume and liquidity to attract new entrants.[17] Problems of collective action exacerbate information externalities and may delay entry into developing markets.[18] Agency costs, including the costs of monitoring and control, can make it difficult to align the corporate interest in profitable lending with the behavior of loan agents if the agents have other interests, such as, for example, a desire not to serve socially excluded classes of households. The social benefits of private lending may exceed the private benefits: for example, expanding lending to homeowners can improve adjacent property values, yet private lenders will take into account only private benefits in making their lending decisions.[19] Network externalities intrinsic to payment systems—such as the electronic infrastructure for retail transactions—may prevent their broad adoption by the private sector despite societal benefits.[20]

Of course, the presence of market failures is an insufficient determinant of policy. The government may be ill equipped to intervene and may choose strategies that make the problem worse or whose costs exceed the value of their benefits. Government agencies might not possess the information needed to regulate effectively, or they may not be able to induce the private sector to respond as they wish; the bureaucracy might not faithfully execute the laws; or the political process might lead the legislature to create laws that improperly favor the regulated entities or some other preferred groups.[21] A proposed government policy might make sense, but that does not tell policymakers whether it ought in fact to be pursued in any given context.

---

14. Stiglitz and Weiss (1981).
15. Petersen and Rajan (1995).
16. Lang and Nakamura (1993).
17. Allen and Gale (2001, p. 147).
18. Petersen and Rajan (1995).
19. Ellen and others (2001); Schill and others (2002).
20. Barr (2004a).
21. See, generally, Stiglitz (2000).

Banking Exclusion

While levels of access and barriers to entering the banking system vary widely across countries in the developed and developing world, some common barriers exist.[22] First, regular checking accounts may not make economic sense for many low-income families. Consumers who cannot meet account balance minimums often pay high monthly fees. In addition, nearly all banks levy high charges for bounced checks or overdrafts, charges that low-income families with little or no savings face a high risk of paying and can ill afford. Moreover, banks hold checks for days before crediting the deposit of funds; for low-income customers, the wait may not be practical. These features of traditional bank accounts are key drivers in keeping the unbanked out of the banking system in both worlds.[23] Banks have weak incentives to offer bank accounts that are tailored to low-income households, because they do not anticipate that the poor will accumulate large enough savings to offset the fixed cost of account provision. Thus a focus of policy has been on reducing the costs of account provision through technology and at times through subsidy.

A second barrier comes from the difficulties that many unbanked persons have in qualifying for conventional bank accounts because of past problems with the banking system. Most banks will not open a regular checking account for an individual who has written too many checks with insufficient funds or failed to pay overdraft fees. While some individuals with past account problems undoubtedly pose high risks, many people could responsibly use no-overdraft bank accounts. By eliminating the possibility of overdraft associated with conventional checking, debit card accounts could help consumers avoid high fees *and* help banks avoid the risk of nonpayment. Debit card accounts also are less costly for banks to offer.

Third, while many communities contain adequate numbers of banks, in some low-income neighborhoods in the developed world and in many communities in the developing world, banks are not readily accessible. Fourth, for some low-income households, lack of financial education is a significant barrier to personal financial stability. Fifth, immigrants in some countries may have difficulty supplying the documentation required to open an account either because they lack documentation or may be reluctant to supply it because they fear that depositories will police immigration laws. As Jennifer Isern pointed out in the conference, documentation requirements may be made stricter by the "know your customer" rules and other bank security provisions that governments have strengthened to

22. Barr (2004a); Kempson (2006).
23. Barr (2004a); Beck, Demirgüç-Kunt, and Martinez Peria (2006).

combat money laundering and terrorist financing.[24] Isern argues that these requirements can result in higher costs and restrictive requirements for serving poor households. Documentation requirements can dissuade prospective customers from moving into the mainstream banking system, or they can simply be impossible for poor households in many countries to meet. The higher costs associated with compliance with the new requirements make the profitability hurdles for financial institutions more difficult to meet in serving poor clientele. Isern suggests that countries adopt more flexible approaches that balance security concerns with the particular needs of low-income clientele. In her judgment, by focusing on higher-risk transactions, governments can more efficiently target enforcement resources, while permitting financial institutions to accept a broader range of documentation for account opening. Isern points to South Africa's success with documentation for the Mzansi account, as well as the decision of the Financial Services Authority in the United Kingdom to provide guidance to banks on more flexible use of documentation to ensure that any uncertainty surrounding documentation requirements did not dissuade banks from serving the poor.

Legal and Financial Infrastructure Reforms

It has long been thought that legal institutions and good governance are important for economic development. Stale discussions about the importance of law in development from a generation ago have largely given way to richly textured debates about what forms of law, of law enforcement, and of public administration and other institutions might improve economic growth and for whom.[25] Unfortunately, however, legal institutions often are quite difficult to change. Part of the problem may stem from the fact that the meaning of "legal institution" encompasses the basic structures of society itself—its norms, values, and social order—which are not directly amenable to change. Part of the problem may stem from the fact that legal reform has political and economic distributional consequences and that elites often block reform for that reason. Part of the problem may stem from the fact that societies lack the competencies required to effectuate reforms and govern, even if policy changes are forthcoming. And part of the problem may stem from the fact that it is often quite difficult to prescribe reforms that would be effective across a wide range of countries. Furthermore, when reform efforts are initiated from outside, they may be seen as especially lacking in normative legitimacy and thus may be more inclined to fail.[26]

24. Isern (2006).
25. Barr and Aviyonah (2004).
26. Pistor and others (2003).

Still, there is agreement that a functioning legal and financial regulatory system is a bedrock requirement for a sound financial system and economic growth.[27] Legal reforms with respect to property rights, contract enforcement, functioning and independent courts, and basic competence and honesty in governance play a major role in financial development. Such broad reforms cannot be fully explored in this chapter, but a few basic observations are in order.

As Ken Dam argued in his presentation to the conference and has subsequently expanded into a brilliant book, functioning credit markets require a functioning legal system, including a system of enforcement of secured credit and bankruptcy.[28] Having enforceable secured credit laws permits lenders to engage in arm's-length transactions with borrowers who have collateral. Commercial law provides creditors with rights that can be enforced against collateral, through both self-help and the aid of courts, under circumstances of nonpayment far short of the bankruptcy of the debtor. Dam demonstrates that secured credit systems often are weak in the developing world with regard to real estate and other assets that businesses often need to pledge to obtain credit, such as machinery and moveable property generally. Dam also shows the importance of having credit registries in which security interests can be recorded.

A legal system also needs reasonable bankruptcy laws that permit creditors to recover debts when appropriate within a reasonable time. Dam demonstrates that in many developing countries, weak bankruptcy laws, delays in the justice system, lack of an independent judiciary, and corruption all work to make bankruptcy systems unworkable. In such countries, lenders cannot recover when loans go bad, so they will not make many loans to the private sector in the first place. Lower levels of credit mean that fewer new businesses enter the market. Moreover, Dam argues, an efficient bankruptcy system facilitates efficient exit of failing businesses from the market, improving overall productivity in the economy. In countries lacking an effective judiciary, having a bankruptcy system that puts great discretionary power in the hands of the courts may be counterproductive, and Dam urges that alternatives be pursued that rely more on workouts led by the private sector.

With respect to the financial sector more specifically, prudential supervision and capital regulation can play a significant part in facilitating access to financial services while maintaining a stable banking and financial system.[29] Again, although broad treatment of prudential matters is beyond the scope of the chapter, it may be useful to analyze the prudential supervision issues that may also arise

---

27. Beck and Levine (2005).
28. Dam (2006a; 2006b).
29. Barr and Miller (2006).

with respect to microfinance institutions. Microfinance institutions have presented challenges to developing country regulatory systems. Because microfinance institutions come in a range of organizational types and sizes and offer a wide variety of different services, regulatory schemes need to be flexible, adaptive, and appropriately tailored to different contexts.[30]

With regard to deposit taking, microfinance institutions are broadly categorized in two groups. For a long time some microfinance institutions have required cash balances to be maintained by borrowers as a form of collateral, earnest money, or a demonstration of ability to repay. Other institutions have served more broadly to mobilize the savings of poor communities as an end in itself or as a source of funding for credit provision and other operations. As microfinance institutions increasingly look to diversify their sources of funding through retail deposit taking, there has been a concomitant rise in interest in the most appropriate ways to supervise and regulate microfinance institutions. Such distinct approaches to lending present challenges for governments in creating fledgling regulatory regimes.

As an initial matter, microfinance regulation, at least in terms of prudential supervision, generally ought to be reserved for institutions that take retail deposits besides the small deposits of earnest money that some of them collect from their borrowers.[31] Moreover, small rural microfinance institutions, even those that accept small levels of deposits, would be difficult to supervise effectively in many countries; such institutions may be better off left unregulated, if the regulations cannot be tailored to be reasonably cost effective for both regulators and the institutions. If regulatory costs make such institutions nonviable, depositors may be forced to invest their savings in higher-risk mechanisms (such as livestock) or to keep cash under their mattress.[32] The volatility, geographic and sector concentration, fast growth, and low capital of many microfinance institutions may mean that regulators would need to require high capital adequacy ratios for deposit-taking institutions.[33] Because prudential regulation is hard to do well, donors, international financial institutions, and microfinance institutions ought to think about strategies that would delay the need for governments to implement such regulation, while long-range planning is undertaken on effective approaches. For example, microfinance organizations could choose not to fund themselves directly with deposits but to serve as deposit takers for supervised depositories that could

30. Barr (2004b); Chaves and Gonzalez-Vega (1994).
31. Vogel and others (2000); Christen and Rosenberg (2000).
32. Christen, Lyman, and Rosenberg (2003); Rhyne and Otero (1994).
33. Vogel and others (2000).

then lend to microfinance institutions more cheaply, or the depositories could pay fees in exchange for deposit funds. Donors could also encourage microfinance institutions to adopt risk-mitigation measures, such as pooled loan loss funds.[34]

The challenges of extending supervision to large numbers of often quite small microfinance institutions would be enormous, given the ineffectiveness of normal supervisory tools. For example, capital calls would be more difficult, given that equity may consist entirely of donor grants, and stop-lending orders would undermine repayment in programs that rely on graduated loan ladders as an incentive for repayment.[35] Moreover, many developing countries with scarce government capacity will have difficulties implementing the new Basel II capital standards even for the largest commercial institutions, let alone for the microfinance sector.[36] Therefore, developing nations should be cautious about extending supervision beyond commercial banking and similar formally regulated depository organizations, perhaps including only large microfinance institutions that take retail deposits. A number of large microfinance institutions already are regulated banks, credit unions, or other licensed entities. The main challenge for regulators will be to adapt prudential supervision to the particular risks and risk-mitigation techniques of microfinance.[37]

In addition to prudential supervision, countries increasingly are focusing on the need to establish sound credit registries. Credit bureaus can help foster financial deepening by reducing information asymmetries, permitting low-income consumers without physical collateral to develop "reputation collateral."[38] Because the private returns to banks from information sharing are lower than the social returns, particularly in thin (developing) markets and because the elites who are current customers of banks benefit from a closed system,[39] it often is difficult for many countries to develop wholly voluntary functioning credit reporting systems. In a number of developing countries, public credit bureaus were created in the 1990s only after massive economic shocks to the financial system or, conversely, only after long periods of economic stability, during which the lack of credit bureaus may have delayed rapid growth.[40]

---

34. See Barr (2004b).

35. Christen, Lyman, and Rosenberg (2003); Christensen (1993).

36. Barr and Miller (2006).

37. Christen, Lyman, and Rosenberg (2003); Vogel and others (2000); Christen and Rosenberg (2000).

38. Miller (2003).

39. For a discussion of private returns in thin markets, see Jappelli and Pagano (1993); Barr (2005a); for benefits for elites in closed systems, see Tressel (2003).

40. Miller (2003).

Moreover, good credit bureaus are hard to build. In many countries, one needs to worry about corruption, erosion of privacy, lack of complete and accurate credit information, and technical capacity as well as fragmented availability of credit information and restrictions on what type of institution may use the data.[41] In the United States, credit bureaus were built up voluntarily over a very long time.[42] Whether choosing a private- or government-sponsored path to creating or strengthening credit bureaus, countries need to ensure that the full range of financial institutions have access to the credit data; that the full range of borrowers are included in the system, including microfinance borrowers; and that both positive and negative credit histories are recorded in the systems.[43]

The conference highlighted a number of examples of countries engaging in wide-ranging legal and financial regulatory reform. For example, Colombian Treasury official Cesar Prado in his presentation analyzed the key barriers to financial access in Colombia: high costs because of a legal framework that requires financial institutions to operate through branches, high costs associated with small transactions, a legal ceiling on interest rates, a lack of reliable information on potential borrowers, and costly security measures.[44] He outlined the key new policy framework adopted by the Colombian government to promote financial inclusion. In particular, Prado described recent regulatory initiatives by the government to open up competition in the banking sector to make it easier for banks to serve the poor.

Prado noted specifically that the government plans to permit banks to offer their services through correspondents and argued that similar strategies by Brazil, Peru, and India have been successful. He suggested that permitting correspondents to act on behalf of banks in account opening, bill payment, remittances, and other services will help build new retail networks. Prado pointed out that the Colombian lottery had more than 5,000 point-of-sale terminals in more than 400 communities and that utilities were already being paid through this delivery channel.

Prado also noted that the government was considering lifting in whole or in part current interest rate ceilings that make it uneconomical for banks to make loans under $500. Colombia also planned to strengthen creditor rights, focusing in particular on secured lending, as Dam suggested; to reform its financial tax laws; and to strengthen credit bureau reporting and consumer credit-reporting rights as

---

41. Miller (2003).
42. Staten and Cate (2005).
43. Barr (2004b).
44. Prado (2006); for the Blue Book, see United Nations (2006).

a way of deepening access to credit. Prado argued that the government's role is to create an enabling environment that permits a broad range of institutions, banking and nonbanking, to serve the poor.

Government Policies Targeting Financial Exclusion

The previous section suggests the types of government policies required to ensure an adequate enabling environment for the financial sector generally, including policies to foster the goal of expanding access to essential financial services for the poor. The following discussion concerns government policies that target financial exclusion directly. Negative prohibitions, disclosure, affirmative obligation, product regulation, subsidy, opt-out rules, and voluntary regimes are considered in turn.

Negative Prohibition

In countries with a history of social exclusion based on race, gender, ethnicity, or other factors, governments have sometimes sought to ban private sector practices that further entrench exclusion. Although competition itself may help to diminish discrimination over the long run, biased lending can persist even in competitive markets.[45] Antidiscrimination laws are enacted to provide a stronger impetus, through legal sanctions, for ending discrimination and to develop social norms against such practices. Antidiscrimination laws might be thought of as being of two types: those that ban discrimination based solely on animus and those that also ban discrimination based on standards that on their face are neutral but that adversely affect socially excluded classes and are not based on business necessity.

In the United States, for example, the Equal Credit Opportunity Act bans discrimination of both types. Empirical evidence suggests that antidiscrimination laws can help to reduce noneconomic barriers to the provision of financial services where they are rooted in stereotypes or bias.[46] However, since such laws focus on racial, ethnic, or gender discrimination rather than on the goal of economic advancement, they often have difficulty getting at hierarchical socioeconomic problems that are highly correlated with social exclusion. Moreover, litigation is costly, and often the expertise and information needed to evaluate whether

---

45. See Becker (1971) for discussion on competition to diminish discrimination; for discussion on biased lending, see Ross and Yinger (2002); Ayres (2001).

46. Barr (2005a).

lenders have discriminated is difficult to obtain, especially when borrowers need to rely on a proprietary credit rating analysis to prove their claim.[47]

Disclosure

There are two types of disclosure regimes: consumer-oriented disclosures and public-oriented disclosures. Consumer-oriented disclosures are designed to improve consumers' ability to shop for products and services. The theory is that the information available in credit markets is imperfect and that disclosures lower the cost of acquiring more information and help consumers negotiate better; that in turn leads to more competition and a more efficient market.[48] In the United States, the Truth in Lending Act embodies this approach. Under the act, creditors have to reveal in a conspicuous and clear manner the annual percentage interest rate of the credit and the key costs of credit.

Two essential problems arise with a disclosure regime of this sort. First, behavioral economics teaches the weakness of relying on consumer understanding to influence consumer behavior; second, many transactions in the financial marketplace involve both complicated legal rules and complicated product structures that even financially sophisticated parties do not fully understand. If consumers are unlikely to understand a financial transaction and in any event are unlikely to behave fully rationally even in the face of disclosed information, then relying on disclosure alone may be an ineffectual response to information asymmetries. Empirical evidence suggests that consumers do have a hard time understanding credit disclosures, and research in behavioral economics confirms that often consumers do not act on available information.[49]

A second type of disclosure regime uses disclosure to reveal information more generally to the market, the general public, the media, and regulators. Such disclosures are not necessarily designed to improve consumer decisionmaking but to further the enforcement of other laws or to communicate social norms. For example, in the United States, the Home Mortgage Disclosure Act requires creditors to reveal information publicly regarding the race, ethnicity, gender, and income of borrowers as well as applicants for a loan who were turned down. The underlying premise is that financial institutions should not base lending decisions on factors other than creditworthiness, loan terms, and property values, and that publicly revealing loan decisions helps outsiders evaluate whether creditors have in

---

47. Ross and Yinger (2002).
48. Schwartz and Wilde (1979).
49. For a discussion of consumers' difficulty understanding credit disclosures, see Barr (2005a); see Bertrand, Mullainathan, and Shafir (2006) about consumers not acting on available information.

fact based their lending decisions solely on those criteria. Public disclosure of this type relies on market reactions, media reporting, consumer and community group activism, legislative oversight, engagement of financial regulators, and other public pressures to alter private sector behavior.

The effectiveness of a public disclosure strategy rests not only on the ability to enforce the disclosure requirement through public remedy or private sanction but also on the other laws and social norms that the law is meant to reinforce and on the strength of the groups and institutions that informally work toward compliance with those norms. In principle, a wholly voluntary public disclosure regime could work, if there were a sufficient social sanction (or private sector group sanction) for failure to comply. However, public approbation alone is unlikely to be sufficient to change corporate conduct unless shareholders and customers have a definite view of exactly what the norm entails and care enough about it to penalize a firm for noncompliance. Such an approach also puts great weight on aligning the interests (and values) of managers and employees of the firm with the societal goal; therefore, internal corporate incentive structures would need to reward those who helped the firm meet its goals with respect to the lending activity being publicly disclosed.

A public disclosure strategy could also risk overenforcement of a social norm or enforcement of a norm other than the one intended. For example, if public disclosure data do not contain information about the creditworthiness of applicants or borrowers, relying solely on those data to assess whether a firm is complying with a norm against discrimination might result in claims of discrimination where none existed. Similarly, if the data do not provide any context for assessing creditors' ability to lend in low-income communities, creditors might face undue pressure to make unsound loans, when a better understanding of market context would suggest otherwise.

Affirmative Obligation

In some contexts, governments have gone beyond disclosure requirements and negative prohibitions on discrimination to impose affirmative obligations on financial institutions to serve specific market segments. In theory, affirmative requirements can help to overcome market failures—for example, by helping overcome collective action problems from information externalities in thin markets. By essentially requiring higher levels of competition, such requirements help markets gain liquidity and volume. Some governments have required financial institutions to provide basic bank accounts to the public. Other jurisdictions have required creditors to seek to serve all creditworthy borrowers in their communities, regardless of the income level of the household or community in which they live.

For example, in the United States, the Community Reinvestment Act of 1977 (CRA) encourages federally insured banks and thrift institutions to meet the credit needs of the entire communities that they serve, including low- and moderate-income areas, consistent with safe and sound banking practices. Federal banking agencies periodically examine and rate banks and thrifts on their CRA performance and make their evaluations and ratings public. Banks and thrifts have an incentive to seek high ratings because regulators consider their CRA record in determining whether to approve any application they make for a "deposit facility," which includes mergers with or acquisitions of other depository institutions. Such applications provide the public with an opportunity to comment on the CRA performance of the institution.

CRA promotes market thickness and solves the problem of underproduction due to externalities by encouraging the banks and thrifts to lend anyway. Under CRA, free riders cannot exploit collective action problems because each bank is, in effect, required to participate in the market. Thus CRA is a form of "precommitment" device that overcomes coordination problems.[50] Banks know that there will be liquidity and volume because other lenders will be looking for lending opportunities in these markets.

Over time, the thicker the market, the less each incremental loan will produce significant information externalities. With lower information externalities, lenders face less of a disincentive to lend because they can capture a larger share of the benefits. Furthermore, as lenders obtain information about creditworthy low-income borrowers and develop expertise in lending to those borrowers, the transaction costs associated with overcoming information asymmetries decrease. With lower information asymmetries, loan prices can be reduced so that they become commensurate with measurable risk, and thus adverse selection and moral hazard pose less of a problem to reaching further into the market in low-income communities.

In addition, CRA encourages banks to support community organizations by giving banks consideration for loans, investments, and services to community development organizations that strengthen and revitalize local communities. Banks need strong institutions in local communities to reduce the risk and increase the effectiveness of their lending operations; stronger institutions, in turn, reinforce the effectiveness of CRA in overcoming market failures. Community-based organizations play roles analogous to those of real estate brokers, developers, and neighborhood associations by stabilizing and improving housing stock, revitalizing local business districts, providing financial counseling, and helping to match creditworthy borrowers with willing banks. Finally, better functioning

---

50. Zinman (2002).

credit markets increase access to homeownership for low-income borrowers, which can increase property values for adjacent neighborhoods.[51]

Experience over the last decade suggests that CRA has been effective in helping to overcome market failures in low-income communities.[52] For example, lenders have formed multibank community development corporations and loan consortia and partnered with third parties to reduce risk, overcome collective action problems, and share the costs and benefits of developing information about low-income markets.[53] Banks have invested in locally based community development financial institutions (CDFI) to develop specialized market knowledge, share risk, and explore new market opportunities. They have engaged in marketing programs to target specific communities and experimented with more flexible underwriting and specialized servicing techniques to determine whether a broader range of applications could be approved without undue risk. Banks also have funded credit counseling to improve the creditworthiness of potential borrowers. Many larger institutions have developed specialized units within their organizations that focus on the needs of low- and moderate-income communities. These units help overcome agency costs by keeping the organization focused on expanding its lending to low-income and minority populations and by sharing expertise on how to do so.

A positive lending cycle has begun in many communities. Once lenders know that others are making loans to a community, they face less liquidity risk, gather information more quickly, and produce positive information externalities. Econometric studies have found evidence that CRA improved access to home mortgage credit for low-income borrowers during the 1990s, when CRA regulations were amended to focus on performance, regulatory agencies stepped up the seriousness of their CRA reviews, and bank merger activity increased.[54] CRA lending appears to be reasonably sound. Most banks find such lending to be as profitable as other lending, but a significant minority faces somewhat higher costs and weaker performance.[55] Although the evidence regarding the performance and profitability of CRA lending is open to conflicting interpretations, it is on balance consistent with the theory that CRA helps overcome market failures and discrimination.

However, there are real costs and dangers involved in pursuing the affirmative obligation approach. Even in countries with a strong "rule of law" tradition, regulatory discretion can add significant costs to implementation. Moreover, in coun-

51. Ellen and others (2001); Schill and others (2002).
52. Barr (2005a).
53. Board of Governors of the Federal Reserve System (2000).
54. Barr (2005a); Litan and others (2000, 2001).
55. Board of Governors of the Federal Reserve System (2000).

tries with significant corruption, government incompetence, or lack of transparency, bureaucratic discretion in implementing the kind of policies discussed above could result in greater bureaucratic power and serious problems with inefficiency, bribery, and kickbacks. Furthermore, a "command and control" approach to affirmative obligation, requiring firms to provide specific products and services, might stifle market innovation. In addition, in many countries, affirmative obligation has been used not to expand access to finance for marginal households but to reinforce crony capitalism through preferential lending to favored political, economic, or social groups. Moreover, directed lending programs, even when undertaken to advance the interests of socially excluded classes, often have been pursued in a heavy-handed way by governments—which may, for example, use quotas to allocate credit, thereby forcing creditors to make unsound loans in a weak market context to uncreditworthy borrowers. No one is helped in the long run by an approach that requires the abandonment of sound lending practices. Bank failures, implosions of government loan funds, defaults, and foreclosures cause real harm to the financial sector and to the real economy.

Product Regulation

In many countries, governments historically have sought to delineate the terms and conditions of financial service products. Usury laws are the most common form of such restrictions. In economic terms, one might argue in favor of usury laws to block the granting of credit at high interest rates because the implied default rates would pose unacceptable social externalities. The concern with usury laws is that they often result in credit constraints on poor (or even middle-income) households that could otherwise afford, and benefit from, credit. Microfinance providers have become increasingly concerned about usury limits because they need to rely on interest rates that are relatively high (but still lower than those of most informal money lenders) to cover the fixed costs of financial intermediation involving small loans.

Another type of product regulation seeks to exclude certain types of loan terms or sales practices. Such restrictions often have two intertwined motivations. On one hand, restrictions on loan terms can enhance price disclosure and competition by focusing borrowers and creditors on the price of credit rather than on other features of the loan that consumers may ill understand. On the other hand, product restrictions may be thought of as a substantive judgment that certain loan terms are inherently unreasonable. In either event, product restrictions are based on the notion that consumers cannot fully understand or act in their own best interests in the face of confusing terms or transactions or deceptive sales practices; moreover, in this view competition alone is insufficient to drive out such practices. In the United States, for example, Congress enacted the Home Ownership and Equity Protection Act to respond to unscrupulous practices in the subprime home equity mortgage market. For certain "high cost" loans, the act restricts loan terms (such as prepayment penalties and balloon payments) and requires enhanced disclosures. Many states in the United States have passed similar antipredatory lending laws.

Product restrictions would tend to drive more of the cost of the loan into the annual percentage interest rate because lenders cannot use prohibited mortgage terms to cover costs. With more of the cost of the mortgage reflected in the rate, it is easier for consumers to understand the costs of the loan and to compare costs. Creditors would then tend to compete more on price and less on other factors as to which consumers have difficulty making and acting on informed choices. However, such product regulations may diminish financial access and harm product competition and innovation to serve low-income households. Governments may easily err by restricting products that would be advantageous or creating new consumer confusion in the form of complicated rules regarding product regulation. For that reason, as discussed below, there is new interest in the possibility of establishing default (opt-in and opt-out) regimes rather than requiring or prohibiting certain financial products and services.

Subsidy

One alternative to government regulation of the types described above is to rely on subsidies, either to the private sector or to households. At some level, subsidies can become substitutes for regulation. If the government pays private sector participants a sufficient amount, for example, they will look harder for creditworthy borrowers in low-income communities in the same way that they would under a regulatory regime. However, developing such a subsidy regime is not without difficulties. Officials would need to determine whether they could provide the amount of subsidy necessary to have the desired effect without generating undesirable windfalls to recipients. In principle, subsidies should be used "to make marginal private costs equal marginal social costs, and to make marginal private benefits equal to marginal social benefits."[56] In practice, that is hard to do. Substantively, it is hard to get private market actors to respond to government subsidies unless the subsidies are robust. Politically, it is hard to prevent the subsidies from becoming too robust. Previous experience suggests both that sufficient incentives are hard to create and that windfalls would be difficult to control if the incentives are sufficient.

---

56. Stiglitz (2000, p. 224).

Subsidies can be paid in a variety of ways: through government-sponsored enterprises and government risk-sharing systems, through supply-side investments, and through the tax system and other means. Some of the trade-offs involved in these various approaches are analyzed below.

GOVERNMENT-SPONSORED ENTERPRISES AND RISK-SHARING MECHANISMS. Bernd Balkenhol suggested in his contribution to the conference that in principle risk-sharing mechanisms can be designed to induce creditors to provide loans to creditworthy borrowers who are not accurately described by traditional measures of creditworthiness.[57] According to this theory, risk-sharing schemes permit lenders to familiarize themselves with low-income clientele, thus lowering information asymmetries, which are a barrier to credit provision, and reducing information externalities that occur when lending provides information to the marketplace about creditworthy borrowers—information whose benefits do not fully accrue to the creditor making the loan. By engaging the private sector in reducing information asymmetries and externalities, risk-sharing schemes can operate more efficiently, in principle, than can government-provided credit or regulation. As Balkenhol points out, however, risk sharing may increase moral hazard and adverse selection and may decrease market incentives for efficient credit provision.

Balkenhol describes four types of ownership and governance of guarantee funds and mutual guarantee associations designed to provide risk sharing: public guarantee funds, private funds, joint ventures of private and public entities, and mutual associations. Even the fully private funds in his models have some government engagement, often including subsidies for capitalization, user fees, loss provision, or operations. Balkenhol's review of the experience under the European Mutual Guarantee Association, a large public-private joint association in Italy, and a wide variety of public and private programs suggests that effectiveness depends on aligning the incentives of banks, borrowers, and guarantors; transparency; low levels of leverage; sound pricing; and a variety of contextual factors. Balkenhol suggests caution in transferring developed country models to the developing world.

Implicit and explicit risk-sharing subsidies are pervasive in the U.S. home mortgage market.[58] Subsidies to home mortgage credit include government insurance through the Federal Housing Administration (FHA) and Ginnie Mae (the Government National Mortgage Association) as well as through government-sponsored enterprises (GSEs), including Fannie Mae (the Federal National Mortgage Association), Freddie Mac (the Federal Home Loan Mortgage Corporation), and the Federal Home Loan Bank (FHLB) system.

57. Balkenhol (2006).
58. See Barr (2005b).

FHA, which operates within the federal government, insures home mortgage loans made by private lenders in the event of default. FHA tends to serve first-time, minority, or low-income borrowers, although at times it competes with conventional lenders. Ginnie Mae, also within the government, provides a credit enhancement to pools of FHA loans and places them for sale on the secondary market. The housing GSEs—Fannie Mae, Freddie Mac, and the FHLBs—are private institutions with government charters, created to provide liquidity to the home mortgage market. Fannie Mae and Freddie Mac issue debt to buy and hold mortgages in portfolio and insure mortgage-backed securities issued to investors. The FHLBs were created to provide short-term loans to thrifts in order to stabilize mortgage lending in local markets. The GSEs benefit from their relationships with the federal government in a variety of ways; most important, they benefit from an implicit guarantee that the federal government will intervene in the event of financial collapse.

Government subsidies can generate windfalls for GSE shareholders and others. GSE subsidies are not transparent, making it difficult for the public to weigh their costs and benefits. In addition, the subsidy programs are not designed solely to overcome the market's failure to provide access to credit for low- and moderate-income borrowers; therefore, some subsidy likely goes to generalized housing consumption. FHA subsidies are transparent because the costs appear in the federal budget. However, the cost of transparency is direct taxpayer liability for the FHA. FHA may not have the management capacity and technical expertise to manage risk as effectively as private market participants. It is certainly possible to design subsidies far better than the ones that the United States has, but past experience advises caution. It is difficult to design general subsidies that are effective, that generate little windfall for recipients, and that protect taxpayers.

PAYMENT SYSTEM SPONSORSHIP. As discussed more fully by David Porteous in chapter 6 of this volume, expanding access to electronic or wireless payment systems and distribution networks is critical to banking poor households. More widespread adoption of these technologies would make electronic banking services more attractive to the unbanked and at the same time make it less expensive and less risky for financial institutions to expand access to the poor. Direct deposit of income is available at low cost to employers, and it provides immediate access to funds for employees. Online debit withdrawal at ATMs, at the point of sale, or over cellphone networks provides a low-cost, convenient means to purchase goods and services without the cost of paper-based systems or the risk of overdrafts. Automatic bill payment and online, cellphone, or other forms of payment also could improve the efficiency of the payment system for low-income households.

Yet research, development, and deployment of these technologies may be lower than is socially optimal. Payment systems carry high fixed costs, and they are characterized by positive network externalities.[59] If many buyers and sellers adopt a given payment system, all users will be better off; however, because public benefits to all users of the payment system exceed private benefits to each individual deciding whether to use the system, this mode of payment may not be adopted or may be adopted more slowly than is socially optimal. For that reason, governments have in many countries sponsored payment systems. A risk of government sponsorship, however, is that a government will choose to sponsor an inefficient technology, helping to lock in a network that does not deliver socially optimal benefits. Government sponsorship also might diminish competition and innovation in payment systems. In other contexts, private parties or associations with sufficient market power have subsidized the network and provided for common rules; the concern there is whether such network sponsorship results in anticompetitive conduct that reduces social welfare.[60] It may be fruitful, therefore, to explore government subsidies to the sector that would foster innovation and deployment in payment systems without locking in one technology through sole sponsorship. Competition in payment systems would mean some greater inefficiencies and cost, but it would likely bring greater innovation.

TARGETED SUPPLY-SIDE SUBSIDIES. In addition to subsidies to the secondary markets or to banks and thrifts, subsidies to specialized community development lenders can be an important means of expanding the reach of these lenders as well as banks and thrifts. Appropriately designed subsidies can, in principle, help to overcome market failures and improve social welfare at a reasonable cost.

One prominent U.S. example of a targeted subsidy is the Treasury Department's Community Development Financial Institutions (CDFI) Fund, established in 1994. The CDFI fund, which was designed to create a national network of financial institutions focused on low-income communities, has provided more than $800 million to locally based, private sector CDFIs as well as to mainstream banks and thrifts. The fund's investments have helped recipients increase their capitalization, develop stronger infrastructure and operations, and expand their reach. The small size and scale of CDFIs suggests, however, that it would be inefficient to switch from relying on the banking system to relying on a system based solely on such specialized lenders; rather, CDFIs work in partnership with banks and thrifts in serving low-income communities. In addition, CDFI funding is subject

59. Katz and Shapiro (1994).
60. Hunt (2003).

to the vagaries of the appropriations process, and it may be hard for community-based institutions to rely on such sources of funding over time. Moreover, government funding may crowd out private sector funding for such institutions and may diminish CDFIs' exercise of market discipline in reaching their goals.

Such targeted community development finance programs also exist in the developing world. For example, at the conference, Prado noted that the Colombian government had recently decided to create a small "Fund of Opportunities" along a similar model. South Africa developed an apex fund to provide financial support to the burgeoning microfinance field in that country. Yet Marié Kirsten argued that the experience in South Africa with its apex fund may suggest caution.[61]

Another means of expanding access to basic banking services would be to provide a tax credit to financial institutions to offer a low-cost, electronic bank account. The tax credit would cover the costs to open an account and to sustain the account on its own cost structure thereafter.[62] In principle, an in-kind supply-side subsidy of this kind could be an efficient means of expanding access to banking services. The supply of low-cost electronic bank accounts is likely to be characterized by a single fixed cost for start-up and low marginal costs for additional accounts. Thus, after provision of the tax credit, supply is likely to be highly elastic. Moreover, the danger is quite small that subsidies for low-cost banking accounts would provide a windfall to banks, because few would offer such accounts without the tax credit. Given that network externalities may slow the adoption of technologies that would better serve the poor, the tax credits are less likely to result in windfalls than to permit market participants to internalize network externalities. The tax credit is likely to generate consumption externalities that benefit society broadly because the fixed investment leads to a new form of low-cost electronic banking accounts. Such accounts would reduce the cost to consumers of cashing income checks, facilitate saving, and provide a means to pay bills into the future.

In sum, governments should consider targeted subsidies as one strategy for expanding access. Yet it is difficult to design such subsidies in a way that targets recipients well, avoids windfalls to the private sector, and deals with the incentive problems of adverse selection and moral hazard. Open-ended government guarantees expose taxpayers to serious liability. The lack of a level playing field for subsidized and nonsubsidized entities also can create real problems for competition and innovation. Subsidies also raise the problem of crony capitalism by favoring entrenched elites, and they can reduce market pressure on the private sector to

61. Kirsten (2006).
62. Barr (2004a).

operate efficiently and soundly. Consideration of all these factors suggests the need, if subsidies are considered, to focus on transparency, targeting, and subsidies that are structured to align private sector incentives with the public purpose—both in risk mitigation and in expanded access. Risk-sharing mechanisms and subsidies can be designed with those principles in mind.

Opt-Out Rules and Other Lessons from Behavioral Economics

Increasingly, countries are beginning to look to other models of government policy that lie between the relatively passive disclosure laws and the more intrusive forms of government regulation. One promising area for future policy development builds on new empirical analysis from behavioral economics. For example, research suggests that individual choices regarding saving are profoundly affected by psychology: mental accounting, starting points, endowment effects, and other psychological frames of mind.[63] Default rules are critical in determining whether and how much individuals will save.[64] By using default rules, governments might encourage welfare-enhancing behavior without prohibiting other market choices.

Behavioral insights may help governments to think more critically about the institutional contexts within which consumer choices are made. A theory of regulating that incorporates behavioral economics might suggest policies that would help to change behavior by using institutional and contextual cues and other techniques to alter consumer attitudes, beliefs, and understanding.[65] Other regulatory techniques would focus on the ways in which default rules can change behavior directly.[66] For example, some countries have used opt-out rules to encourage positive behavior in a variety of areas, from organ donation to retirement contributions. If employers are required to enroll workers in automatic retirement plans unless the worker affirmatively opts out of participating, enrollment rates will be much higher, and net savings may increase.

Similar types of policies can be pursued across a range of financial service products and services that reach lower-income households.[67] For example, employers could be required to deposit worker income checks directly into a low-cost bank account with an automatic savings plan, unless the employee opts out of the arrangement. Governments could provide for making tax refund and benefit payments into a direct deposit account with savings features, again, unless the beneficiary opts out. In the credit arena, borrowers could be provided

---

63. Kahneman and Tversky (2000).
64. Thaler and Benartzi (2004).
65. See Jolls and Sunstein (2005).
66. Thaler and Benartzi (2004).
67. Barr (2007).

with a basic, easy-to-understand credit product with a realistic payment plan, unless they opt out.

Such opt-out rules have the potential to help encourage positive saving and credit behaviors without strong government intervention. This approach does, however, have key problems. Default rules may be too weak, particularly in the face of market pressures that may favor something other than the default opt-out rule. Opt-out rules do not in and of themselves encourage the financial services sector to provide the services that poor households need if such products are too expensive to offer to low-income households; governments may have to provide subsidies to encourage sufficient supply. For low-income households, opt-out rules would likely need to be combined with public subsidy to provide meaningful access or to generate savings at levels that would matter in their lives.

Tightly linked to advances in behavioral economics, Michael Sherraden's presentation focused on the role of government policy in helping low-income households increase their savings rate and their asset holdings.[68] Sherraden's pioneering work on asset-development policy in the United States has confirmed that poor households can and do save.[69] Sherraden shows that "individual development accounts" can encourage low-income households to save for such goals as education, small business development, and homeownership. In particular, Sherraden demonstrated that institutional constructs—incentives, expectations, making saving easy, and other factors—meaningfully contribute to household decisionmaking to save. Sherraden's institutional design experiments complement pathbreaking work in behavioral economics demonstrating that default-rules, framing, and heuristics—not simply incentives—have powerful influence on consumer behavior. Despite Sherraden's finding that low-income households could save if given the appropriate opportunities to do so, government policy on asset development has historically focused on rewarding saving by middle- and upper-income households.[70] Sherraden has helped change that, with important successes, for example, in the United Kingdom with the development of the Child Trust Fund, which is a universal, progressive matched savings program for every child starting at birth.

Sherraden and his colleagues have now begun to experiment with asset-building policies in the developing world, showing promising results in early work among the poor in Uganda, Peru, Colombia, and elsewhere and generating interest in such programs in Indonesia and South Korea. Sherraden suggests that the key next steps include figuring out how to go to scale in vastly different political, economic, and cultural environments—particularly when the formal financial sector is weak, badly

68. Sherraden (2006).
69. Schreiner and Sherraden (2007).
70. Sherraden and Barr (2005).

regulated, or dishonest. Moreover, experimental research continues to yield new insights into the institutional constructs required to promote savings in different contexts. In an evolving amalgam of factors, Sherraden suggests that savings outcomes are linked to access, information, incentives, facilitation, expectations, restrictions, security, and perhaps simplicity. Further refining these constructs through real-world applications, both in the developed and developing world, is an important challenge ahead. Sherraden and his colleagues are demonstrating how disciplined, engaged social science research can help to transform government policies to promote the financial services poor households want and need.

Voluntary Regimes

In some contexts, financial services trade organizations have developed voluntary charters and codes to expand access to finance. In her presentation to the conference, Elaine Kempson described such systems in the United Kingdom, France, Belgium, Germany, and other developed countries.[71] In her judgment, the wholly voluntary systems have had limited success because financial institutions have weak incentives to promote the accounts on a wide scale and compliance with voluntary codes is not aggressively monitored. She suggested that the Canadian and U.K. approaches, under which voluntary incentives are stimulated by formal legislation and enforced by regulatory or industry bodies, are preferable. Kempson highlighted the work of the U.K. Treasury Financial Inclusion Taskforce, and the conference also heard from the Taskforce's Chairman, Brian Pomeroy, in a keynote address. The Taskforce is helping to call attention to the problems of financial exclusion in the United Kingdom and to galvanize government and private sector responses. The high visibility of the Taskforce helps to put pressure on financial institutions and government agencies alike to respond effectively. In Kempson's view, voluntary codes can work, but they need to be carefully monitored and enforced by an independent body with real power, whether in industry or in government.

William Knight, then commissioner of the Financial Consumer Agency of Canada, echoed this view at the conference.[72] He described Canada's experience under its Access to Basic Banking Service Regulations. Before Canada's new legislation, compliance with voluntary codes was "not impressive." Under Canadian law, consumers have a right to open a personal bank account and to have a Canadian government check cashed for free at any bank, whether or not they are a customer. The Canadian Financial Consumer Agency also conducts extensive

71. Kempson (2006).
72. Knight (2006).

financial education and outreach. Canada is now studying the effectiveness of this new approach.

Marié Kirsten's presentation at the 2006 conference described South Africa's experiences, with particular regard to the Financial Sector Charter of 2003, a voluntary arrangement among major financial services firms to expand access. The charter sets out specific goals for improving access in key areas, including transaction accounts, savings products, life insurance products, investment pools, and shorter-term risk insurance products. As part of the initiative, major banks committed to offer a low-cost basic bank account, the Mzansi account, now held by more than 1.5 million poor South Africans.

Conclusion

Trade-offs among regulatory regimes affecting financial access are unavoidable. Experience suggests, moreover, that different policies ought to be pursued for different problems in different countries at different stages of legal and financial development. Many policies that are effective in the developed world would not work in the developing world, and many policies pursued in the developing world would be misplaced in the developed world. Furthermore, the long history of the "law and development" movement suggests the appropriateness of maintaining a degree of humility in offering advice on the direction of government policies.

In countries with weak legal and financial infrastructure, priority perhaps ought to be placed on removing government obstacles to private sector competition in providing microfinance to the poor. Long-term reforms of the legal and financial regulatory environment are critical to economic growth and poverty alleviation and should be pursued, but because they are so difficult, immediate attention should be paid to aspects of government policy that prevent effective delivery of microfinance, both by mainstream and by specialized providers. With respect to long-term legal reforms, each country needs to develop systems that rely on an honest assessment of government capacity, private sector market structure, and the potential role of nongovernmental organizations. With respect to targeted policies to promote financial access, the trade-offs involved among the approaches suggest the need again for a nuanced understanding of government capacity, market context, and private sector initiative.

Cross-modal strategies—using one mode of government policy to reinforce other norms—are one promising approach.[73] For example, governments can use public disclosure to reinforce norms in favor of equal access to credit for credit-

73. Barr (2005b).

worthy borrowers if affirmative obligation or negative prohibition is not likely to be as fruitful or efficient in a particular country. As another example, governments can use opt-out policies to move markets toward more socially optimal savings and credit products rather than prohibiting disfavored products entirely.

This chapter explores the theoretical and practical bases for a range of government policies. By analyzing the different modes of financial access policy—the enabling environment, negative prohibition, affirmative obligation, disclosure, subsidy, opt-out rules, and voluntary codes—the chapter provides a starting point for assessing the trade-offs among these policies. Future research and experimentation will enable policymakers to refine the trade-offs in particular cultural and market contexts.

References

Allen, Franklin, and Douglas Gale. 2001. *Comparing Financial Systems*. MIT Press.

Ayres, Ian. 2001. *Pervasive Prejudice? Nontraditional Evidence of Race and Gender Discrimination*. University of Chicago Press.

Balkenhol, Bernd. 2006. "Access to Finance: The Place of Risk-Sharing Mechanisms." Paper prepared for "Access to Finance: Building Inclusive Financial Systems." Brookings Institution and World Bank, Washington, May 30–31.

Barr, Michael S. 2004a. "Banking the Poor." *Yale Journal on Regulation* 21, no. 1: 121–237.

———. 2004b. "Microfinance and Financial Development." *Michigan Journal of International Law* 26, no. 1: 271–96.

———. 2005a. "Credit Where It Counts: The Community Reinvestment Act and Its Critics." *New York University Law Review* 80, no. 2: 513–652.

———. 2005b. "Modes of Credit Market Regulation." In *Building Assets, Building Credit: Creating Wealth in Low-Income Communities*, edited by Nicolas P. Retsinas and Eric S. Belsky, pp. 206–36. Brookings.

———. 2006a. "Modes of Government Policy." Paper prepared for "Access to Finance: Building Inclusive Financial Systems." Brookings Institution and World Bank, Washington, May 30–31.

———. 2006b. "Summary of Proceedings." Paper prepared for "Access to Finance: Building Inclusive Financial Systems." Brookings Institution and World Bank, Washington, May 30–31.

———. 2007. "An Inclusive, Progressive National Savings and Financial Services Policy." *Harvard Law and Policy Review* 1, no. 1: 161–84.

Barr, Michael S., and Reuven Aviyonah. 2004. "Globalization, Law, and Development: Introduction and Overview." *Michigan Journal of International Law* 26, no. 1: 1–12.

Barr, Michael S., and Geoffrey Miller. 2006. "Global Administrative Law: The View from Basel." *European Journal of International Law* 17, no. 1: 15–46.

Barth, James R. 2001. "Banking Systems around the Globe: Do Regulation and Ownership Affect Performance and Stability?" In *Prudential Supervision: What Works and What Doesn't*, edited by Frederic Mishkin, pp. 31–95. University of Chicago Press.

Barth, James R., Gerard Caprio Jr., and Ross Levine. 2001. "Financial Regulation and Performance: Cross-Country Evidence." Working Paper 118. Santiago: Central Bank of Chile.

Beck, Thorsten, and Ross Levine. 2005. "Legal Institutions and Financial Development." In *Handbook of New Institutional Economics,* edited by Claude Menard and Mary M. Shirley, pp. 251–78. New York: Springer Press.

Beck, Thorsten, and Augusto de la Torre. 2006. "The Basic Analytics of Access to Financial Services." Policy Research Working Paper 4026. Washington: World Bank.

Beck, Thorsten, Asli Demirgüç-Kunt, and Maria Soledad Martinez Peria. 2006. "Banking Services for Everyone? Barriers to Bank Access and Use around the World." Policy Research Working Paper 4079 (December). Washington: World Bank.

Beck, Thorsten, and others. 2000. "Finance and the Sources of Growth." *Journal of Financial Economics* 58, no. 1: 261–300.

Beck, Thorsten, and others. 2004. "Finance, Inequality, and Poverty: Cross-Country Evidence." Working Paper 10979. Cambridge, Mass.: National Bureau of Economic Research.

Becker, Gary S. 1971. *The Economics of Discrimination.* University of Chicago Press.

Bertrand, Marianne, Sendhil Mullainathan, and Eldar Shafir. 2006. "Behavioral Economics and Marketing in Aid of Decision-Making among the Poor." *Journal of Public Policy and Marketing* 25, no. 1: 8–23.

Board of Governors of the Federal Reserve System. 2000. *The Performance and Profitability of CRA-Related Lending.* Report by the Board of Governors of the Federal Reserve System, submitted to Congress pursuant to section 713 of the Gramm-Leach-Bliley Act of 1999. Washington.

Chaves, Rodrigo, and Claudio Gonzalez-Vega. 1994. "Principles of Regulation and Prudential Supervision and Their Relevance for Microenterprise Finance Organizations." In *The New World of Microenterprise Finance: Building Healthy Financial Institutions for the Poor,* edited by Maria Otero and Elizabeth Rhyne, pp.11–26. West Hartford, Conn.: Kumarian Press.

Christen, Robert Peck, and Richard Rosenberg. 2000. "The Rush to Regulate: Legal Frameworks for Microfinance." Occasional Paper 4. Washington: Consultative Group to Assist the Poor.

Christen, Robert Peck, Timothy R. Lyman, and Richard Rosenberg. 2003. "Microfinance Consensus Guidelines: Guiding Principles on Regulation and Supervision of Microfinance." Washington: Consultative Group to Assist the Poor.

Christensen, Garry. 1993. "Limits to Informal Financial Intermediation." *World Development* 21, no. 5: 721–31.

Clarke, George, and others. 2003. "Finance and Income Inequality: Test of Alternative Theories." Policy Research Working Paper 2984. Washington: World Bank.

Dam, Kenneth. 2006a. "Credit Markets, Creditors' Rights, and Economic Development." Paper prepared for "Access to Finance: Building Inclusive Financial Systems." Brookings Institution and World Bank, Washington, May 30–31.

————. 2006b. *The Law-Growth Nexus: The Rule of Law and Economic Development.* Brookings.

Ellen, Ingrid Gould, and others. 2001. "Building Homes, Reviving Neighborhoods: Spillovers from Subsidized Construction of Owner-Occupied Housing in New York City." *Journal of Housing Research* 12, no. 2: 185–216.

Greenwood, Jeremy, and Boyan Jovanovic. 1990. "Financial Development, Growth, and the Distribution of Income." *Journal of Political Economy* 98, no. 5: 1076–107.

Haber, Stephen. 1991. "Industrial Concentration and the Capital Markets: A Comparative Study of Brazil, Mexico, and the United States, 1830–1930." *Journal of Economic History* 51, no. 3: 559–80.

Hunt, Robert M. 2003. "An Introduction to the Economics of Payment Card Networks." *Review of Network Economics* 2, no. 2: 80–96.

Isern, Jennifer. 2006. "Balancing Access to Finance with AML/CFT Considerations." Paper prepared for "Access to Finance: Building Inclusive Financial Systems." Brookings Institution and World Bank, Washington, May 30–31.

Jappelli, Tullio, and Marco Pagano. 1993. "Information Sharing in Credit Markets." *Journal of Finance* 48, no. 5: 1693–718.

Jolls, Christine, and Cass Sunstein. 2005. "Debiasing through Law." Working Paper 11738. Cambridge, Mass.: National Bureau of Economic Research.

Kahneman, Daniel, and Amos Tversky. 2000. *Choices, Values and Frames*. Cambridge University Press.

Katz, Michael L., and Carl Shapiro. 1994. "Systems Competition and Network Effects." *Journal of Economic Perspectives* 8, no. 2: 93–115.

Keijzers, Jennifer. 2006. "UNCDF: The Blue Book and Lessons Learned on Obstacles to Finance." Paper prepared for "Access to Finance: Building Inclusive Financial Systems." Brookings Institution and World Bank, Washington, May 30–31.

Kempson, Elaine. 2006. "Policy-Level Responses to Financial Exclusion in Developed Economies: Lessons for Developing Economies." Paper prepared for "Access to Finance: Building Inclusive Financial Systems." Brookings Institution and World Bank, Washington, May 30–31.

Kirsten, Marié. 2006. "Policy Initiatives to Expand Outreach in South Africa." Paper prepared for "Access to Finance: Building Inclusive Financial Systems." Brookings Institution and World Bank, Washington, May 30–31.

Knight, William. 2006. "Canada's Access to Basic Banking Regulation." Paper prepared for "Access to Finance: Building Inclusive Financial Systems." Brookings Institution and World Bank, Washington, May 30–31.

Lang, William W., and Leonard I. Nakamura. 1993. "A Model of Redlining." *Journal of Urban Economics* 33, no. 2: 223–34.

La Porta, Rafael, Florencio López-de-Silanes, and Andrei Shleifer. 2002. "Government Ownership of Banks." *Journal of Finance* 57, no. 1: 265–301.

Levine, Ross. 2004. "Finance and Growth: Theory and Evidence." Working Paper 10766. Cambridge, Mass.: National Bureau of Economic Research.

Litan, Robert E., and others. 2000. "The Community Reinvestment Act after Financial Modernization: A Baseline Report." Washington: U.S. Department of the Treasury.

Litan, Robert E., and others. 2001. "The Community Reinvestment Act after Financial Modernization: Final Report." Washington: U.S. Department of the Treasury.

Miller, Margaret J., ed. 2003. *Credit Reporting Systems and the International Economy*. MIT Press.

Petersen, Mitchell A., and Raghuram G. Rajan. 1995. "The Effect of Credit Market Competition on Lending Relationships." *Quarterly Journal of Economics* 110, no. 2: 407–43.

Pistor, Katharina, and others. 2003. "Economic Development, Legality, and the Transplant Effect." *European Economic Review* 47, no. 1: 165–95.

Prado, Cesar. 2006. "Policy Initiatives to Increase Financial Access in Colombia." Paper prepared for "Access to Finance: Building Inclusive Financial Systems." Brookings Institution and World Bank, Washington, May 30–31.

Rajan, Raghuram. 2006. "Opening Remarks." Paper prepared for "Access to Finance: Building Inclusive Financial Systems." Brookings Institution and World Bank, Washington, May 30–31.

Rajan, Raghuram, and Luigi Zingales. 2003. "The Great Reversals: The Politics of Financial Development in the Twentieth Century." *Journal of Financial Economics* 69, no. 1: 5–50.

Rhyne, Elizabeth, and Maria Otero. 1994. "Financial Services for Microenterprises: Principles and Institutions." In *The New World of Microenterprise Finance: Building Healthy Financial Institutions for the Poor*, edited by Maria Otero and Elizabeth Rhyne, pp. 55–75. West Hartford, Conn.: Kumarian Press.

Ross, Stephen, and John Yinger. 2002. *The Color of Credit: Mortgage Discrimination, Research Methodology, and Fair-Lending Enforcement.* MIT Press.

Schill, Michael H., and others. 2002. "Revitalizing Inner-City Neighborhoods: New York City's Ten-Year Plan." *Housing Policy Debate* 13, no. 3: 529–66.

Schreiner, Mark, and Michael Sherraden. 2007. *Can the Poor Save? Saving & Asset Building in Individual Development Accounts.* New Brunswick, N.J.: Transaction Publishers.

Schwartz, Alan, and Louis L. Wilde. 1979. "Intervening in Markets on the Basis of Imperfect Information: A Legal and Economic Analysis." *University of Pennsylvania Law Review* 127, no. 3: 630–82.

Sherraden, Michael. 2006. "Schemes to Boost Small Savings: Lessons Learned." Paper prepared for "Access to Finance: Building Inclusive Financial Systems." Brookings Institution and World Bank, Washington, May 30–31.

Sherraden, Michael, and Michael S. Barr. 2005. "Institutions and Inclusion in Saving Policy." In *Building Assets, Building Credit: Creating Wealth in Low-Income Communities*, edited by Retsinas and Belsky, pp. 286–315.

Staten, Michael, and Fred Cate. 2005. "Accuracy in Credit Reporting." In *Building Assets, Building Credit: Creating Wealth in Low-Income Communities*, edited by Retsinas and Belsky, pp. 237–65.

Stiglitz, Joseph. 1994. "The Role of the State in Financial Markets." In *Proceedings of the World Bank Annual Conference on Development Economics*, pp. 19–52. Washington: World Bank.

———. 2000. *Economics of the Public Sector.* 3rd ed. New York: Norton.

Stiglitz, Joseph, and Andrew Weiss. 1981. "Credit Rationing in Markets with Imperfect Information." *American Economic Review* 71, no. 3: 393–410.

Thaler, Richard H., and Shlomo Benartzi. 2004. "Save More Tomorrow: Using Behavioral Economics to Increase Employee Saving." *Journal of Political Economy* 112, no. 1: 164–87.

Tressel, Thierry. 2003. "Dual Financial Systems and Inequalities in Economic Development." *Journal of Economic Growth* 8, no. 2: 223–57.

United Nations. 2006. *Building Inclusive Financial Sectors for Development* (Blue Book). New York: Department of Economic and Social Affairs and United Nations Capital Development Fund.

Vogel, Robert C., Arelis Gomez, and Thomas Fitzgerald. 2000. "Microfinance Regulation and Supervision Concept Paper." Working Paper. Bethesda, Md.: Microenterprise Best Practices.

Zinman, Jonathan. 2002. "The Efficacy and Efficiency for Credit Market Interventions: Evidence from the Community Reinvestment Act." Working Paper CRA02-2. Cambridge, Mass.: Harvard University Joint Center for Housing Studies.

MICHAEL S. BARR
ANJALI KUMAR
ROBERT E. LITAN

8

Conclusion

THE CONFERENCE PAPERS on which this volume is based and the discussions that took place during the conference explored seven central themes concerning financial inclusion:

—Building financial access is a process of gradually establishing meaningful inclusion; it cannot be achieved in a single dimension or measured in simple terms of "having" or "not having" access.

—Work toward building an appropriate spectrum of indicators of access has increased rapidly in recent years, but meaningful multicountry and multidimensional measures that have more direct policy relevance still need to be developed.

—Research is making it increasingly clear that expanded financial access can increase growth, increase incomes of the poor, and reduce income inequality, but the mechanisms by which it creates those effects remain uncertain.

—Microfinance institutions offer one path toward expanding financial access; other "double bottom line" institutions, which adopt both profit-seeking and social goals, can also help to expand access, using different designs to reach different market segments.

—Commercial and savings banks and other regulated depository institutions can be part of the solution, as shown by successful, profitable models that rely on innovations in delivery techniques and product design.

—Financial access is supported by innovation, competition, scale, and efficiency in technology and payment infrastructure, but these goals may conflict and may be difficult to achieve simultaneously. For example, achieving scale may be at odds with maintaining competition. Trade-offs are required, at least initially, to launch new products and processes.

—Government policies can help foster or hinder financial access in a variety of ways. There has been a paradigm shift in government support, away from direct provision of access through government-run institutions or heavy subsidies and toward newer methods that focus on the enabling environment and more targeted approaches deploying a range of tools.

Moving Forward: An Action Plan

Integrating the messages of this conference volume into a policy agenda going forward is the concluding challenge. What is the future role of governments, private financial institutions, international agencies, and researchers in fostering expansion of financial access? Our proposals for action follow from the findings listed above and together provide a framework for building inclusive financial systems.

Map a Path toward Meaningful Inclusion in Financial Access

First, there is a need for better monitoring and measurement of financial access that takes account of its multidimensional nature, looking not only at whether a member of society has access to an account in an institution or some specific financial service but also at the appropriateness of the product for the segments of society to be served. While researchers or international institutions may be well placed to undertake this work, they would need the support of financial institutions and governments and their work would need to be integrated with institutional and governmental efforts.

For too long, many policymakers and researchers have tended to view financial access as something to be achieved through a single act or measure or, metaphorically, by flipping an "on/off" switch. We have measured financial access by whether an individual has an account relationship or has received a loan without inquiring about the nature of the account or the pricing or terms of the loan. We have not inquired deeply enough into whether the product or service is well designed to meet the financial needs of low-income households. Indeed, until recently we rarely asked low-income households what financial services they actually wanted.

All that is changing, as researchers and policymakers—and financial services providers, an important part of the picture—increasingly focus on understanding the financial service needs of low-income households.[1] Financial access, after all, is about the customer. When one asks whether financial access is improving, the question should be framed in terms of what households or firms want and need from financial services. There has been a good deal of progress in that regard. For example, during the conference we heard about the work of the World Bank and the FinMark Trust in conducting global or country-specific surveys of financial access. The World Bank has become increasingly involved in survey work in a number of countries and also in measuring access on multiple dimensions through information provided by regulators or financial institutions. In the United States, new survey work has been done regarding the financial needs of low-income households.[2] Financial services firms are looking to meet the needs of low-income households in new ways because they can focus on what such households really want from their financial service providers.

In the coming years, researchers, policymakers, and financial services providers will have an opportunity to work together to develop household surveys and market research designs that could enable deeper penetration into the financial service marketplace with products that are better tailored to the needs of lower-income households. Given that information is a public good, it would make sense for governments and international agencies to participate in sponsoring such research. If a market-based focus is to be maintained, private financial sector institutions also must be key partners in the effort.

Understand the Impact of Financial Access on Growth and Poverty

The second area for future action is that impact evaluations must continue, not only in terms of aggregate access and its impact on poverty and inequality but also in terms of the impact of changes in micro-level policies and in product design, which can help shape appropriate products for different segments of society. As Raghuram Rajan, the chief economist at the International Monetary Fund, reminded us at the outset of the conference, those who are concerned about financial exclusion must be willing to "fight to improve access." Financial reforms can favor both growth and the poor, but they do not necessarily do so. In many countries, financial reforms have been used to entrench the power of elites rather than to open up access for excluded households.[3] In some countries, weak legal institutions keep lending focused on those with bank relationships, and in other countries, crony capitalism

---

1. See chapter 2, this volume.

2. Michael S. Barr, Detroit Area Household Financial Services Study, Survey Research Center, University of Michigan, available at www-personal.umich.edu/~msbarr/ [May 14, 2007].

3. See Rajan and Zingales (2003).

and other modes of financial repression dominate. Corruption, excessive government regulation, overly weak government institutions, and similar government failures can block financial development.

Economic theory suggests that financial development can contribute to economic growth[4] and that growth can contribute to poverty alleviation.[5] Financial development could contribute directly to poverty alleviation by easing credit constraints on the poor and indirectly by fostering economic growth that benefits the poor. However, there is wide disagreement about whether and under what circumstances it might have those effects. Whether financial development promotes poverty alleviation may depend in part on broader economic circumstances and trends in a country, on financial sector structure, and on government polices regarding legal, economic, and financial infrastructure.

Support Sustainable Microfinance Services

Third, sustained support to microfinance is to be valued and should be broadened to include other institutions that adopt the double bottom line of social support and economic viability. It should be recognized that microfinance is a form of financial service, which can be delivered through multiple institutional forms. There are inherent limitations to using only microfinance institutions to expand access. The need for sustainable microfinance to evolve into or partner with other institutional forms should be recognized from the outset.

Microfinance encompasses the full range of financial products, which can permit poor households to receive income, store value, make payments, and protect themselves against economic risks through access to credit, savings, insurance, and transactional services. Many microfinance institutions specialize in providing one form of microfinance—microcredit or microcredit linked to savings mobilization—but increasingly they are offering a broader array of financial products and services to meet the needs of poor households. Moreover, different institutions offer microfinance products to different segments of underserved households and firms.

Microfinance is not provided solely by self-defined microfinance institutions but also by a range of other providers, including in some instances commercial banks and other regulated depository institutions. Market actors need to develop and implement institutional structures, products, and services that meet the range of low-income households' financial needs. In developing regulatory policy, governments need to be sensitive to the particular form of a microfinance institution.

---

4. See Levine (2004).
5. Beck and others (2004).

Some forms of regulatory policy in the financial sector, especially regarding smaller players, could stifle innovation and make lending to the poor unprofitable. At the same time, a purely hands-off attitude toward the microfinance sector as a whole is unlikely to be appropriate, given prudential concerns associated with institutions involved in savings mobilization and consumer protection concerns regarding credit provision.

Research suggests that as microfinance grows in scale and sophistication, both profitability and greater outreach are possible. Although many institutions continue to struggle to achieve financial self-sustainability, a number of significant microfinance providers have succeeded in reaching those on the lower rungs of the income ladder and appear to be operating sustainably and on a relatively large scale.

Microfinance today is beginning to look like an industry, with a market structure seen elsewhere in finance, including concentration ratios, market segmentation, and market discipline. As the top microfinance institutions increasingly operate sustainably and at scale, they may be able to attract increasing private financial flows. Such private sector funding offers the prospect of expanding microfinance beyond what would be available through reliance on donor and government funding and of increasing market discipline in the industry. There are downsides to reliance on private flows, however; for example, private funds can quickly flow out, just as they flow in, as the financial crises of the 1990s showed. Moreover, given the cost-intensive nature of microfinance provision and the difficulty that many microfinance institutions have in reaching self-sustainability, it is likely that private sector foreign capital flows will not be a panacea for microfinance funding in the near future.

Recognize That Commercial Banks, Thrifts, and Credit Unions Can Contribute

Fourth, recent efforts of major commercial financial institutions to expand access to the poor on a for-profit basis offer promise for the large-scale expansion of appropriately adapted financial services for the poorest people. Those efforts should be supported. Intensive investigation into multiple product features and delivery mechanisms is needed if they are to be successful.

In principle, regulated depository institutions can play an important role in expanding access to finance among low-income households. Such entities often have specialized expertise in financial institution management, and they are exposed, to a greater or lesser extent (depending in part on government prudential policies and deposit insurance), to market discipline. They often have the scale and scope of services to permit greater efficiencies in reaching a larger customer base.

In practice, however, many regulated depository institutions in many countries serve only the elites in their societies. Even in countries where such institutions reach a broad segment of middle-income households, regulated depository institutions often do not reach further, into low- and moderate-income households. While broad access to financial services is certainly a major step in the right direction and far superior to having financial systems serve only the well off, in such societies there is still much progress to be made in completing the market.

What will be required to further encourage such institutions to serve low-income households? Innovation—in products, cost, technology, and people—that helps firms serve households at lower cost and risk. Such institutions need to engage in outreach—as one of the conference panelists put it, "bringing the bank closer to people." Firms will need to focus on low-income clients and build internal incentive structures and specialized units within the bank to develop the expertise needed to serve such a clientele. Taking those steps will require the commitment of the most senior management to changing the corporate culture and attitudes toward serving the poor.

Introduce Innovations in Payment Systems and Technology to Lower Costs

Fifth, as described above, new technologies to expand financial access—through branchless banking, mobile and other communication methods, and computerized or card-based banking— should be encouraged, along with the use of technologies such as credit rating and scoring. These technologies help build the infrastructure to support the expansion of financial access.

New forms of electronic payment systems, in combination with new communications technologies, can help countries reach further into their populations with financial services at lower cost and sometimes at lower risk than entailed in the traditional form of doing business through brick-and-mortar branches, tellers, and paper checks. Key products include electronic, debit-card-only access accounts that lower the cost of transactions and can reduce the risk of overdraft.[6] Increasingly international remittances can be sent using international automated clearinghouse transfers among banks, dual-ATM cards, and similar lower-cost electronic technology. Banks are moving toward electronic accounts that let low-income households receive income, pay bills, store value, and save over time.

Moreover, developing countries may be able to leapfrog over older technologies and go directly to new, lower-cost forms of delivering financial access, which might include, for example, mobile banking using cell phones as well as wireless payment system infrastructure. How to foster innovation, efficiency, and scale in

6. See Barr (2004a).

meeting the needs of low-income households with these new technologies remains the key question. Given the societal interest in broadly expanding access to financial services, how can governments help to sponsor newer payment system technologies without stifling innovation? It remains essential to overcome these challenges in the next few years in order to increase the likelihood that new technologies serve the needs of low-income households rather than further excluding them by fostering a new technological divide.

Adopt Government Policies That Foster Sustainable Financial Access

Finally, governments can play a proactive role in promoting the new paradigm by building an appropriate legal and regulatory structure to enable expansion of financial access. They also can support access by helping to create a conducive macroeconomic environment with low inflation and low public borrowing. In addition, governments can undertake other supportive policies that seek to harness market forces in positive ways.

If financial development may foster poverty alleviation and government policies may affect the extent to which financial development serves that purpose, what should governments do? One strategy is to view financial reforms through the lens of microfinance clients by asking whether reforms will help financial institutions in their country serve poor borrowers.[7] Financial reforms that build the legal, regulatory, and financial infrastructure essential to supporting savings mobilization, credit markets, insurance, and payment systems can serve as the backbone of a strategy to improve access to financial services. After all, as microfinance institutions have shown, it is not impossible—difficult, but not impossible—to mobilize efforts to serve the poor if the financial sector cannot serve the broader society. Prudential regulation of depository institutions serves the goal of financial stability, which is a prerequisite to sound provision of financial services to the poor.

Countries can go beyond these essential market reforms to focus directly on questions of access. By using a range of strategies—disclosure, obligation, product regulation, prohibition, subsidy or taxation, voluntary codes, and behavioral default rules—countries can increase the likelihood that the financial sector will serve a broad cross-section of society, including those at the bottom of the income ladder.[8] In our judgment, it is time to move beyond a sole focus on financial market liberalization toward a deeper understanding of the role of government in fostering financial access. A greater sensitivity to market incentives that permits

7. See Barr (2004b).
8. See chapter 7, this volume.

market competition to work; more supple forms of government intervention when needed; and a commitment to transparency may make it more likely that government policies, when implemented, will encourage broad expansion of access to financial services.

Finally, let us return to where we started. If indeed we must "fight to increase access," then we hope that this volume contributes to our understanding of how to do so effectively. Financial development can help lead to economic growth and poverty reduction, but it need not do so. The actions of private sector firms, nongovernmental organizations, and governments themselves help decide whether financial development improves the lives of the poor. In our judgment, ensuring that financial development benefits society in general, including the poor, is essential to ensuring that global economic integration and growth continue. At bottom, what will it take to make globalization work for all of us? This volume attempts to begin to answer that question.

References

Barr, Michael S. 2004a. "Banking the Poor." *Yale Journal on Regulation* 21, no.1: 121–237.

———. 2004b. "Microfinance and Financial Development." *Michigan Journal of International Law* 26, no. 1: 271–96.

Beck, Thorsten, and others. 2004. "Finance, Inequality, and Poverty: Cross-Country Evidence." Working Paper 10979. Cambridge, Mass.: National Bureau of Economic Research.

Levine, Ross. 2004. "Finance and Growth: Theory and Evidence." Working Paper 10766. Cambridge, Mass.: National Bureau of Economic Research.

Rajan, Raghuram, and Luigi Zingales. 2003. "The Great Reversals: The Politics of Financial Development in the Twentieth Century." *Journal of Financial Economics* 69 (1): 5–50.

Contributors

Conference Organizers

Michael S. Barr
*University of Michigan
Law School*

Anjali Kumar
World Bank

Robert E. Litan
*Brookings Institution and
Kauffman Foundation*

Collen Mascenik
World Bank

Contributors to Conference Presentations and Summary Papers

Robert Annibale
Citigroup

Hany A. Assaad
International Finance Corporation

Bernd Balkenhol
International Labor Organization

Michael S. Barr
University of Michigan Law School

Thorsten Beck
World Bank

Carolyn Blacklock
ANZ Banking Group

Cesare Calari
World Bank

Suvalaxmi Chakraborty
ICICI Bank

Anne-Marie Chidzero,
FinMark Trust

Massimo Cirasino
World Bank

Stijn Claessens
World Bank

Robert J. Cull
World Bank

Ken Dam
University of Chicago Law School

Asli Demirgüç-Kunt
World Bank

Annie Duflo
*Institute for Financial Management
and Research, India*

Karen Ellis
*U.K. Department for International
Development*

Enrique Errazuriz
Banco Estado, Chile

Jose Antonio Garcia
World Bank

Murray Gardiner
DBS Global Solutions

Xavier Gine
World Bank

Adrian Gonzalez
Consultative Group to Assist the Poor

Mario Guadamillas
World Bank

Martin Hagen
KfW

Jim Hanson
World Bank

Patrick Honohan
World Bank

Jennifer Isern
Consultative Group to Assist the Poor

Julia Johannsen
Institute of Rural Development

Mukta Joshi
Consultant to the World Bank

Dean Karlan
Yale University

Henriette Keijzers
*United Nations Capital Development
Fund*

Elaine Kempson
University of Bristol

Marié Kirsten
Development Bank of Southern Africa

William Knight
Financial Consumer Agency of Canada

Doris Koehn
KfW

Anjali Kumar
World Bank

Ross Levine
Brown University

Jeff Liew
UNDP Pacific Sub-Regional Centre

Robert E. Litan
*Brookings Institution and Kauffman
Foundation*

Elizabeth Littlefield
Consultative Group to Assist the Poor

Maria Soledad Martinez Peria
World Bank

Katherine W. McKee
*U.S. Agency for International
Development*

Jose Antonio Meade
Financiera Rural

Jose Mena
Banco Estado

Fernando Montes-Negret
World Bank

Jonathan Morduch
New York University

Herman Mulder
ABN Amro Bank

Gida Nakazibwe-Sekandi
Bank Windhoek

Ajai Nair
Consultant to the World Bank

Mark Napier
FinMark Trust

Steve Peachey
World Savings Banks Institute

Brian Pomeroy
Her Majesty's Treasury, United Kingdom

David Porteous
Bankable Frontier Associates

Cesar Prado
*Ministerio de Hacienda y Crédito
Público, Colombia*

Raghuram Rajan
International Monetary Fund

Elizabeth Rhyne
ACCION International

Marguerite S. Robinson
Harvard University

Loraine Ronchi
World Bank

Richard Rosenberg
*Consultative Group to Assist
the Poor*

Stuart Rutherford
University of Manchester

Bharat Sarpeshkar
*Citigroup Corporate and Investment
Bank*

Mark Schreiner
Washington University in St. Louis

Moumita Sensarma,
ABN AMRO Bank

Khalid Sheikh
ABN AMRO Bank

Michael Sherraden
Washington University in St. Louis

Nancy Todor
Citigroup

Augusto de la Torre
World Bank

Carlo Tresoldi
Banca d'Italia

Konstantinos Tzioumis
Consultant, World Bank

Marilou Uy
World Bank

Maria Iride Vangelisti
Banca d'Italia

J.D. von Pischke
Frontier Finance International

Flavio Weizenmann
Real Microcredito Assessoria Financiera

Bing Xiao
Wells Fargo

Maria Carmela Zaccagnino
Banca d'Italia

Manfred Zeller
University of Hohenheim

Index